The Great Sports
Documentaries

The Great Sports Documentaries

100+ Award Winning Films

MICHAEL PETERS

McFarland & Company, Inc., Publishers
Jefferson, North Carolina

LIBRARY OF CONGRESS CATALOGUING-IN-PUBLICATION DATA

Names: Peters, Michael, 1969– author.
Title: The great sports documentaries : 100+ award winning films / Michael Peters.
Description: Jefferson, North Carolina : McFarland & Company, Inc., Publishers, 2017. | Includes bibliographical references and indexes.
Identifiers: LCCN 2017049694 | ISBN 9781476669595 (softcover : acid free paper) ∞
Subjects: LCSH: Documentary films—United States—Catalogs. | Sports in motion pictures.
Classification: LCC GV704 .P475 2017 | DDC 070.1/8—dc23
LC record available at https://lccn.loc.gov/2017049694

BRITISH LIBRARY CATALOGUING DATA ARE AVAILABLE

ISBN (print) 978-1-4766-6959-5
ISBN (ebook) 978-1-4766-3048-9

© 2018 Michael Peters. All rights reserved

No part of this book may be reproduced or transmitted in any form or by any means, electronic or mechanical, including photocopying or recording, or by any information storage and retrieval system, without permission in writing from the publisher.

Front cover image from *More Than a Game*, 2008; LeBron James, center (Lionsgate/Photofest)

Printed in the United States of America

McFarland & Company, Inc., Publishers
  Box 611, Jefferson, North Carolina 28640
    www.mcfarlandpub.com

CONTENTS

Preface and Acknowledgments   1

Introduction   3

The Filmography   11

Bibliography   187

Index   189

Preface and Acknowledgments

In recent years, documentary films have become more important and more prevalent than ever. The reasons for the boom in documentary film production in the new millennium may boil down to the fact that film-making equipment is more accessible and more affordable than ever before or perhaps that documentaries can be shot on tiny budgets compared to fictional films, making them more appealing to film companies. Another possible reason why documentaries seem to have gained more prominence in the 21st century is that the avenues for distribution of films have widened so much that the traditional route can be bypassed altogether. One interesting explanation that often goes overlooked is a simple one—the audience for documentary films has grown. The reasons that more people are choosing nonfiction today over other genres may be related to increasingly poor options in the latter, but more than likely it has to do with both filmmakers and viewers seeking out narrow topics that interest them. Arguably, sports (and to a lesser extent various other forms of competition) has grown as subject matter for documentary films more so than any other topic over the last two decades.

This book came about simply out of curiosity and a basic love of research and cataloging. And, of course, what I felt was a need to group some of the older sports documentaries together with some of the newer ones as a guide for others interested in the topic. It began several years ago as I was spending lots of time with my father and re-watching *Baseball*, the epic nine-part documentary series by Ken Burns that originally aired on PBS in the mid–1990s. I appreciated the series far more than I had previously primarily because of my viewing companion, but also because I was viewing it for the first time as someone who had recently taken an interest in sociology and especially in all aspects of sport in society. I began to seek out and watch every documentary film dealing with sports that I could find and then branched out to see documentary films dealing with other forms of competition, which had become wildly popular on the heels of *Spellbound* in 2002, the film chronicling the 1999 Scripps National Spelling Bee.

It was only natural for me to catalog the films that I had watched and list those that were yet unwatched. At its zenith, the list was well over 300 films, with brief summary notes for some of my favorites. The next thing I knew, I was diving deeper into the production side of the films and creating something of an annotated filmography. Noticing that the inclusion criterion for my list was extremely broad, or even non-existent aside from "feature documentaries and sports/competition," I began to narrow it down and include films based on their importance to their topic and to the genre. Awards and accolades for the films was a major factor in determining their overall importance, but certainly not the only factor. Needless to say, the list of films not included in this book that easily could have been is a long one. I hope that some of those filmmakers will not feel slighted, nor will readers looking for a specific sport or competition that might not be included.

Following its introduction to the topic of sports and competition documentaries, this book includes summaries of award-winning nonfiction films. Although nowhere near an all-inclusive list, the entries represent what I feel are the most historically important sports documentaries and many newer titles that have been received with acclamation. Some of the summaries are clearly more detailed than others, but all provide a basic overview of the film and the film's topic. I hope that it will in fact serve as a guide for viewers interested in the exploding relationship of sports and competition to documentary film. I would like to thank my friends and family for their support and patience and Matthew Carroll, a photographic and photo-editing guru, for his help in that area. I owe many other people a great deal of thanks as well, which I will do personally.

Introduction

The Sports Documentary, Past

When heavyweight champion James J. Corbett lost his title to Bob Fitzsimmons in Carson City, Nevada, on St. Patrick's Day, 1897, the entire 14-round bout was filmed by a man named Enoch Rector. Using 11,000 feet of film and three different 63mm movie cameras that he had invented, Rector was able to film the fight continuously. *The Corbett-Fitzsimmons Fight* (1897) was soon being screened all over the country and at 90 minutes was the longest film that had ever been released to date (Niemi 190). Not only was this the first feature-length motion picture, it could also be called the first feature-length documentary and the first-ever sports documentary. Other major boxing matches that followed Corbett-Fitzsimmons would be filmed and screened in the same fashion over the next several years.

Most notable of the boxing matches being screened in theatres in the early 20th century were those involving Jack Johnson, the first African American heavyweight champion. These films featuring Johnson defeating white opponents received incredible media attention, simultaneously stirring racial animosity and immense pride. Author Dan Streible suggests that Johnson's screen presence made him, "in essence, the first black movie star" (195). Billed as "The Fight of the Century," Johnson's 1910 victory against James J. Jeffries and the film that followed led to race riots across the country and a ban on the distribution of fight films across state lines. By the time that motion pictures became talkies in the 1930s, boxing was a staple genre in the narrative fiction film as well, but sports in general as a primary subject for documentary films was still decades away.

Leni Riefenstahl's *Olympia* (1938), the two-part film documenting the 1936 Summer Games in Berlin, began the tradition of an official film being made for each Olympiad. Although the film and Riefenstahl herself would become controversial a few years later when the world learned more of Nazi ideology and war crimes, it was considered a cinematic masterpiece at the time. Aside from the official Olympic films and *The Conquest of Everest*, the 1953 British film documenting Sir Edmund Hillary's famous expedition, and perhaps *Torero!*, the 1956 Mexican film about bullfighter Luis Procuna, the 1940s and 1950s were largely devoid of noteworthy feature-length sports documentaries. Perhaps signaling that sport was indeed a worthwhile subject matter for documentary filmmakers, three of the official Olympic films from the 1960s—*The Grand Olympics* (1961), *Tokyo Olympiad* (1965), and *The Olympics in Mexico* (1969)—all received critical praise, and two were nominated for the Documentary Feature Academy Award.

Further reinforcing the notion that sports and athletics made for interesting nonfiction subject matter, *The Horse with the Flying Tail* (1960), a Walt Disney Productions film about championship equestrianism, won the Oscar at the start of the decade. Near the close of the decade, filmmaker-turned-singer/songwriter Harry Chapin earned an Oscar nomination for his 1968 film *Legendary Champions*, documenting the first several heavyweight champions of the world. The 1960s may have been when the sports documentary gained its footing, but the following decade was when it truly blossomed as a nonfiction genre, with a total of five such films receiving an Oscar nomination during the 1970s.

Sports continued to become a legitimate subject for American nonfiction filmmakers during the 1960s and 1970s thanks in large part to the expanding role of documentaries on network television. The relatively new medium of television provided an outlet for aspiring filmmakers and all three major American television networks featured popular documentary programming in the pre-cable years, often venturing into the world of sports. CBS's *The Twentieth Century* series, hosted by Walter Cronkite, produced the short film *The Violent World of Sam Huff* in 1960, which was integral to the growing popularity of the NFL. In 1965, legendary producer David L. Wolper used a young director named William Friedkin (*The French Connection, The Exorcist*) to shoot an innovative film for ABC about professional football. Both *Violent World* and Friedkin's film, *Pro Football: Mayhem on a Sunday Afternoon*, heavily influenced the future work of Ed Sabol and NFL Films (Vogan 136).

Robert Drew, a filmmaker who is often called the father of the cinéma vérité style in America, was a pioneer of television documentaries. Drew and a group of talented filmmakers including Richard Leacock, D.A. Pennebaker, James Lipscomb, and Albert Maysles (as Drew Associates) made a number of important television documentary films dealing with sports: *On the Pole* (1960), about driver Eddie Sachs at the Indianapolis 500; *Mooney vs Fowle* (1961), about high school football rivals in Miami; *The Big Guy* (1965), about boxer Jim Beattie; *The Sun Ship Game* (1970), about the sport of competitive soaring; and *Men of the Tall Ships* (1976), about a trans-Atlantic sailing race of tall ships during the United States Bicentennial celebration. Author Ian Aitken explains that the documentary methodology pioneered by the Drew team "would have considerable influence on documentary films over several decades" (318).

It could be said that longer form television documentaries of the 1960s and 1970s were natural successors to the newsreels of previous decades, which provided moviegoers with a small taste of nonfiction before their feature film presentation. The short documentary subjects common to newsreels prior to the 1960s often delved into sports, so naturally the longer form television documentaries that came later did as well. More contemporary television documentaries, often offered by public broadcasters such as PBS, in the United States, or the BBC, in the United Kingdom, also ventured into the world of sports on occasion. For example, *Hoop Dreams* (1994), often hailed as one of the greatest documentaries of all time, first aired on PBS. Likewise, PBS also aired *Baseball*, the nine-part documentary miniseries by filmmaker extraordinaire Ken Burns in 1994.

The Sports Documentary, Present

In examining how it has come to be that so many new documentary films dealing with sports and competition are being made today as compared to the 20th century, a few different explanations come to mind. Documentary films in general began to take on new importance in the final decade of the last century, and that importance has only grown since. In his insightful article "Situating the Sports Documentary," Ian McDonald argues that a shift in emphasis in the documentary format emerged in the late 1990s, in which documentaries began applying the fiction film techniques of story-led and character-led narratives (209). Because of this shift, the appeal and audience for theatrically-released documentaries has clearly grown, and with that the subject matter for nonfiction films has grown as well. This shift also represents a new idea that documentaries are no longer perceived as dull and gloomy, but rather can be just as entertaining as they are educational (McDonald 215).

Feature-length documentary films dealing with sports and competition are more prevalent than ever before primarily because filmmakers are exploring the subject more than ever before. While maverick filmmakers such as Warren Miller have been documenting activities now considered "extreme sports" for more than 50 years, it is a relatively new phenomenon to find so many different contemporary films dedicated to the outdoor pursuits of trekking, mountaineering, running, biking, and snow-play. Similar to Miller's snow-play films, the nonfiction surf film has been around for decades and had a very dedicated, yet relatively small, audience. Add to that the door that was opened when skateboarding aficionados began documenting their exploits in narrative fashion during the 1990s and you have a vast collection of documentaries to fit the niche of so-called adventure or extreme sports.

The athletic endeavors more commonly associated with sports have a clear place in the recent documentary tradition as well, but theatrically-released films dealing with traditional sports were infrequent up until the 1990s. Although a number of documentary films dealing with sports such as boxing, football, soccer, and track and field had achieved success and critical acclaim prior to the mid–1990s, it was the groundbreaking work of directors Steve James and Leon Gast, with *Hoop Dreams* (1994) and *When We were Kings* (1996), that truly opened the door to the attention we see sports documentaries getting today. Whereas Michael Moore's ultra-successful films *Bowling for Columbine* (2002) and *Fahrenheit 9/11* (2004) serve as a good dividing line between the general documentary past and general documentary present, these seminal mid–1990s films of James and Gast serve as the dividing line between the sports documentary past and the sports documentary present.

A number of films from the first decade of the 21st century played a pivotal role in not only bringing nonfiction sports films into the mainstream, but also in stretching the definition of sports and athletics into other areas that are just as fiercely competitive. *Spellbound* (2002), an Oscar-nominated film following eight young competitors at the Scripps National Spelling Bee, takes an observational approach to the competition, as does *Word Wars* (2004), about the National Scrabble Championship, and *Mad Hot Ballroom* (2005), about a ballroom dance competition for fifth graders in New York City. *The King of Kong: A Fistful of Quarters* (2007), about a rivalry between classic arcade gamers, similarly blurs the line between sports and hobbies, but the competition and intensity is as strong as in any traditional sport.

The prevalence of sports as subject matter in documentary films has grown even steadier over the last decade. In the fall of 2009, the television network ESPN began airing documentary films under the name *30 for 30* (meaning 30 films on subjects taking place during the 30 years of the network's existence). In the seven years since then, the project has been expanded and the list of films has swelled to more than 100. Although the overwhelming majority of the films were not theatrically released, some of the best known documentary filmmakers dealing with sports have been involved in the project and a number of the films have been presented at various film festivals. The *30 for 30* series has brought in a whole new audience by mixing contemporary sports history with the storytelling of documentary filmmaking.

The worldwide importance and popularity of sports and athletics has been obvious for some time, but the resurgence of importance in documentary filmmaking that has been taking place since the 1990s perhaps represents the most significant era since the documentary movement led by John Grierson in Great Britain in the 1930s. Along with this resurgence of importance in documentary films, the subject matter being examined in films has expanded, as has the sort of recognition and celebrations for the films. Neither film festivals nor film awards are anything new, but both have grown exponentially in number over the last two decades, and now there are both festivals and awards specifically catering to and honoring nonfiction films, viewers, and filmmakers. Taking into consideration the historical tradition of sports documentaries and the ever-growing viewership and importance of more contemporary nonfiction sports films, an annotated list of films is sorely needed. I have attempted to provide that with this book. I hope that it guides readers to films that they will enjoy.

How to Use This Guide

The basic structure of this book is fairly straightforward. The films are listed alphabetically by their official titles, with alternate titles in parentheses. Foreign-language titles will use the English translation or English alternative, but will have their the original foreign title in parentheses. For example, *The Olympics in Mexico* (1969), the official film of the 1968 Summer Olympics, will appear like this: *The Olympics in Mexico (Olimpiada en México)*, 1969. Also listed with the title will be the year of release, the director(s), the film's running time, and the film's country of origin or production.

Each film included has been synopsized or summarized to some degree, so the obligatory warning about spoilers is needed here. Some film summaries are far more divulging than others, but great effort was put into each one to avoid spoiling some of the fairly rare surprise twists that a few documentaries contain. While the entries steer clear of recommending or not recommending that the films be sought out for viewing, many do suggest similar titles and most mention the film's availability. Although the list is often not exhaustive, each entry also includes a list of awards or accolades that the film has won or been nominated for. Along with the standard alphabetical listing of entries, there are also indexes by sport (basketball, soccer, gymnastics, tennis, etc.) and issues (human rights, sexuality, gender, race, etc.) that can be cross-referenced.

A Word about Entries, Inclusions and Exclusions

Defining sports documentary is simple enough—a documentary film with a sport, game, or athletic endeavor as its primary subject matter. Determining what qualifies as a sport within the documentary is the more difficult task. For the most part, the notion of what is and what is not a sport is easy to grasp. The previously-mentioned endeavors often classified as adventure or extreme sports typically make the cut, even when there is no real competition involved. For example, activities such as mountaineering and trekking (mountain climbing, hiking), surfing, skiing, skating, biking, running, exercising in almost any fashion, and occasionally even fishing are almost universally considered athletic even when competition is not involved. The concept of competition, however, expands our definition a great deal. Almost any activity can be included in this definition when it is applied to a contest or competition. Some of these examples include brain games, such as trivia or spelling, board games, arcade games, dance or art competitions, and even quirky physical endurance tests, as is the case with *Hands on a Hard Body* (1997).

Similarly, defining documentary film is relatively simple—a nonfiction film capturing reality with actual participants instead of actors with staged and scripted scenes. Due to the fact that virtually anything can be displayed as moving visual media nowadays thanks to video-capturing technology, the definition of film is a bit stricter. Inclusions are limited only to feature-length films, defined by the Academy of Motion Picture Arts and Sciences as films with running times of more than 40 minutes. The entries in this book are predominantly theatrically-released films, which should primarily explain the exclusion of many good films aired as part of ESPN's *30 for 30* series, with *The Two Escobars* (2010) being a prominent exception. Direct-to-video and television-only documentaries have largely been excluded also, but there are exceptions there as well—*Fallen Champ: The Untold Story of Mike Tyson* (1993), for example. Likewise, episodes within a documentary series have been excluded in favor of singular films, despite how good some of those have been. *Baseball* (1994), *Hockey: A People's History* (2006), and Ezra Edelman's Academy Award–winning *O.J.: Made in America* (2016) come to mind.

As the title of this work implies, the great majority of the films included have won awards or other accolades of some variety. In the few cases that included films have not been recognized with awards, they have been included because they hold a certain historical significance in the documentary tradition or within their topic. Finally, the simple fact is that a work such as this would be virtually impossible if it were to include every significant documentary film dealing with sports or competition, so, needless to say, plenty of great films have been excluded from my list. Because both sports and documentary film should always be inclusive instead of exclusive, I strongly recommend that readers seek out films not included here, and they do exist! Regardless of what sporting passion you may have, a nonfiction film exploring that passion likely exists. The number of films summarized in this guide was not an arbitrary one; it simply represents important, award-winning sports documentaries that this researcher has found, viewed, and written about over the last year.

THE FILMOGRAPHY

The Armstrong Lie, 2013
Director: Alex Gibney; Running Time: 124 minutes; U.S.

Oscar-winning filmmaker Alex Gibney (*Taxi to the Dark Side*, 2007, *Enron: The Smartest Guys in the Room*, 2005) set out to document Lance Armstrong's return to cycling in 2009 following the seven-time Tour de France champion's retirement from the sport four years earlier. Gibney's original unscreened film, titled *The Road Back*, was completed, but found a unique obstacle when news broke in 2012 that Armstrong had used performance-enhancing drugs. Despite years of doping allegations by rival competitors, Armstrong vehemently and aggressively denied it. The fact is Armstrong had been doping since his first (of seven consecutive) Tour de France titles in 1999, and possibly even longer. The United States Anti-Doping Agency, in its 2012 report, went so far as to suggest that Armstrong's U.S. Postal Service Pro Cycling Team "ran the most sophisticated, professionalized, and successful doping program that sport has ever seen." Armstrong finally came clean and admitted to doping throughout his entire span of Tour de France victories in a January 2013 interview with Oprah Winfrey. Gibney was present at the televised interview with Winfrey and within hours had the same personal admission for his film that had originally intended to celebrate the champion who beat cancer and raced clean in a time when few others did. As one interview subject explains in the film, those who knew the truth were scared that Gibney was "buying into the bullshit" with his original focus.

The Armstrong Lie reinforces what virtually everyone already knew—that doping had been rampant in professional cycling for more than a decade. Rampant may not even be a correct description; the film actually gives rise to the notion that no rider had truly been clean during the 2000s. The fact that cheating by way of blood-doping and testosterone injections was so widespread does not lessen the disgrace that came to Armstrong

The Armstrong Lie, 2013

Alex Gibney's original intent was to celebrate Lance Armstrong's return to cycling, but he changed his focus to document the seven-time Tour de France champion's fall from grace in *The Armstrong Lie* (2013).

after his admission of guilt. As Gibney so effectively explores, the primary scandal with Armstrong is both that he had been treated as a true American hero after defeating testicular cancer and returning to dominate the European-based sport, *and* that he had been so belligerent in his repeated decade-long denials of cheating. Armstrong's denials were so strong that they often came with lawsuits and threats of lawsuits, separate accusations about his accusers, and general attempts to destroy anyone who dared to challenge his truthfulness. In particular, the way he went after former teammate Frankie Andreu and his wife, Betsy, after their 2005 testimony was especially personal. The lies and abuse of power of Lance Armstrong became personal to Gibney as well, perhaps prompting him to change focus and tackle the lies so strongly because his original film would have been humiliating in its own right. One aspect that is left purposely unexplored, but strongly hinted at during the film, is that the International Cycling Union, the sport's governing body, was complicit in Armstrong's cheating. Released in 2014, the DVD features deleted scenes and an interesting commentary track with the director.

Awards: 2014 Golden Trailer Awards: Best Documentary TV Spot; 2013 Chicago Film Critics Association Awards: Best Documentary (nominated); 2013 Copenhagen International Documentary Festival: Audience Award (nominated); 2013 London Film Festival: Grierson Award (nominated); 2013 San Francisco Film Critics Circle: Best Documentary (nominated); 2014 BAFTA Awards: Best Documentary (nominated); 2014 Gold Derby Awards: Documentary Feature (nominated); 2014 Moscow International Film Festival: Best Film of the Documentary Competition (nominated); 2014 Online Film & Television Association: Best Documentary Picture (nominated).

The Barkley Marathons: The Race That Eats Its Young, 2014
Director: Annika Iltis, Timothy James Kane; Running Time: 89 minutes; U.S.

Located just outside of Knoxville, Tennessee, within the Cumberland Mountains, Brushy Mountain State Penitentiary was a maximum security prison that once housed James Earl Ray, the man who assassinated Martin Luther King in 1968. Ray made an ill-fated escape attempt from Brushy Mountain in 1977, but was captured within three days after traveling only eight miles from prison grounds. This may prove that Ray was a poor trekker, poor outdoorsman, or even poorly motivated, but if definitely proves that the terrain of the area is not for the average hiker. The supposed escape route that Ray attempted has taken on new meaning over the last 30 years as it is the origin for what has become one of the most grueling trail races in the world. Every spring, 40 athletes receive a letter of condolence from either "Lazarus Lake" or "Raw Dog" after they are accepted to compete in the Barkley Marathons, but that only occurs after their $1.60 application fee and completed essay explaining why they should be allowed to compete has been received. It is the annual rituals such as this that make the Barkley Marathons an unforgettable experience, as well as a nearly unfinishable ultramarathon. In fact, in the race's first 25 years, only ten runners had even completed the full course, which consists of five marathon-distance loops (26 miles) full of surprises and mountainous terrain.

Filmmakers Annika Iltis and Timothy James Kane document the 2011 race in their film with the fitting title and subtitle: *The Barkley Marathons: The Race That Eats Its Young*. As is the case each year, competitors have come from all over the world to test themselves against this race designed by Gary "Lazarus Lake" Cantrell, a colorful Tennessean who looks more like a woodsman that one may encounter on the course rather than the experienced distance runner that he actually is. Other unique features of the race that Cantrell and co-designer Karl "Raw Dog" Henn have implemented include playing taps each time an entrant quits and requiring that a page from several strategically-placed books on the course be torn out and returned after loops. The book pages (which match the runners' numbers) assure the truthfulness of their completion of the loop and are always themed in some way, such as *Southern Discomfort* or *A Time to Die*. With the race being documented for the film, 88 percent of the runners had already bowed out by the 40-hour mark, but a few are still going strong even as they approach 100 total miles. Iltis and Kane's participatory mode approach to the filming of the actual race make for interesting viewing of the competition, but also for sympathetic viewing when the pain and disappointment is so clear. Available via DVD and streaming options, the film enjoyed a very successful festival run.

Awards: 2014 Austin Film Festival: Documentary Feature Audience Award; 2015 Kansas City Film Fest: Heartland—Best Documentary Feature Festival Prize; 2015 Sheffield Adventure Film Festival: Audience Award; 2015 Hot Docs Canadian International Documentary Festival: Best Documentary (nominated); 2015 Nashville Film Festival: Documentary Grand Jury Prize (nominated).

Baseball Girls, 1995

Director: Lois Siegel; Running Time: 82 minutes; Canada.

Produced by the National Film Board of Canada and directed by Lois Siegel, *Baseball Girls* is an interesting examination of women's participation in baseball and softball. The film features a mixture of historical analysis and contemporary documentation of women involved in both baseball and softball. In the same way that Ken Burns did with his fantastic nine-part documentary series, *Baseball*, which aired on PBS in 1994, Siegel makes great use of archival material in exploring the historical role that women have played in Major League Baseball. It is also interesting that Burns's work and Siegel's quirky, gender-specific film both came at roughly the same time as the MLB player's strike, which shortened the 1994 and 1995 seasons and cancelled the 1994 postseason altogether. Another interesting aspect of Siegel's film is that she turns it into something of a nonlinear narrative, at one moment focusing on contemporary women's fast pitch softball then tying in historical anecdotes such as Effa Manley, a Negro Leagues team owner and the first woman inducted into the Baseball Hall of Fame.

Prior to visiting a recreational slow-pitch softball league team in Canada, where the women play for camaraderie and relaxation, Siegel provides some interesting history about the "Bloomer Girls," the popular baseball teams of women who barnstormed the country playing male teams in the early part of the 20th century. From there, a look at more serious fast-pitch softball is provided with a visit to the first annual Canada Cup International Fast-Pitch Championships at the Softball City complex in Surrey, British Columbia. Michelle Granger, one of the game's most dominant pitchers and a four-time NCAA All-American, is featured here. Former big league pitcher Bill "Spaceman" Lee is interviewed concerning his aunt, Annabelle Lee, who was a star in the All-American Girls Professional Baseball League. Featured in the 1992 hit movie *A League of Their Own*, the AAGPBL existed from 1943 to 1954 while many big leaguers were fulfilling military duty. The final segment of the film provides a nice piece of 1990s nostalgia with a visit to tryout camps for the Colorado Silver Bullets, the all-female professional baseball team (managed by Hall of Famer Phil Niekro) that existed from 1994 to 1997. The film is available for streaming online and in DVD from the director's website or the National Film Board of Canada's website

Awards: 1996 Athens Ohio International Film and Video Festival: Documentary Film Award; 1996 Palermo International Sport Film Festival: Targa Citta' Di Palermo Award; 1998 Toronto Film Critics: Bronze Apple Award.

The Battered Bastards of Baseball, 2014

Director: Chapman Way, Maclain Way; Running Time: 73 minutes; U.S.

"Major League Baseball teams have farm clubs for one reason only, and that's to develop players. They don't care if the farm club wins, they don't really care about the team, they don't care about the city, and they have no investment in the city." That is the way one interview subject in the wildly entertaining 2014 film *The Battered Bastards of Baseball* describes the system of professional baseball across America in which minor league teams are contractually affiliated with the clubs of Major League Baseball. Within that farm system structure, there are different classification levels and players frequently move up or down depending on their development and talent. This system wasn't always the case, though. At one time, many minor league teams were unaffiliated with clubs at a higher level, operating independently, which meant that they had a steadier presence and a greater connection to the city in which they played. By the 1970s, however, as baseball had become more business-oriented and franchises wanted to widen their player pools through the farm system, the number of independent minor league clubs had dwindled from hundreds down to zero. Brothers Chapman and Maclain Way, in their first feature film, revisit a captivating piece of sports history with their examination of the independent Portland Mavericks baseball club and the five-year shaking that it caused within the business of organized professional baseball.

The Way brothers are nephews of actor (and former minor league player) Kurt Russell and grandsons of actor Bing Russell, who had played and studied baseball so much that he produced instructional videos for kids during the 1960s. In 1973, Russell found himself with lots of free time after the TV show *Bonanza* had been cancelled (on which he played lawman Clem Foster) so he turned to his true passion of baseball and began the noble experiment of bringing an independent minor league team to the city of Portland, Oregon, which had just seen its team of 70 years, the class Triple-A Portland Beavers, relocate to Spokane, Washington. The Beavers had left because of lackluster play and poor attendance, so Russell's notion of a class Single-A team being successful there was laughable to most, and especially absurd considering that his independent team would be playing against the well-paid, top draft choices of major league clubs ("No Wonder They're Called Mavericks" 1B). Instead, Russell held tryouts open to anyone, but particularly wanted players that were castoffs and rejected by the baseball establishment. Despite the fact that they would be playing for peanuts compared to typical minor leaguers, players came from all over to try out and a certain collective personality began to take shape as Russell built his team. The Way Brothers add plenty of wrinkles to their typical underdog theme with anecdotal evidence of the team's antics, but also provide lots of archival footage to prove that the stories are true.

Beginning with Russell as the team's owner, former player-turned night club impresario Frank Peters as its manager, and even future Academy Award-nominated filmmaker Todd Field (*In the Bedroom*, 2001, *Little Children*, 2006) serving as its batboy, the team itself carried a theme of outsiders bucking the system. With the freewheeling team built around speed, Russell shook the foundation of the establishment in everything he did, including the hiring of the first female and later the first Asian-American to serve as general manager of a professional team. Russell even signed former big league pitcher Jim Bouton in 1975. Bouton had effectively been blacklisted by MLB clubs after the publication of his controversial tell-all book *Ball Four* in 1969 (the title of the film comes from a passage Bouton uses in *Ball Four*). The many interview subjects all seem to agree that the other clubs in the Northwest League were so bent on beating Russell that they sent double and Triple-A players down to their Single-A clubs for the playoffs just to prevent Russell from winning the pennant. After the Mavericks five winning seasons with record-setting attendance, Major League Baseball took a renewed interest in Portland and invoked territorial rights, which they were allowed to do by not being subject to anti-trust laws, but they would have to buy Russell out. The notion of winning the battle but losing the war might apply to Russell and the Portland Mavericks. Following a Sundance premiere, the film was purchased by Netflix for distribution and its rights for a possible narrative feature adaptation were highly sought after as well.

Awards: 2013 Tribeca Film Institute/ESPN Prize; 2014 Sundance Film Festival: Film Selected.

Bending Steel, 2013

Director: Dave Carroll; Running Time: 92 minutes; U.S.

Chris Schoeck is a New York City personal trainer with a peculiar obsession and a unique existence. He readily admits that he really has no friends or relationships outside of his parents, and even acknowledges that he doesn't want any because he finds getting involved to be onerous and too effort-consuming. He discusses his alienation by explaining that he's always felt extraterrestrial to everyone and everything around him. Schoeck's single-minded determination to become a professional strongman (or "old-time strongman") seems to be his lone focus in life and is what finally brings him out of his shell. This quest, the subject matter for the film *Bending Steel* by director Dave Carroll, becomes oddly inspiring and thoroughly fascinating. The title refers to the most common feat of strength performed by the small fraternity of muscle men who harken back to Vaudeville days with their performances, but otherwise look like run of the mill middle-aged men. Schoeck first reaches out to Chris "Haircelues" Rider, an advanced and actively performing strongman, who in turn introduces Schoeck to a whole community of like-minded individuals. Very likeable, but obviously vulnerable, Schoeck finds a support group and surrogate family within this subculture, and through them he conquers his fears of performing live and reforms his misanthropic ways.

Carroll primarily explores the themes of community and family, but also offers a more simplistic and personal introspective journey. While there may be some question as to how sports-oriented the sideshow concept of *Bending Steel* really is, the feats of strength and the training that goes into them is most certainly in the realm of sports and competition. Schoeck, for example, practices this craft routinely in a cage in his basement, bending nails, steel bars, horseshoes, and ripping apart phone books. At well under six feet tall and roughly 150 lbs., the fact that Schoeck does not have the hulking frame of a bodybuilder makes his obsession all the more compelling. Rider, who quickly becomes a mentor to Schoeck, does have a more physically-imposing build, but still not that of a bodybuilder's, as one may expect with a professional strongman. With his long red hair and beard aiding his persona, Rider begins to teach Schoeck the important aspect of showmanship. Before Schoeck and Rider begin to organize an old-time strongman exhibition at Coney Island, just like the ones from a century ago, they visit Schoeck's parents to explain their plans. It is here that viewers gain an extra insight into some of the self-esteem issues that seem to be at the heart of Schoeck's reclusiveness. While his parents do not necessarily seem unloving, they are obviously not supportive of his strongman aspirations.

Part of the allure of *Bending Steel* is that this community of performers all regularly acknowledge the historical roots of what they are doing, and even speak about the strongmen of old in the same vein as pioneering Hall of Famers in traditional sports. Schoeck and Rider pay a visit to Slim "The Hammerman" Farman, who is now 76 years old, but can still perform the leverage lift that made him famous—balancing two 26-pound sledgehammers inches from his head using only his wrist strength. Perhaps the

Chris Schoeck, the subject of *Bending Steel* (2013), has a unique obsession relating to sports and competition.

most revered strongman of all was Farman's mentor, Joseph "The Mighty Atom" Greenstein, who stood only five feet, four inches tall and weighed 145 pounds, but performed feats so astonishing throughout the 20th century that he was regularly featured in "Ripley's Believe It or Not." Also featured is Dennis Rogers, who appeared on various television shows performing an assortment of strength feats in the 1990s and has been considered "pound-for-pound" the strongest man in the world. Rogers, in particular, seems to connect with and inspire Schoeck to reach new heights in his quest. It is in a conversation with Rogers that Schoeck reveals another one of his demons: he is a recovering alcoholic, who was drinking heavily by the age of 12. Connecting the overarching theme of community and illuminating the close bond that Schoeck has made with his new family, the film's final scenes take place at the Coney Island show, where Carroll focuses in on the empty seats reserved for Schoeck's parents. The film is widely available in streaming format, but has yet to be released via DVD.

Awards: 2013 Camden International Film Festival: Audience Award, Emerging Cinematic Vision Award (Dave Carroll, Ryan Scafuro); 2013 Key West Film Festival: Audience Award; 2014 Cinema Eye Honors Awards: The Unforgettables Award (Chris Schoeck), Spotlight Award (nominated); 2014 Fargo Film Festival: Best Documentary Feature, Best in Show; 2014 Oxford Film Festival: Best Documentary Jury Award; 2013 BendFilm Festival: Best Documentary Jury Prize (nominated); 2013 Calgary International Film Festival: Best International Documentary (nominated), Maverick Award (nominated); 2013 Hot Springs Documentary Film Festival: McKinnis Sports Documentary Award (nominated); 2013 Indianapolis International Film Festival: Best Documentary Grand Jury Prize (nominated); 2013 Kansas International Film Festival: Best Documentary Audience Award (nominated); 2013 Sidewalk Film Festival: Best Documentary (nominated); 2013 Woods Hole Film Festival: Best Documentary Feature Jury Prize (nominated).

Beyond the Mat, 1999

Director: Barry Blaustein; Running Time: 102 minutes; U.S.

Barry W. Blaustein's 1999 award-winning film begins on a very personal level, with the filmmaker explaining that he is not really sure why he likes it, but he does. He also explains that it is no longer just a childhood obsession with him; he still watches it today, though he doesn't tell a lot people nowadays. The "it" that Blaustein is referring to is the sport of professional wrestling, which he quite openly acknowledges that he knows is nothing more than choreographed theatre with athleticism. In fact, he argues that most fans of professional wrestling know this as well, but it is this sense of theatre mixed with pageantry, "cheesy acting," and athleticism that is the sport's allure. And yes, most of its fans will argue that it is indeed a sport, even if the winners of the matches are predetermined. Blaustein spends quite a bit of time following the lives of three well-known professionals, but also focuses in on the corporate side of the business, by examining the World Wrestling Federation (WWF, now World Wrestling Entertainment or WWE) and Extreme Championship Wrestling (ECW) entities. Headed by CEO Vince McMahon, the former of these is a publicly-traded company worth nearly $1 billion that even employs writers, composers, and costume designers. The latter is described as an incredibly violent renegade company just starting out, a promotion where "old wrestlers go to be reborn and young wrestlers go to be discovered."

The wrestlers that Blaustein follows include Terry Funk, a 32-year veteran whose body is clearly breaking down from the physical demands of the sport. Funk knows that he should retire, and hears as much from his family and doctor, but cannot seem to do so. He has agreed to wrestle for ECW and help that promotion get off the ground. Mick Foley, known in the wrestling world as "Mankind," is truly a unique man who was one of the biggest stars in the business when the film was made. Blaustein says that his willingness to punish his body would be understandable if he were crazy, but he is actually the most normal of any wrestler he had met. Foley himself wishes to be referred to as "the world's most polite wrestler." One of the film's more controversial elements was that Foley's children can be seen being visibly upset and crying as their father takes a staged beating (from a young Dwayne "the Rock" Johnson). Finally, Jake "the Snake" Roberts was one of the biggest stars in the business during the 1980s, but is now dealing with substance abuse and is estranged from his family. Rather than focusing only on these three main characters, Blaustein offers a personal look at several other wrestlers who had yet to make it big, and generally examines what it is that makes them want to get into the sport. *Beyond the Mat* does a fantastic job of lending a sympathetic ear to fans of the sport who want to ignore the ridicule and enjoy the spectacle. Shortlisted for an Academy Award, the film is available via streaming and in DVD format with special features including commentary tracks by the director, Funk, and Foley.

Awards: 2000 Cinequest San Jose Film Festival: Best Documentary, Audience Favorite Choice Award, Documentary; 2000 South by Southwest Film Festival (SXSW): Documentary Feature, First Film Audience

Award; 2000 Directors Guild of America: Outstanding Directorial Achievement in Documentary (nominated); 2000 Las Vegas Film Critics Society Awards: Best Documentary (nominated).

Bicycle Dreams, 2009

Director: Stephen Auerbach; Running Time: 104 minutes; U.S.

The Race Across America is the world's longest human-powered race, in which bicyclists will each follow the same course from a designated starting point on the West Coast to a point on the East Coast. The 2005 edition of the race, which filmmaker Stephen Auerbach chronicles for his 2009 award-winning film *Bicycle Dreams*, is exactly 3,051.7 miles, from San Diego, California, to Atlantic City, New Jersey. The race has no planned rest stops or time stages, so the clock is always running for these extraordinary athletes who will typically finish the journey in eight or nine days after biking an average of roughly 375 miles per day. That is, of course, the averages for those who actually finish the race, and as the film explains in its first few minutes, only 48 percent of the 288 entrants since its inaugural year of 1982 have done so. Because the race takes place across the United States, riders not only have to deal with drastic changes in weather, altitude, and terrain, but also must do so while dealing with motorists on the road. This scenario, a grueling endurance race in which sleep deprivation and exhaustion are the norm, mixed often with auto traffic, is far more dangerous than it sounds.

Auerbach's participatory documentary technique works beautifully, as he cuts away to profile interviews with many of the riders and less formal interview commentary from members of their respective pit crews traveling along in vehicles. The early focus in the first several days is on the early leaders, Jure Robič, a Slovenian who is the defending champion, and Marko Baloh, another Slovenian who had dropped out of the 2003 race due to a blood clot in his lungs. The fact that Auerbach is still introducing new riders late in the film is just one aspect of his technique that separates it from other sports documentaries which chronicle a competition. His interesting choice of music is another aspect that really adds to this exceptionally well-made film. The inherent danger involved in the Race Across America becomes painfully apparent when tragedy strikes and a rider is killed in Colorado. This shocking tragedy not only creates a filmmaking hurdle for Auerbach, but also strikes viewers with a dose of reality that separates it from typical nonfiction. The film was released via DVD in 2009 amidst a strong festival run and worldwide screenings.

Awards: 2009 Breckenridge Festival of Film: Best Documentary Audience Award; 2009 Grand Rapids Film Festival: Best Documentary; 2009 Red Rock Film Festival: Best Documentary Feature Grand Jury Prize; 2009 Yosemite Film Festival: Best Director (Auerbach); 2010 Canada International Film Festival: Royal Reel Documentary Competition; 2010 Lake Arrowhead Film Festival: Best Documentary Feature; 2011 International Festival of Sports Movies Krasnogorski: Best Foreign Film.

Bigger, Stronger, Faster*, 2008
Director: Chris Bell; Running Time: 105 minutes; U.S.

Director Chris Bell grew up in an all–American, sports-minded family. He idolized Arnold Schwarzenegger, Sylvester Stallone, and Hulk Hogan—each a symbol of American values, patriotism, and hard work. What a shock it was when he learned that all three used steroids to help them achieve their success. Not only that, but Bell's older brother, Mike, a former college football player and professional wrestler, and his younger brother, Mark, a record-setting power lifter, have both used steroids for years. But is it really cheating, or is it downright American to try to be the best? The questions which Bell poses to the viewer don't end there. How is corrective eye surgery or pain-killing injections for athletes not considered cheating, or amphetamines for fighter pilots, or performance anxiety drugs for musicians, or even Viagra for porn stars? The scandal that ensued when it became known how widespread steroid usage was in Major League Baseball might have been the tipping point, but America has long had a culture of finding a competitive advantage, even when condoned steroid usage helped its Olympic teams in the 1950s. The issues are explored in whirlwind fashion, and from every possible angle, but eventually end up as a very personal dilemma. From the cute asterisk and play on words in the title (referring respectively to baseball's tainted home run record and the Olympic motto), to the self-deprecating narration, *Bigger, Stronger, Faster** is a clever film.

In participatory documentary fashion, Bell blurs the lines between, sports, science, pop culture, entertainment, and news in a way that few filmmakers ever do. He takes dead aim at America's obsession with winning and body image, selective morality, and even consumerism. Ultimately, Bell's debut film serves multiple purposes and can be used to straddle the fence, reinforcing positions on either side of the steroids debate. Largely, what it does is examine American values and asks the viewer to examine their own values. While it goes a long way in exposing the hypocrisy of some anti-performance enhancing drug campaigns and calling hogwash on many health risks associated with steroid usage, it also serves a cautionary role and doesn't exactly place users, or the whole muscle industry, in the best light. It is for certain, though, as entertaining and engrossing as nonfiction filmmaking gets. Only months after the film's release, Bell's dilemma became even more personal with the death of his older brother at only 37 years old, which according to Bell had a lot to do prescription drugs (Kilkenny). Sparked by both his brother's death and his own struggles with addiction that developed later, Bell completed a follow-up film in 2015, *Prescription Thugs*, which switches focus from steroids and the muscle industry to prescription drug abuse and Big Pharma. Additionally, Bell explored the world of overbearing parents and child athletes with his 2013 film *Trophy Kids*. After premiering at the 2008 Sundance Film Festival, *Bigger, Stronger, Faster** had a limited theatrical release and DVD release later in the year.

Awards: 2008 Houston Film Critics Society Awards: Best Documentary Feature (nominated); 2008 Karlovy Vary Fresh Films Fest: Special Mention; 2008 Karlovy Vary International Film Festival: Best Documentary Special Mention; 2008 Sundance Film Festival: Grand Jury Prize (nominated); 2008 Warsaw International Film Festival: Best Documentary (nominated); 2009 Cinema Eye Honors Awards: Outstanding Achievement in a Debut Feature Film (nominated); 2009 Prism Awards: Feature Film (nominated).

In his participatory documentary, *Bigger, Stronger, Faster** (2008), filmmaker Chris Bell examines how easily one can legally obtain human growth hormone.

Broken Noses, 1987
Director: Bruce Weber; Running Time: 75 minutes; U.S.

Renowned fashion photographer Bruce Weber's foray into feature filmmaking is full of the same artistic sexuality that his famous Calvin Klein underwear ads featured. By the mid–1990s, Weber had become well known for his black and white, nostalgic style of photographing chiseled male models, and controversial for his use of adolescent boys as models. That controversial element is evident in this poetic-mode boxing documentary, but will largely go undetected by the unsuspecting. Weber's use of black and white cinematography, covered with a smooth jazz soundtrack, provides a nostalgic feel and an artistic look at youngsters participating in the combat sport. The primary subject is former pro boxer Andy Minsker, who was once boxing on ESPN and an alternate for the 1984 U.S. Olympic Team, but is now past his prime in his mid–20s and coaching young pugilists at the Mount Scott Boxing Club in Portland, Oregon. Perfectly willing to show off his sculpted body, and always full of giddy, playful masculinity, Minsker is a perfect fit for the lens of Weber.

Though the film begins by introducing and nicknaming each of the club's young boxers as they pose for photographs, it soon diverts fully to a profile of their charismatic, and sometimes inappropriate, mentor. Minsker's boxing career is not explored as much as his mentoring and training techniques or the complex relationships he has with the people around him. It is alleged that Minsker suffered abuse from his stepfather, and it is clear that the relationship with his real father (also a former boxer) is strained, but he continues to be on good terms with both sets of parents. Interestingly, the relationships he has with Ed, his former trainer, and the children he now trains seem to be the most rewarding. The film's final scene is an artistic venture into an exhibition match between youth boxing clubs; as the youngsters swing wildly at one another, Joni James croons away with the soft rendition of "Too Young." The music of jazz icon Chet Baker (who was the subject of Weber's Oscar-nominated film *Let's Get Lost* the following year) features prominently as well. A festival hit in 1987 and 1988, including Sundance and Toronto, the film was released for home video by Kino International during the early 1990s and has recently made it to DVD.

Awards: 1988 International Documentary Association: IDA Award; 1988 Sundance Film Festival: Grand Jury Prize (nominated).

Brooklyn Castle, 2012
Director: Katie Dellamaggiore; Running Time: 101 minutes; U.S.

More than half of the students at Intermediate School 318 in Brooklyn, New York, come from homes falling well below the federal poverty level. Despite this, the school has an extra-curricular program that ranks as one of the best in the nation. But the extra-curricular stars at I.S. 318 are not athletes, they are chess players. To illustrate just how good the chess program has become, John Galvin, an assistant principal and coach of the chess team, says that they are thought of as the New York Yankees of chess. It is a good comparison considering that I.S. 318 has won just as many national chess titles since getting the program started in the 1990s as the Yankees have won World Series titles (27). Another illustration would be that Albert Einstein's chess rating of 1800 would make him only fourth-best on their team. *Brooklyn Castle,* by filmmaker Katie Dellamaggiore, takes a close look at the lives of a few of the team's key players while also exploring the issue of school funding for such programs. Dellamaggiore began chronicling the students in 2009, but during her filming public schools across the nation were faced with deep budget cuts due to the economic recession, and this was especially true in New York. The film's focus changed only slightly to include the aspect of how the students and the school deal with this dilemma.

From a sporting and competition aspect, chess makes for an interesting comparison to traditional activities because of the concentration required and commitment necessary to become a master. The students profiled in *Brooklyn Castle* lack neither. They include Patrick, a 7th grader who uses chess to overcome ADHD, Justus, a soft-spoken 6th grade prodigy who has some trouble with all the attention he's getting, Alexis, a 7th grader who is already mapping out his future, Rochelle, an 8th grader who plans on becoming the first African American female master, and finally Pobo, a 7th grader who is simply far too charming and charismatic to not win the student body presidential election. When the chess matches end, there are no celebrations or even cheers, only a simple handshake. Viewers unfamiliar with chess may not even be able to recognize who the winner was. Soon after though, away from the board, the disappointment of a loss is very clear. Obviously, these students are in it for more than just the perks of the many school-sponsored trips to competitions. Their commitment to the game and their passion to succeed in life thanks to the academic doors that may open to them because of their skill is truly uplifting. Following a festival run and limited theatrical release in 2012,

In *Brooklyn Castle* (2012), the chess team members are the extra-curricular stars at Intermediate School 318 in Brooklyn, New York.

the film was aired via the POV film series on PBS. The film has also been acquired by Sony Pictures with a narrative feature remake reportedly in the works.

Awards: 2012 Newport Beach Film Festival: Documentary Audience Award; 2012 Philadelphia Film Festival: Documentary Showcase Audience Award; 2012 South by Southwest Film Festival (SXSW): Documentary Spotlight Audience Award; 2013 Golden Trailer Awards: Best Documentary; 2012 Hot Docs Canadian International Documentary Festival: Top Ten Audience Favorite; 2013 Black Reel Awards: Best Documentary (nominated); 2013 Image Awards: Outstanding Documentary (nominated); 2014 News and Documentary Emmy Awards: Outstanding Coverage of a Current News Story, Long Form (nominated).

Chasing the Horizon, 2006

Director: Markus Canter, Mason Canter; Running Time: 88 minutes; U.S.

Life is a journey, not a destination. The journey of three men, Milo Brown, Jeff Lloyd, and Toby O'Mara, as they form Team Horizon and compete in the SCORE Baja 1000 is documented in the 2006 film *Chasing the Horizon* by directors Markus and Mason Canter (as "the Flying Canter Brothers"). The Baja 1000 is the longest point-to-point race in the world. It has been an officially-sanctioned race since 1967 and takes place every year in the Baja California Peninsula of Mexico. Some of the famous names from outside the world of off-road racing that have competed in the Baja 1000 include NASCAR's Robby Gordon and Jimmie Johnson, actors Steve McQueen, Paul Newman, James Garner, and Patrick Dempsey, motorcyclists Malcolm Smith and Travis Pastrana, and musicians Ted Nugent and Michael Nesmith. In their participatory mode film with a perfectly fitting hard rock soundtrack, the Canter Brothers do not spend too much time on the race's unique history, but instead focus on the firestorm of personalities that have come together to form Team Horizon. Brown, the team's captain, is an ex-con who owns a junkyard; Lloyd, the main driver and financer has been both homeless and a millionaire in his lifetime; and finally O'Mara, a plumber by trade, is the team's chief mechanic.

As the team tries to ready the truck for racing, the pressure very clearly starts to mount and tempers flare multiple times during filming. With Lloyd being the financer of the team and Brown and O'Mara being the ones building the truck, things get tense first when the truck isn't ready for testing, next when a night of drinking during a test run leads to a flat tire and stranded truck, and finally when Lloyd finds expensive international phone calls from the Mexican hotel on his bill. Despite the multiple times that tempers flared almost to the point of punches, it is clear that the team is something of a family, albeit a highly dysfunctional one. As intertitles in the film keep viewers aware of the looming race day, it serves the purpose of highlighting the pressure that exists in the situation. Not only is this pressure easy to sense, it also becomes somewhat painful to realize the money that Lloyd is putting into his dream of racing the Baja 1000—a dream that could very easily end with nothing to show for it except the story. When race day finally rolls around, Lloyd's family shows up for support and the film's theme of family is stressed even more. Ultimately, lady luck did no favors for Team Horizon and their race ends prematurely. The Canter Brothers turn what might have been an overly emotional final scene into more of a prime documentary film moment by briefly visiting scores of other teams who suffered the same fate. The film is difficult to locate in DVD format, but is available for streaming online.

Awards: 2006 Great Lakes Film Festival: Best Documentary Feature Festival Prize, Best Documentary Grand Jury Prize; 2006 Newport Beach Film Festival: Best Documentary; 2006 San Diego Film Festival: Best Documentary Festival Award; 2006 Valley Film Festival: Best Documentary 10 Degrees Hotter Award.

The Conquest of Everest, 1953

Director: George Lowe; Running Time: 78 minutes; U.K.

One of the earliest feature length English language sports documentaries, *The Conquest of Everest* was named the best British documentary film of 1953 and was nominated for an Academy Award in the United States. Documenting the first successful ascent to the summit of the earth's highest peak, Mount Everest in Nepal, the film's director was George Lowe, a New Zealand-born mountaineer who was Oscar-nominated a second time for his 1958 film *Antarctic Crossing*. The film begins with the unique piece of history that the coronation of Queen Elizabeth II was taking place on the same day, June 2, 1953, when news broke in London of the successful ascent. Newspaper headlines are shown reading "The Crowning Glory: Everest is Climbed." Before focusing in on the 1953 expedition that made New Zealander Edmund Hillary and Nepalese Sherpa Tenzing Norgay internationally famous, the film first provides some background on previous attempts to summit Everest. Among these was the infamous 1924 expedition of George Mallory and Sandy Irvine, who both disappeared during their attempt. As for the ninth known attempt and the first successful ascent, the 1953 expedition was led by British Colonel John Hunt and totaled over 400 people, including 362 porters and 20 Sherpas. Although dated, the film offers a solid documentation of the expedition and is fascinating for those interested in mountaineering or history. It can be found for online streaming and also was released in DVD format in 2014.

Awards: 1953 National Board of Review: Top Foreign Film; 1953 New York Film Critics Circle Awards: Special Citation, Best Film (2nd place); 1954 BAFTA Awards: Best Documentary Film, Certificate of Merit (Thomas Stobart); 1954 Academy Awards: Best Documentary Feature (nominated).

The Crash Reel, 2013

Director: Lucy Walker; Running Time: 108 minutes; U.S.

The inspirational story of Kevin Pearce is told in unique fashion by filmmaker Lucy Walker (*Blindsight*, 2006, *Waste Land*, 2010) using a mixture of archival footage and present-day observational, fly-on-the-wall filming. By 2009, snowboarding had not only moved from simply a recreational activity to an Olympic sport, but it had also become a sport in which very young, highly-specialized extreme sports athletes could become very wealthy through professional sponsorships. Kevin Pearce was one of those athletes, who by 2009 had developed an intense rivalry with Shaun White for American snowboarding supremacy. On New Year's Eve of 2009, Pearce was critically injured while training in Park City, Utah, and spent the next five months rehabilitating from a traumatic brain injury. The jarring non-linear narrative begins with the months leading up to the 2010 Winter Olympics in Vancouver. Pearce and a group of fellow professional snowboarders are training for the games when Pearce suffers a near-fatal head injury while being filmed. Immediately cutting from scenes of partying and lighthearted snowboarding fun to a soundless, black screen before revisiting the scene's aftermath with his friends visually shaken, Walker's filmmaking recreates the seriousness of the situation.

The mixture of archival footage from Pearce's early years as a non-professional daredevil and the more recent footage of him becoming one of the best snowboarders in the world are especially effective in not only introducing him, but also in introducing the sport that had skyrocketed in popularity during the 2000s. The remarkable recovery that Pearce made over the next several months is documented, as is the love and support he received from his friends and family over that time. Especially unique in Pearce's story is that one of his three brothers, David, has Down Syndrome and has struggled himself to come to grips with the fact that his disability is not going away. When Pearce begins to recover even more fully, his desire is to snowboard again, but his recovery is nowhere near as advanced as he thinks it is. David's ability to accept his limitations doesn't exactly inspire Kevin to do the same as his push to return to boarding places an obvious strain on the family. While the story of Pearce's injury and recovery may be the film's primary focus, the aspect of the inherent danger in the way that the sport continually pushes the boundaries of safety is a clear issue as well.

Walker's film has a lot going on, but the various avenues that she goes down are not gratuitous or arbitrary; they are needed for the full picture of Pearce. Each of the subjects that *The Crash Reel* embraces could easily become their own film, but the complexity of Pearce's story requires them to be tied together. The emotional aspect of Pearce's recovery and his desire to board again despite doctors' orders, traumatic brain injury itself, the strange friendship-turned-rivalry between Pearce and White, the safety of the increasingly-dangerous sport and the culpability of sponsors, and the loving relationship that Pearce has with his intellectually-disabled brother are all subjects worthy of a more thorough examination. Likewise, the film may miss another worthy examination by not approaching professional extreme sports as actual occupations, akin to any other sporting or athletic profession. Granted, such a job is extremely atypical, and it appears that many professional snowboarders may be fortunate in that affluence allows for their chosen profession to begin with, but the fact remains that a catastrophic injury ends that career and income. Regardless, *The Crash Reel* is a fantastic film about serious subjects in a sport that has largely failed to be taken seriously in nonfiction filmmaking. Following a festival run across the world, limited theatrical release, and an HBO premiere in 2013, the film was shortlisted for the Documentary Feature Academy Award and released in DVD format in 2014.

Awards: 2013 Dallas International Film Festival: Audience Award; 2013 Melbourne International Film Festival: Most Popular Documentary; 2013 New Hampshire Film Festival: Best Documentary Film; 2013 Port Townsend Film Festival: Best Documentary Film; 2013 Seattle International Film Festival: Documentary Special Jury Award, Documentary Award (nominated); 2013 South by Southwest (SXSW) Film Festival: Festival Favorites Audience Award; 2013 Telluride Mountain Film Festival: Student Film Award; 2013 Whistler Film Festival: Best Mountain Culture Film; 2014 Cinema Eye Honors Awards: Outstanding Achievement in Nonfiction Filmmaking for Television, Audience Choice Prize (nominated); 2014 News and Documentary Emmy Awards: Outstanding Informational Programming—Long Form; 2013 Gotham Awards: Best Documentary (nominated); 2013 Miami Film Festival: Knight Documentary Competition Grand Jury Prize (nominated); 2013 Milwaukee Film Festival: Best Film (nominated); 2013 Moscow International Film Festival: Best Film of the Documentary Competition (nominated). 2014 Directors Guild of America: Outstanding Directorial Achievement in Documentary DGA Award (Walker, nominated).

Dark Horse: The Incredible True Story of Dream Alliance, 2015

Director: Louise Osmond; Running Time: 85 minutes; U.K.

As an English figure of speech, "the sport of kings" first came into existence referring to war, but in the 19th century it began to be used as way to describe the primarily English aristocracy that participated in the sport of horse racing. As one historian explains in the 2015 film *Dark Horse: The Incredible True Story of Dream Alliance*, horse racing grew out of challenges from one wealthy person to another. It was very much the sport of the "rich, landed gentry," he adds. Just as she did in her 2006 film *Deep Water*, about yachtsman Donald Crowhurst and the 1968 *Sunday*

Times Golden Globe Race, filmmaker Louise Osmond becomes an extraordinary raconteur in order to tell the story of a South Wales mining village and the racehorse jointly owned by some of its citizens. The unique twist to the story is that the community owners of the horse were not only novices to the sport, but they most certainly were not the wealthy elites that have come to be associated with racehorse ownership.

The story begins with Jan Vokes, who was working as a barmaid at a Cefn Fforest pub in 1999 when she took an interest in breeding a racehorse after hearing one of the patrons discussing the sport and business of thoroughbred horse racing. It wasn't exactly a notion out of the blue as she had bred show budgies, champion racing pigeons, and whippets in her younger days. The only problem, however, is that because of the costs associated with the affluent sport, working-class people have never been able to really take part. As Vokes explains, she knew that these sorts of people liked to keep their sports to themselves and "keep us commoners out." Her plan was relatively simple—create a syndicate to share the costs. The community had seen its share of depression, as the mine closures had left many out of work, but it remained close-knit. Vokes was able to bring in 30 neighbors willing to pay £10 per week. Howard Davies, the one member who had any experience in the sport, explains that "the syndicate came together for one simple reason: they wanted to see if it could work."

Starting from square one and having already purchased a "cheap, but cheerful" broodmare (£300) with her husband Brian, Vokes then began looking for a stallion with stud fees closer to £3,000 than the typical fees more than double that amount. The appropriate name Dream Alliance was decided upon for the foal, and by the time that the syndicate began paying for his training, he certainly looked the part of a racehorse-to-be. While Osmond's themes of community and bucking the system take shape, the classical underdog story comes together just as one may expect. As Dream Alliance began winning, he became the community's horse, and for a community that had once enjoyed the mining boom but more recently had been exploited and abandoned by the industry, his winning ways were welcomed as a source of pride. Although Osmond takes no unfair shots at the sport of horse racing, the underlying theme of class differences is evident as the exclusivity and snobbery become apparent at some of the more prestigious races. Despite the fact that Vokes and the Dream Alliance syndicate did not set out to strike a blow for the working class, or even to prove some sort of point to the racing establishment, it is hard not to see their achievement as one to be celebrated on behalf of the have-nots in the well-to-do world of horse racing. Following a premiere at the 2015 Sundance Film Festival, the film was released on DVD and is also widely available for streaming.

Awards: 2015 British Independent Film Awards: Best Documentary; 2015 Golden Trailer Awards: Best Foreign Documentary Trailer; 2015 Sundance Film Festival: World Cinema Documentary Audience Award, World Cinema Documentary Grand Jury Prize (nominated); 2016 Critics Choice Documentary Awards: Best Sports Documentary (nominated).

Deep Water, 2006

Director: Louise Osmond, Jerry Rothwell; Running Time: 93 minutes; U.K.

The disturbing story of yachtsman Donald Crowhurst and the *Sunday Times* Golden Globe Race is retold in this award-winner from the same production team that brought the sporting adventure-turned-disaster story *Touching the Void* (2003) to film. Spurred by the public reception to Sir Francis Chichester's 1967 voyage, becoming the first person to sail around the world single-handed via the Great Capes of Africa, Australia, and South America, the *Sunday Times* sponsored and promoted this first-of-its-kind competition in 1968. The race differed from Chichester's accomplishment in that it must be a non-stop, solo circumnavigation (Chichester had stopped in Australia). Offering a trophy to the first finisher and a cash prize for the fastest time, the event was open to all comers, stipulating that they must set sail before October 31. Knowing that the real prize was fame similar to what Chichester had attained, several of the world's best sailors announced their intentions and sought sponsorship. The least well-known and experienced among nine contenders was Donald Crowhurst, a British businessman who had achieved little success manufacturing and selling navigational aids for sailors. Crowhurst found a wealthy sponsor, but had to sign a contract stipulating that he must repay the funding if he fails to start the race or drops out early. Essentially, Crowhurst had bet his life on winning, or at least finishing, a challenge that no one had ever undertaken and many thought impossible.

Despite starting at the last moment allowable in his custom-built, woefully-unprepared 41-foot trimaran and encountering early difficulties, Crowhurst suddenly began to report amazing progress in December, even claiming a single-day speed record. In reality, his trimaran was suffering severe damage and soon it became clear that going forward into the dangerous Southern Ocean would be a certain death. Crowhurst stopped all radio contact for months while he faced his dilemma and options:

dropping out of the race not only meant financial ruin for his family, but also humiliation because of his falsely reported positions, but traveling forward meant death. Using chilling archival material and interviews with his family, directors Louise Osmond and Jerry Rothwell piece together the amazing story of a man who chose a deceptive third option and saw things spiral out of control. Fellow competitors Robin Knox-Johnson, the race's eventual winner, and French author Bernard Moitessier, whose journey became spiritual and also ended with an odd twist, are heavily featured as well. *Deep Water* unfolds in the same gripping fashion as *Touching the Void*, but uses the traditional documentary techniques of narration (by Oscar-winner Tilda Swinton) and archival material to tell this story of fame and desperation. The DVD features include an eerie look at Crowhurst's boat, along with actual tape recordings, and separate short films on the other sailors, journalists covering the race, and the Crowhurst family.

Awards: 2006 Rome Film Fest: Best Documentary; 2007 San Diego Film Critics Society: Best Documentary; 2007 Australian Film Critics Association Awards: Best Documentary (commended); 2007 British Independent Film Awards: Best British Documentary (nominated).

Derby, 1971

Director: Robert Kaylor; Running Time: 93 minutes; U.S.

Director Robert Kaylor (*Carny*) and producer William Richert (*My Own Private Idaho*) set out to make a documentary about roller derby in 1970, but ended up with a film more about a young man following his dreams. With a narrative feel and lots of banked-track action, *Derby* was released as a feature presentation during the height of America's roller derby craze in the early 1970s. Although the sport has seen something of a revival and increased notoriety with women's leagues at the grassroots and regional levels in recent years, the nationwide popularity of roller derby in the late 1960s and early 1970s is almost hard to fathom nowadays. With millions of television viewers each week and crowd-sizes rivaling that of the traditional professional sports, the sport and spectacle of roller derby was indeed a large part of American culture at the time of the film's release.

The film's central character is Mike Snell, a cocky and philandering Ohio man, who dreams of leaving his blue-collar job for roller derby stardom. When not focusing on the cultural phenomena of roller derby through the lives of Snell and his family, Kaylor glimpses in on the professional skaters themselves as they speak about their craft. In particular, the sport's biggest star, Charlie O'Connell, is profiled as the serious athlete in a spectacle sport similar to professional wrestling and the singular inspiration for Snell because of his $50,000 salary. *Derby* explores the themes of following one's dream and fandom in this unique sport, but also provides a sociological examination of lower middle class life in a dying Rust Belt town. Chock full of 1970s nostalgia, the rare original director's cut of the film, with its original R-rating, has been released on DVD by Code Red and features two insightful commentary tracks.

Awards: 1972 National Society of Film Critics: Special Award (Kaylor).

Dogtown and Z-Boys, 2001

Director: Stacy Peralta; Running Time: 91 minutes; U.S.

Dogtown is an economically-depressed area of Santa Monica, where Pacific Ocean Park once resided. The Z-Boys are a group of young surfers-turned-skateboarders who formed the Zephyr Competition Team and revolutionized the sport and industry of skateboarding in the 1970s. As skateboarding was inspired by surfing culture on the California coast, the surfing-to-skating transition is integral not only to the Z-Boys story, but to the sport itself. What started as a surfer's land hobby in the late 1950s grew into organized competitions by the mid–1960s, but it soon disappeared and was considered only a passing fad. By the early 1970s, however, new advances in equipment prompted a rebirth in the popularity of skateboarding, and the Zephyr team became true pioneers of a burgeoning movement. Almost by accident, the young skaters introduced the freestyle and aerial movements when they began skating and filming themselves in swimming pools left empty because of the 1976 California drought. Full of ego and attitude, the team largely consisted of street kids who found sponsorship and guidance in Skip Engbloom, Jeff Ho, and photojournalist Craig Stecyk, co-owners and founders of the Jeff Ho Surfboards and Zephyr Productions Shop.

Using actual footage of the event, the film tracks how the Z-Boys began to gain notoriety at the 1975 Del Mar Nationals competition, where their surfing style of skating was in complete contrast to the upright style from the 1960s. Thanks largely to a series of articles written by Stecyk for *Skateboarder Magazine*, the Z-Boys became famous and soon began to leave the Zephyr team for more lucrative sponsorships. With a pace and editing similar to the action it details, the story most prominently profiles

Z-Boys Jay Adams, who missed his opportunity to cash in and wound up in prison, Tony Alva, who is widely regarded as the most important skater of all time, and the filmmaker himself, Stacy Peralta. Viewing skateboarding as his "ticket," and ultimately parlaying his fame into the business, management, and videography side of the sport, Peralta was clearly the visionary of the group. Narrated by Sean Penn, the award-winning film not only tells the Z-Boy story, but also provides a history of skateboarding with lots of interaction, personal reflection, archival footage, and a classic rock soundtrack that was nominated for a Grammy Award. In terms of critical acclaim, box office, and DVD sales, *Dogtown and Z-Boys* is one of the most successful sports documentaries of all-time.

Awards: 2001 AFI Fest: Best Documentary; 2001 Denver International Film Festival: Best New Feature-Length Documentary; 2001 Sundance Film Festival: Documentary Audience Award, Documentary Directing Award, Grand Jury Prize (nominated); 2002 Independent Spirit Awards: Best Documentary; 2002 Newport Beach Film Festival: Best Documentary; 2003 Grammy Awards: Best Compilation Soundtrack Album for a Motion Picture (nominated); 2003 Online Film and Television Association: Best Documentary (nominated); 2003 Online Film Critics Society Awards: Best Documentary (nominated); 2003 Phoenix Film Critics Society Awards: Best Documentary (nominated); 2003 Satellite Awards: Best Motion Picture, Documentary (nominated).

Doin' It in the Park: Pick-Up Basketball, New York City, 2012

Director: Kevin Couliau, Bobbito Garcia; Running Time: 83 minutes; U.S.

Serving as a videographic encyclopedia of pick-up or street basketball ("streetball"), *Doin' It in the Park* is an entertaining film focusing on outdoor playground basketball in various locations of New York City. Filmmakers Kevin Couliau and Bobbito Garcia explore this sporting subculture and how it relates to the city that is known as the worldwide Mecca of basketball. Couliau is a French photographer and Garcia is a New York DJ, radio host, and author. In their participatory mode documentary, the filmmakers examine the current basketball scene on a number of famous playgrounds, interviewing a host of contemporary players, while also providing a historical analysis, interviewing legendary players such as Pee Wee Kirkland and James "Fly" Williams. Altogether, Couliau and Garcia visit 180 different courts throughout the city's five boroughs to film over a single summer, but first they provide enough background to explain how this subculture came about. In 1934, as basketball was first beginning to be so closely associated with New York City, there were 119 playgrounds there. By 1960, there were nearly 800 playgrounds. The growth of playground basketball is obvious enough, but an aspect that often goes overlooked is that it has always been, and still is, free recreation for the masses.

Commonly referred to as "pick-up" basketball because teams are formed organically, and certainly not limited to the Big Apple, streetball employs a slew of unwritten rules and codes, but those often vary from playground to playground. With an emphasis on physical post play and slick ball handling, with moves such as the crossover, the culture of pick-up basketball has had a great influence on organized basketball. Likewise, the culture of pick-up has also given rise to nearly universal specialty games such as H-O-R-S-E and twenty-one that have been played for decades. Prior to zeroing in on the many locally-famous courts and playgrounds and the numerous well-known players who have been regulars there, Couliau and Garcia explore the origins and meanings of these specialty games. The courts featured most prominently include West 4th Street, known as "the Cage" due to the surrounding fence, Goat Park, named after legendary player Earl "The Goat" Manigault, and Rucker Park, which is the most famous of all due to legendary players such as Connie Hawkins, Tiny Archibald, and Julius Erving having been regulars there. Narrated by Garcia, and perhaps at times a little too enthusiastically, *Doin' It in the Park* is a film about basketball and New York City, but mostly a film about history and culture. The film is available in DVD or streaming format.

Awards: 2012 New Jersey International Film Festival: Best Documentary; 2012 Urbanworld Film Festival: Best Feature Audience Award; 2012 San Francisco Back Film Festival: Best Documentary (runner-up).

The Eagle Huntress, 2016

Director: Otto Bell; Running Time: 87 minutes; U.K./Mongolia/U.S.

Eagle hunting is a form of falconry in which trained golden eagles are used to catch small game such as foxes and rabbits. Practiced by the Kazakhs in Mongolia and other nomadic societies of Central Asia, it is a centuries-old tradition that is passed down from father to son and from one generation to the next. One of the most successful documentaries of 2016, *The Eagle Huntress* tells the story of Aisholpan Nurgaiv, a 13-year-old Kazakh girl from Mongolia who seeks to become one of the first females to master the skill. Although the elder eagle hunters of the area are very much against the female empowerment message represented in the film, Aisholpan's father ignores the built-in boundaries relegating women in their society to the home. In fact, he strongly supports Aisholpan's desire to hunt and allows her to enter the annual Golden Eagle Festival after they capture an eaglet for her to train and hunt with. First-time feature filmmaker Otto Bell found a great story and effectively explores this little-known cultural pursuit with the added aspect of sports and competition. The scenes taking place at the prestigious Golden Eagle Festival in the provincial capital of Olgii in the foothills of the Altai Mountains unfold in a way not at all uncommon to other sports stories, but it represents only a small portion of the overall story.

Similarly, the sequences in which Aisholpan and her father train her eagle can be thought of in the exact way that training occurs for virtually any sport or competition. However, the added aspect of having to first capture the yet-unable-to-fly bird, which they do during a nerve-racking early scene by climbing a mountain and scaling down a rocky cliff via rope, clearly connects this sport to nature and the physical environment in a way that few others could do. Aside from the gender barrier-breaking that Aisholpan eventually does, she is a very typical 13-year-old girl, as viewers see her interacting with other girls at the boarding school she attends through the week and even painting her fingernails while watching over her growing eagle. When the competing begins, Aisholpan does indeed set herself apart from other 13-year-olds as her eagle records the fastest time in one of the competitions and she wins the overall prize. Suggesting that the competition proves nothing, some of the older men are still opposed to the idea and now say that actual hunting is the only real test. As supportive as her father is, he may agree with this sentiment and soon takes Aisholpan on a hunt. The film's final sequence documents their grueling hunt deep into the freezing, snow-covered mountains.

The Eagle Huntress succeeds in finding a great story and delivering it with cinematic flare, but the film itself has a certain feel that defies the tradition of cinéma vérité, or fly-on-the-wall, observational documentaries. Regardless of whether or not Bell took some liberties for dramatic effect, as some have suggested in the months since it was released and shortlisted for an Academy Award, the story highlights a unique sport and competition from a unique culture. Bell's examination of gender is not heavy-handed, but clearly present throughout. His central theme is that of breaking gender barriers, but secondary themes of cultural traditions, father-daughter relationships, and even man's relationship with nature are present as well. With a film examining a cultural tradition that rejects modernity, it is especially interesting that a thoroughly modern trend of filmmaking (drone photography by Simon Niblett) was so effectively used to capture some of the breathtaking scenes. While never fully committing to expository mode documentary narration, the film does feature voice-over descriptions for some scenes that are provided by actress Daisy Ridley, of *Star Wars: The Force Awakens* (2015) fame. Popular Australian singer/songwriter Sia provides an original song for the film *Angel by the Wings*, which accompanies the end credits and really brings home the female empowerment theme. Following a successful festival run and wide theatrical release, *The Eagle Huntress* was released in streaming and DVD format.

Awards: 2016 Denver International Film Festival: Documentary Film People's Choice Award; 2016 Hamptons International Film Festival: Documentary Feature Golden Starfish Award; 2016 Hawaii International Film Festival: Best Documentary Feature Audience Award; 2016 Middleburg Film Festival: Documentary Feature Audience Award; 2016 Mill Valley Film Festival: Valley of the Docs Audience Award; 2016 National Board of Review: Top Five Documentaries; 2017 Cinema Eye Honors Awards: The Unforgettables (Aisholpan Nurgaiv), Outstanding Achievement in Production (Otto Bell, Sharon Chang, Stacey Reiss—nominated), Outstanding Achievement in Cinematography (Simon Niblett—nominated), Outstanding Achievement in a Debut Feature Film (Bell—nominated); 2016 Amsterdam International Documentary Film Festival: Audience Award (3rd Place); 2016 Aspen Filmfest: Best Documentary Audience Award (2nd Place); 2016 Critics Choice Documentary Awards: Best Song in a Documentary (Sia: "Angel by the Wings," nominated), Best First Documentary (Bell—nominated), Best Sports Documentary (nominated); 2016 Las Vegas Film Critics Society Awards: Best Documentary, nominated), 2016 Melbourne International Film Festival: Most Popular Documentary (2nd Place); 2016 Satellite Awards: Best Motion Picture, Documentary (nominated); 2016 St Louis Film Critics Association: Best Documentary Film (nominated); 2016 Women Film Critics Circle Awards: Best Documentary by or About Women (nominated); 2017 BAFTA Awards: Best Documentary (nominated); 2017 Directors Guild of America: Outstanding Directorial Achievement in Documentary (nominated); 2017 London Critics Circle Film Awards: Documentary of the Year (nominated); 2017 Producers Guild of America Awards: Outstanding Producer of Documentary Theatrical Motion Pictures (Bell, Reiss—nominated).

The Endless Summer, 1966

Director: Bruce Brown; Running Time: 95 minutes; U.S.

Narrative feature films about beach culture became popular with moviegoers during the 1960s as an extension of the surfing craze on the West Coast during the same time. The activity and later sport of surfing, however, was rarely ever a focal point of these so-called "beach party films," which instead relied on campy teenage humor to define the genre. At the same time, a serious examination of surfing was indeed taking place through documentary films, defining a separate genre known as "surf films" and delighting enthusiasts of the budding recreational sport. Although these sort of surf films were popular with surfers themselves during the 1950s, it wasn't until Bruce Brown's *The Endless Summer* was released theatrically across the nation in 1966 that a truly groundbreaking surfing documentary was made. Despite initially being rejected by major distributors, *The Endless Summer* grossed over $20 million worldwide upon its release and has a legacy arguably as important as any sports documentary.

As for the film itself, Brown follows and narrates as two young surfers go from location-to-location across the globe in search of waves and the never-ending summer climate. The surfers, Robert August and Mike Hynson, find waves in Australia, Hawaii, New Zealand, South Africa, and Tahiti. All the while, August and Hynson interact with the locals and take in the scenery and culture of the respective locales. The legacy of Brown's film is not only that it introduced this relatively new sport and culture to so many people, or that it introduced new locations to already-seasoned surfers, but rather that it did so with a fun and carefree narrative approach rather than the typical documentary technique of straight-faced information and evidence. Working alongside his son Dana, Brown's follow-up sequel, *The Endless Summer II*, was released in 1994. In addition to his many surf films, Brown also explored motorcycle racing with his 1971 Oscar-nominated feature *On Any Sunday*.

Awards: 2002 National Film Preservation Board: Selected for preservation in the National Film Registry at the Library of Congress.

Facing Ali, 2009

Director: Pete McCormack; Running Time: 100 minutes; U.S.

With the myriad of documentary films focusing on the life and boxing career of Muhammad Ali, it was a surprise that a contemporary film could cover the subject in such a refreshing way. Filmmaker Pete McCormack does this by examining Ali through the perspectives of ten famous heavyweights who faced the three-time world champion throughout his 20-year career. Credit for this unique concept goes to author Stephen Brunt, whose 2003 book of the same title was the basis for the film. Canadian producer Derik Murray knew immediately that the approach of having Ali's most famous opponents tell their stories would translate into a feature documentary. The end result was a film which not only provides a new look at Ali by allowing other champions to speak for and about him, but also one which allows those other champions to equally shine. In essence, it is a series of short biographical sketches of some of the greatest heavyweights of the 1960s and 1970s. Loaded with special features, the DVD was released following the film's run through several film festivals.

The ten interview subjects have more of a common bond than being the best opponents Ali ever faced in the ring, they also agree that facing Ali was the pinnacle of their respective careers. Likewise, the matches discussed represent the full spectrum of Ali's career: from British champion Henry Cooper, whose first match with Ali was in 1963 just before he became world champion for the first time, to Larry Holmes, who defeated Ali so badly in 1980 that it left no doubt his career was at the end. Canadian bruiser George Chuvalo and the singing boxer Ernie Terrell discuss their respective matches in 1966 and 1967, when Ali was first becoming a controversial figure. Joe Frazier, Ken Norton, George Foreman, Ron Lyle, Earnie Shavers, and Leon Spinks discuss their great bouts with Ali during the 1970s. Chuvalo, Foreman and Lyle, in particular, are captivating in telling their stories: Chuvalo has lost two sons to drug overdoses and his wife and another son to suicide; Foreman charismatically shares his conversion experience of becoming a born-again Christian; and Lyle speaks about his life in prison and a near-death experience after he was stabbed. Most poignantly, though, is Frazier, who finally seems willing to drop his guard a little when speaking about his fierce rival. *Facing Ali* is widely available in streaming format and was released on DVD in 2009.

Awards: 2009 Vancouver Film Festival: Most Popular International Documentary Film; 2010 Leo Awards: Best Cinematography in a Documentary Program or Series (Ian Kerr), Best Direction in a Documentary Program or Series, Best Feature-Length Documentary Program (Derik Murray and Paul Gertz), Best Picture Editing in a Documentary Program or Series (Jesse James Miller); 2010 Vancouver Film Critics Circle: Best British Columbia Film.

Fallen Champ: The Untold Story of Mike Tyson, 1993

Director: Barbara Kopple; Running Time: 93 minutes; U.S.

Although even more bizarre and dramatic chapters of his life would unfold later, two-time Academy Award-winning filmmaker Barbara Kopple (*Harlan County, USA,* 1976, *American Dream,* 1990) was tasked with summing up the meteoric rise and fall from grace of controversial heavyweight champion Mike Tyson to this point in his career. In February of 1993, just less than a year after Tyson was sentenced to six years in prison for a rape conviction, NBC aired *Fallen Champ: The Untold Story of Mike Tyson,* conspicuously billing it as a reality movie rather than a documentary film. A mix of unique archival footage of Tyson as an amateur and candid interviews with those few people closest to the future champ reveal a truly confounding teen, showing ominous and disturbing signs of what might lay ahead, while at the same time showing a shy and sensitive young man. The film documents the champ's brutal dominance at the top of the sport, in which he captivated the world with his streak of 27 consecutive victories in route to becoming the youngest heavyweight champion in history. Tyson's first 19 professional bouts from March of 1985 to March of 1986 all resulted in either knockouts or technical knockouts, and 12 of those came in the first round.

Only a few years before becoming one of the most recognizable sports figures in the world, Tyson was a petty criminal whose willingness to learn the art of boxing impressed a counselor at the Tryon School for Boys in Johnstown, New York. The impression he made with the youth counselor led to his tutelage under legendary fight manager Cus D'Amato, which proved to be the first loving guidance of his life. D'Amato passed away just before Tyson won the title in 1986, and perhaps the one person who could have kept the champ grounded and viewed him as more than a money-maker was gone. Before long, Tyson was involved in a media storm with his tumultuous marriage to actress Robin Givens and his career was being questionably managed by controversial promoter Don King. Following his shocking upset loss of the title to Buster Douglas in 1990, Tyson seemed to unravel and fall into the cult of celebrity, where few people said no.

In September of 1991, Tyson was indicted on charges of raping an 18-year-old beauty contestant in Indianapolis and, following a high-profile trial, was convicted the following February. Although Tyson could be viewed sympathetically through some of the film, ultimately it is a disturbing portrait of the boxer. Most disturbing is some misogynistic support of Tyson during the trial and the fact that his slow implosion was predicted by some of those close to him years before due to his previous interactions with girls and young women. *Fallen Champ* was thought to be a divergence for the acclaimed filmmaker, who had primarily dealt with the issues of labor strife, gender, and class, but it winds up allowing Kopple to effectively and fairly tackle other hot-button societal issues such as race, sex, and celebrity. After garnering critical acclaim and several awards, *Fallen Champ: The Untold Story of Mike Tyson* was released for home video by Columbia Pictures (VHS). The film can be found online for stream viewing as well.

Awards: 1993 Television Critics Association Awards: Outstanding Achievement in Movies, Miniseries, and Specials; 1994 Directors Guild of America: Outstanding Directorial Achievement in Documentary (Kopple); 1993 American Television Awards: Best News, Information, or Documentary Special (nominated); 1993 Primetime Emmy Awards: Outstanding Individual Achievement in Informational Programming (Kopple, nominated).

Finding Traction, 2014

Director: Jaime Jacobsen, Charles Dye; Running Time: 57 minutes; U.S.

The fast-growing sport of trail running is explored in the 2014 film *Finding Traction*, which documents one of the sport's stars, Nikki Kimball, as she attempts to break an established record for a 273-mile trail running through the state of Vermont. Filmmakers Jaime Jacobsen and Charles Dye craft a personal film that allows viewers an extremely intimate look at a superb athlete and the inner workings of this unique sport. While Kimball shines as the centerpiece of the film, the trail itself that she is attempting to conquer in record time emerges as something of a character as well. Running vertically across the state, from the Massachusetts state line to the Canadian border, Vermont's Long Trail is especially meaningful to Kimball because she grew up only miles away and began her athletic career there as a cross-country skier. Constructed a century ago, it is America's oldest recreational trail falling under the "long distance" category. Its distance of 273 miles is the equivalent of more than ten marathons, which Kimball will need to complete in less than four days, 12 hours, and 46 minutes in order to become the new record-holder. Jacobsen and Dye largely forsake the Long Trail's history and the beauty of Vermont's Green Mountains to zero in on Kimball's personality and the technical aspects of the sport, but its prominence in the story is evident throughout. Among the technical aspects in this burgeoning sport are a runner's aid stations, which one of Kimball's crew compares to NASCAR pit stops, where the runner receives medical attention, eats, and sleeps, if needed.

Another interesting aspect that becomes clear with Kimball is the motivational element, which differs from typical ultra-running because one is racing against a clock instead of being pushed by competitors leading or following. Part and parcel to the film is the theme of gender, but not necessarily because Kimball is attempting to break a record held by a man. Rather, the competition being documented is the rare instance of the biological differences between men and women involved in the same sport being nullified by the technical components of that sport. As an evolutionary biologist explains in the film, the fastest men are faster than the fastest women, but only by a small degree and that difference decreases as the distance becomes longer, and that is especially the case with distances exceeding 100 miles. Despite this particular competition holding no real biological advantage for men, gender equity in athletics is something that Kimball pulls no punches in speaking about. She acknowledges that women have come a long way in sports in her lifetime, but also points out that women get paid less and receive far less media attention. Additionally, the theme of overcoming adversity arises as Kimball divulges that she has suffered with depression and found running as a means of battling the crippling lows that she was once dealing with. In addition to an effective soundtrack by the indie band Cloud Cult, the filmmakers are able to capture intimate moments with Kimball on the trail by utilizing mounted GoPro cameras carried by her crew and pacers. Following a successful festival run in 2014 and 2015, the film was released for streaming and in DVD format.

Awards: 2014 Danish Adventure Film Festival: Best Action Sports Film; 2015 Sheffield Adventure Film Festival: Best Women in Adventure Film, Gold Award, Best Running Film, Silver Award; 2015 Vancouver International Mountain Film Festival: Best Mountain Sports Film; 2014 Banff Mountain Film Festival: Mountain Film Competition, Finalist.

Fire in Babylon, 2010

Director: Stevan Riley; Running Time: 80 minutes; U.K.

The West Indies cricket team, which dominated sport from the late 1970s until the 1990s, is the subject for filmmaker Stevan Riley (*Listen to

Me Marlon, 2015) in his 2010 film *Fire in Babylon*. The West Indies team was unique in several regards, but primarily in the fact that it was made up of players from a number of different Caribbean islands that all had differing attitudes, lifestyles, and politics. The various island nations only came together under the banner of West Indies cricket, and that was reflected in the excitement and pride that the team generated throughout the Caribbean region. Another bonding feature of the different island nations is the common legacy of slavery and colonialism, as almost all of the nations had been British colonies until later in the 20th century. Throughout the century, cricket was seen as an English aristocratic sport, so when the descendants of slaves began excelling at the sport in the 1970s, it was symbolic of these Caribbean territories asserting their independence from colonialism, most of which had only gained that independence in the previous decade. This symbolic breaking away from colonialism into a postcolonial era of autonomy and freedom is represented by the fact that up until the 1960s, a white man was always captain of the West Indies team. Although the film may be seen more as an examination of racial politics through sport, the transition to post-colonialism through sport is likely Riley's primary goal.

Riley details how the teams of the early 1970s were seen as talented, but not as winners. The term "Calypso cricketers" was often used to describe the West Indies teams of the late 1960s and early 1970s that entertained fans but were never taken too seriously. That stigma began to change when Clive Lloyd took over as team captain in 1974. After being intimidated and humiliated by Australia's pace bowling tactics during the team's 1975–76 tour, Lloyd determined that the West Indies needed to employ the same techniques in order to be competitive. He found a quartet of intimidating bowlers in Michael Holding, Colin Croft, Joel Garner, and Andy Roberts who were just as fast and aggressive as the Australians and who would collectively become known as "the four horsemen of the apocalypse." In addition to the quartet of fast bowlers, Viv Richards, who is regarded as one of the greatest batsmen of all time, exemplified the team's newfound confidence amid escalating racial tension. Using a mixture of archival cricket footage and present-day interviews with team members, Riley examines the role that race played within the team's new identity and how that identity carried over into the 1980s as the controversial Rebel Tours in apartheid South Africa took place. Although American viewers may not be intimately familiar with cricket, the themes of cultural assimilation and cultural identity should be universal, as should be the notion of a previously marginalized group rising up against its oppressor.

Along with Bunny Wailer serving as an interesting interviewee in the film, the soundtrack features reggae legends Bob Marley and Gregory Isaacs. It is available in both streaming and DVD formats.

Awards: 2011 Jamaica International Reggae Film Festival: UNESCO Award Feature Documentary; 2010 British Independent Film Awards: Best Documentary (nominated); 2012 Evening Standard British Film Awards: Best Documentary (nominated); 2013 Broadcasting Press Guild Awards: Best Single Documentary (nominated).

First Position, 2011
Director: Bess Kargman; Running Time: 90 minutes; U.S.

In her 2011 documentary film *First Position*, first-time feature filmmaker Bess Kargman examines the high stakes world of competitive youth ballet. The competition in this case is the Youth America Grand Prix, the world's largest and one of the most prestigious ballet competitions for children between the ages of nine and 19 years old. The stakes are high because the Youth America Grand Prix is not only the world's largest such competition, but it also awards full scholarships and job contracts to winners. An intertitle early in the film reads that ballet competitions are the most effective way for aspiring dancers to be seen by the world's elite dance schools and companies. The YAGP's founder explains further the importance and controversial nature of this particular competition by pointing out that these young dancers already know exactly what they want to do in life and they must succeed early in order to follow those dreams. With more than 5,000 dancers entering each year, the competition's semi-finals are held in a number of cities across the globe and less than five percent of the entrants advance to the finals in New York City. Kargman herself is a former dancer and her familiarity with the topic shines through as she focuses in on the training and commitment required.

The larger themes of cost and sacrifice really shine through as well. As a single costume for a single routine can cost over $2,000 and proper training can be just as expensive as a college education, the painful foot-stretching exercises, battered feet, and missing out on typical activities are not the only costs and sacrifices that must be made by the kids and their supportive families. In chronicle fashion similar to many other competition-themed documentaries dealing with children, the film follows six skilled and motivated dancers as they prepare for the event that could truly change their lives. Kargman's usage of the families and dance teachers in building the personal story of each kid is top rate, as are her choices with music and which kids to profile and follow. They represent a unique mixture of teens and pre-teens that all defy the stereotypes associated with ballet in some way. Although the comparisons to films such as *Spellbound, Mad Hot Ballroom*, and *Racing Dreams* are inevitable, *First Position* would likely succeed even without following their narrative paths because it closely examines a highly-competitive world for highly-trained artists that most people know very little about. Unlike those other films, however, it does not feel as though these kids can walk away unfazed and find a new interest if their talent in ballet falls short of their ambition.

Among the kids profiled is Aran, an athletic 11-year-old who lives in Italy where his American Naval officer father is stationed. He is clearly a gifted dancer, but one gets the idea that he would be just as successful at football or baseball. Joan Sebastian is a 16-year-old Colombian living alone and training in New York. With his ultimate goal being to help provide for his family back in Colombia, his maturity level is as evident as is his powerful dancing. Miko and Jules are siblings from California who seem to fit the mold of kids being pushed to succeed by an over-bearing parent. It doesn't take long, however, for viewers to catch on to the fact that Jules shares neither the enthusiasm nor talent for dancing as does his older sister. Rebecca is a 17-year-old cheerleader from Maryland who plans to forego college in favor of landing a spot in a company. If those plans work out, her parents expensive investment in her training will have been fruitful. Perhaps the most engaging profile is that of Michaela, who was adopted from a Sierra Leone orphanage at age four after her parents were killed in the country's civil war. Now 14 and living with her adoptive family in Philadelphia, she not only shrugs off the whispers that black girls cannot be ballerinas, but also the limitations that one may encounter due to a noticeable skin pigmentation disorder. Distributed nationally by IFC Films, *First Position* has grossed over $1,000,000 since its 2012 theatrical release. It is available in both DVD and streaming format.

Awards: 2011 San Francisco DocFest: Staff Prize; 2012 Dallas International Film Festival: Best Documentary Feature Audience Award; 2012 Portland International Film Festival: Best Documentary Audience Award, Best New Director; 2011 Hamptons International Film Festival: Best Feature (nominated); 2011 Toronto International Film Festival: Documentary People's Choice Award (2nd Place); 2012 Miami Film Festival: Knight Documentary Competition Grand Jury Prize (nominated); 2012 Palm Springs International Film Festival: Best Documentary Feature Audience Award (nominated), John Schlesinger Award (Kargman, nominated); 2012 Sarasota Film Festival: Best Documentary Feature Jury prize (nominated); 2013 Chlotrudis Awards: Best Documentary (nominated); 2013 Image Awards: Outstanding Documentary (nominated).

Football Under Cover, 2008
Director: David Assmann, Ayat Najafi; Running Time: 86 minutes; Germany/Iran.

The Iranian Women's National Football Team has lots of spirit and love for the game, but what it lacks is support from its country and, most importantly, an opponent. Marlene Assmann, a German film student and amateur footballer, took it upon herself to remedy that situation by attempting to arrange a match between the Iranian team and her squad, BSV Al-Dersimspor. A truly multicultural club with players of European, Asian, and Middle-Eastern origin, BSV Al-Dersimspor is an amateur team from the Berlin district of Kreuzberg that resembles something of a close-knit family on and off the pitch. Filmmakers David Assmann (Marlene's brother) and Ayat Najafi document the entire process of making the match come about, which turns out to be far more difficult than actually training or playing. Najafi, along with Marlene, who also serves as the film's editor, take a heavy participation role as the two travel to Iran to meet with possible sponsors and learn about the strict "moral codes" that the German players must abide by in order to play there. Therein lays the major theme of *Football Under Cover*: the love of soccer as a bridge between cultures, religions, and traditions. The differences in gender roles between Islam and Western culture can be shocking, but the universality of soccer may be able to break down those barriers. The cultural oppression of women in fundamentalist Islam is most evident when viewers first meet some of the Iranian players and learn that a few dress as men in order to train in public.

Serving as a narrator throughout the film, Marlene's introduction is quite introspective and tone-setting, as she explains that she rarely ever finishes things that she begins, but her latest project is something that she intends to complete. After bringing the idea to her teammates, they quickly jump on board, but also discuss some of their reservations, with the notion of wearing headscarves and pants seeming to be the major issue. While reading through the Islamic codes regarding "indecent behavior," it becomes clear that the German women begin to realize that the freedoms of their liberal society must be suspended in order for their match to take place. From there, Marlene and Ayat begin the search for a sponsor and visit the oil company Iranol, which is receptive at first but later backs out. FIFA finally comes through to back the historical match as the German team arrives and begins to prepare. One scene which really highlights the religious dogma restrictions of a non-secular society is when one of the mothers of an Iranian player explains that she was a member of the national team in the early 1970s, but their dreams of playing internationally ended later in the decade when the Iranian revolution took place. Although no men are allowed into the stadium to watch the match, the strict dress and conduct codes for women must continue to be followed and female members of the "morality police" are there to keep close watch on spectator behavior. As disturbing as that may be to Westerners, it is also nice to see Iranian women in the stadium challenge those rules and express their displeasure of the double standard for men. The film is available for streaming, but is difficult to locate in DVD format for non–European viewers.

Awards: 2008 Berlin International Film Festival: Best Documentary Film Teddy Award, Audience Award; 2008 L.A. Outfest: Freedom Award; 2008 Molise Film Festival: Highest Honor; 2008 Pink Apple Film Festival Zurich: Audience Award; 2009 Prix Europa: Iris Award Best Multicultural Television Program of the Year; 2008 First Steps Awards, Germany: Documentary Film (nominated).

Fordson: Faith, Fasting, Football, 2011

Director: Rashid Ghazi; Running Time: 92 minutes; U.S.

Dearborn, Michigan, has the largest concentration of Muslims in any city in the world outside of the Middle East. In a perverse way, that fact became widely known in the United States in the weeks and months following the 9/11 terrorist attacks. The Arab-American community in Dearborn at first prayed that 9/11 was not terrorism perpetrated by Muslims, and then braced for a backlash when it became clear that it was. The backlash came in the form of suspicion and bigotry toward this community that had previously been accepted as part of the diverse American fabric. Threats directed at mosques in the United States were fairly common in the weeks following 9/11, as were threats toward individuals thought to be Muslim and even to certain businesses and schools. Fordson High School in Dearborn, which has a student body that is roughly 95 percent Muslim, was one of these schools. It is one of the oldest and largest public high schools in the state of Michigan, and according to Principal Imad

Fadlallah, it has the same issues, problems, and ideals as any other high school in the United States. In *Fordson: Faith, Fasting, Football*, first-time feature filmmaker Rashid Ghazi profiles the Fordson Tractors football team for a week in 2009 as they prepare for their rivalry game with crosstown Dearborn High School. Ghazi's examination, which also happens to take place during Ramadan, when Muslims practice fasting during daylight hours, serves as a reminder that the uniquely American sport of football is so ingrained into certain communities that it can act as a natural bridge and barrier-breaker.

The Arab-American community is important to Dearborn because of the role it played in building the city, and especially so with their work ethic after the downturn in the automobile industry during the 1980s. This fact is not lost in the film, but Ghazi also doesn't shy away from working in the more controversial aspects of cultural assimilation, the blurred line between church and state as it relates to the school's football program, and the sort of insularity that the community advocates. After hearing some of the harsh rhetoric heard in the aftermath of 9/11 that begins the film, that insularity among Dearborn Muslims is understandable, but the concept of young adults keeping their hometown so centric in their lives—even when great opportunities for them lie elsewhere—is a little surprising. *Fordson* is a complex film exploring the major issues out in the open, but also exploring themes such as communal insularity that are not so obvious. Although the assimilation efforts may seem to be lacking because of the community's insularity, the one cultural area which the community has clearly embraced is high school football. Among the four players that Ghazi focuses on most closely, all are the sons or nephews of past players, obviously talented on the field, and also devout in their faith. By mixing those aspects together, and viewing the kids as they prepare to play their bitter rival from the more affluent part of Dearborn, it shows how truly normal they are among American teenagers. Written by documentarian Ruth Leitman, the film is available for streaming or in DVD format.

Awards: 2011 Dead Center Film Festival: Special Grand Jury Award; 2011 Detroit-Windsor Film Festival: Best Documentary; 2011 Manhattan Film Festival: Best Feature Documentary; 2011 Politics on Film Festival: Audience and Founders Award; 2011 Slamdance Film Festival: Documentary Feature Special Jury Prize; 2011 Traverse City Film Festival: Best U.S. Documentary Grand Jury Award; 2011 World Cup Film Awards: Champion.

Forever Pure, 2016
Director: Maya Zinshtein; Running Time: 85 minutes; Israel/UK/USA

In the first few moments of the 2016 film *Forever Pure,* one can easily grasp that the fan base of Beitar Jerusalem Football Club is far from ordinary. Decked out in the team colors, the fans chase down the bus carrying players, show up en masse to the initial training session of the 2012–13 season, and chant to the players, "I love you, I swear! The police won't stop me; my heart will always stay yellow and black!" In her directorial debut, filmmaker Maya Zinshtein follows the Israeli Premier League club during the tumultuous season, examining the nexus of soccer, politics, religion, and hatred. Over that single season, the cheers of love and support change drastically to jeers and serious threats from the very same fans, all brought on because the club's owner, Russian-born Jewish oligarch Arcadi Gaydamak, brought in two players from Chechnya who are Muslim. There are plenty of Arab players in the league and at least one club is majority Arab, but the lone team that had never signed an Arab or Muslim player was Beitar. The reason that this is the case becomes crystal clear throughout the film, and even though Zinshtein attempts to keep the focus on the team's season, the real story here is the ultra-right-wing nationalist fan base of the club and the lengths it will go to in order to keep the team what it considers ethnically and religiously "pure."

Known as La Familia and sometimes resembling a militant political organization more than football supporters, the club's fan base is easily the most controversial in the IPL due to their outspoken nationalism and frequent racist chants from the east stands of Teddy Stadium. As one commentator explains, since its founding in 1936, Beitar has truly been about much more than football. It is the club that represents Mizrachi Jews, which are Jewish descendants from countries in the Middle East and Northern Africa (as opposed to Jews coming to Israel from European countries). Additionally, it is also the club that represents the underclass of Israel and the political right. That connection of Israeli football to political ideology, political parties, and even political opportunism is an important theme touched upon by Zinshtein as well. Beitar has long counted right-wing politicians such as Menachem Begin and Benjamin Netanyahu as supporters and it is widely thought that Gaydamak himself purchased the club in 2005 in order to help in his bid to become mayor of Jerusalem a few years later. Gaydamak's mayoral bid was wildly unsuccessful, but it seems that his controversial signing of Chechen players Dzhabrail Kadiyev and Zaur Sadayev had the profound political impact that he was searching for. He even admits in the film that he had no illusions of the players helping the team win, but rather the move was meant to expose the racism and actions of La Familia.

With the arrival of Kadiyev, a baby-faced 19-year-old, and Sadayev, a more experienced 23-year-old, one really has to feel sorry for them as the jeers and taunts start immediately and they are forced to travel everywhere with bodyguards. Upon their arrival, team captain and goalkeeper Ariel Harush somewhat reluctantly welcomes them publicly and he is soon branded a traitor. A similar fate occurs with Itkiz Korenfein, the club's general manager and former star player, who receives death threats from crowds outside his home. Despite the fact that many supporters claim that La Familia is an extreme minority, the midseason boycott initiated by the group reduces the crowd size at Teddy Stadium from the regular 20,000-plus to a mere 200. The gut-wrenching sociopolitical sports story even incorporates technology and social media as one player takes to Facebook to sympathize with La Familia and quickly becomes a hero to the fans despite being suspended by the club. Keeping in mind that "fan" is shortened from the word "fanatic," Zinshtein paints a very dark portrait of extremist political elements intermingling with the business of sports. *Forever Pure* enjoyed a successful festival run in 2016 and early 2017 and has aired as part of the *Independent Lens* film series on PBS in the United

Forever Pure (2016) examines racial and religious intolerance within La Familia, a notorious group of Beitar Jerusalem Football Club supporters in the Israeli Premier League.

States and the *Storyville* film series on the BBC in the United Kingdom. A streaming and probable DVD release will be coming in 2017.

Awards: 2016 Jerusalem Film Festival: Best Editing Haggiag Award, Lia Van Leer Award, Best Director of a Documentary Van Leer Group Foundation Award (Zinshtein); 2017 River Run International Film Festival: Documentary Feature Special Jury Prize, Best Documentary Feature Jury Prize (nominated); 2017 Tromsø International Film Festival: Faith in Film Award; 2016 Chicago International Film Festival: Documentary Gold Hugo Award (nominated); 2016 DOC NYC: Viewfinders Grand Jury Prize (nominated); 2016 Zurich Film Festival: Best International Documentary Film Golden Eye Award (nominated); 2017 Cleveland International Film Festival: Greg Gund Memorial Standing Up Award (nominated); 2017 Copenhagen International Documentary Festival (CPH:DOX): F:ACT Award (nominated); 2017 Dallas International Film Festival: Documentary Grand Jury Prize (nominated).

Freedom's Fury, 2006

Director: Colin Keith Gray, Megan Raney; Running Time: 90 minutes; U.S./Hungary.

Despite being a landlocked nation, Hungary has a great tradition of competitive swimming and water polo. In fact, the Hungarian Men's National Water Polo Team has won nine of the 26 gold medals in Olympic competition, more than twice as many as any other nation. One of the great teams in its history was the 1956 squad, which captured the gold medal at the Melbourne Olympics after unthinkable chaos had taken place on the streets of Budapest, its capital city. Hungary had been occupied by Germany during World War II, but was liberated when the Soviet Union invaded and pushed Germany out. That liberation was short-lived, however, as the Soviets were an occupying force from that point on and Hungary became a Soviet satellite state lacking any real aspects of autonomy. By 1956, Hungarian hostility toward its Soviet occupiers had reached a boiling point and a bloody student-led uprising began taking shape in October. In a semifinal water polo match between Hungary and the Soviet Union at the 1956 Summer Olympics, that hostility would play out and lead to what became known as the "blood in the water match." Marked by intense, rough play with frequent bursts of violence, the infamous match was allegorical for a nation striking back against its oppressors.

In *Freedom's Fury*, the sibling filmmaking team of Colin Keith Gray and Megan Raney revisit this classic piece of sports history and the symbolic

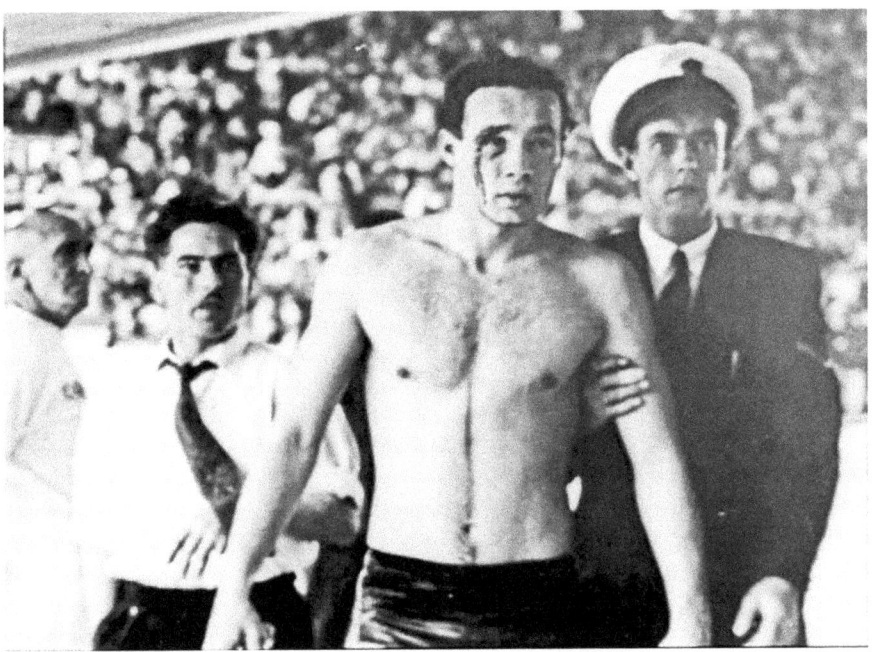

Hungary's Ervin Zádor being led away from the pool at the infamous "blood in the water" match at the 1956 Summer Olympics, documented in *Freedom's Fury* (2006).

role that it played in the Cold War. Narrated by nine-time gold medal-winning American swimmer Mark Spitz (who had once been coached by Ervin Zádor, one of Hungary's great players in 1956), the film tells a story that is strikingly similar to the one in the 2012 film *The Other Dream Team*, which documents Lithuania's struggle to break free of the Soviets in 1990 and how that struggle was manifested through the performance of its basketball team at the 1992 Sydney Olympics. Whereas Lithuania was annexed by the Soviets and its athletes were forced to represent the Soviet Union in international competition, Hungary was autonomous during the Cold War in that its athletes still represented their own country. Despite that semblance of autonomy, the Soviet Union controlled Hungary on both the political front and on the sports front, as they took advantage of that control and forced the Hungarian water polo team to train with the Soviet team. In doing this leading up to the 1956 games, the Soviet team transformed itself from one that had only started competing a few years earlier into one that was now a medal contender.

Due to their training and isolated location away from Budapest, the

Hungarian team was largely unaware of the bloodshed in the uprising taking place in late October, which had grown to include factory workers and was now numbering in the hundreds of thousands. With freedom fighters on the streets of Budapest demanding democratic reforms and attempting to destroy any symbol of Soviet control over Hungary, the archival footage compiled by Gray and Raney is stunning to see. Although a few of the early demands were met, the Soviet Union had successfully suppressed the revolution by the time that the Olympics opened in Melbourne on November 22, leaving more than 3,000 dead and hundreds of thousands more fleeing as refugees. In front of a decidedly anti–Soviet crowd, the Hungarian team became symbolic freedom fighters in the pool when the two teams met in the semifinals. The match nearly turned into a riot and produced one of the most indelible images in Olympic history as Zádor was photographed leaving the pool with blood streaming from his face. Following their semifinal win, Hungary defeated Yugoslavia to win gold and many of their key players chose to defect to the West rather than continue to live under Soviet oppression. The film ends with members of both the Hungarian and Soviet Union teams from 1956 meeting to reminisce about their infamous match. Executive produced by actors Quentin Tarantino and Lucy Liu, the film premiered at the 2006 Tribeca Film Festival. DVD features include a making of featurette and director's commentary.

Awards: 2006 Order of the Knights Cross by the Hungarian Government (Colin Keith Gray, Lucy Liu, Megan Raney, Quentin Tarantino, Andrew Vajna); 2007 United States Congressional Screening and Special Mention.

The Game of Their Lives, 2002

Director: Daniel Gordon; Running Time: 80 minutes; U.K.

Held in England for the first time, the 1966 FIFA World Cup was one of the first truly global events because live television transmissions of the matches were now traveling around the world. World Cup viewers in 1966 were not only witnessing a fantastic tournament full of surprises, they were also likely getting their first glimpses at people from the mysterious, secretive nation of North Korea. The nation had remained completely isolated from the West since the beginning of the Cold War and the subsequent Korean War that had split the country into the communist North and capitalist South. Little was known about North Korea at the time, and most nations in the West (including Great Britain) had not diplomatically recognized it since the beginning of the Korean War more than 16 years earlier. Retold by British filmmaker Daniel Gordon in *The Game of Their Lives*, the story of the 1966 North Korean World Cup team captivated football fans across the world and remains as one of the greatest international sports moments ever.

The fact that the North Korean team was even in the field of 16 to begin with was surprising; what they were able to accomplish was downright shocking. Because FIFA had determined that only one spot was available to all of Africa, Asia, and Oceania, the African nations in turn boycotted altogether and that left only Australia and North Korea to earn the lone contested spot. The larger and much more experienced Australians were heavy favorites, but North Korea won both head-to-head qualifying matches held in Cambodia. Relating to economic development, speed and energy were dominant themes in North Korea at the time. This was typified in the Chollima Movement, named after the winged-horse in Korean mythology. The team played a Chollima style of football, focusing on speed, energy, and teamwork, and even called themselves "the Chollima football team" in a song still heard in North Korea today. Despite an average height of only five-feet and five-inches tall, their Chollima style certainly took their Western opponents by surprise at the 8th World Cup.

Drawing a spot in Group Four with the Soviet Union, Chile, and heavy cup favorite Italy, the North Koreans were written off completely after losing the first match to the much more physical Russians. By the team's next match, versus Chile, North Korea had earned strong support from the fans at Middlesbrough by virtue of their underdog status. The working class town of Middlesbrough was serving as the home base for the team and its locals immediately fell in love with the team of mysterious communists due to their politeness and style of play. After a draw with Chile, North Korea shocked the world when it upset Italy and became the first Asian team to advance to the quarterfinals. The fascinating story didn't end there, as the team began brilliantly versus Portugal with three early goals. From that point, however, Portugal star Eusebio took control of the match and scored four consecutive goals. Using access provided by Koryo Tours, a travel company specializing in North Korean tourism, Gordon was the first person to be given permission to interview the team that the world has not heard a peep from since 1966. He gathered the seven living members of the team for present-day interview segments and mixed that with archival footage of their matches for a great historical documentary. Gordon revisited North Korea in a similar fashion with his 2004 film *A State of Mind*, about the Pyongyang Mass Games, and his 2006 film *Crossing the Line*, about a U.S. soldier who defected to North Korea in 1962.

The Game of Their Lives can be found for online streaming or ordered in DVD format from Gordon's production company, Very Much So Productions.

Awards: 2003 Royal Television Society: Best Sports Documentary; 2003 Seville Film Festival: Best Documentary; 2004 Seattle International Film Festival: Documentary Award; 2003 British Independent Film Awards: Best British Documentary (nominated); 2003 Grierson Awards: Best Historical Documentary (nominated).

Generation Iron, 2013

Director: Vlad Yudin; Running Time: 106 minutes; U.S.

In 1977, the commercially-successful film *Pumping Iron* not only introduced viewers to future TV star Lou Ferrigno and future movie star Arnold Schwarzenegger, it also introduced them to the relatively-unknown sport of bodybuilding. Russian filmmaker Vlad Yudin's 2013 film *Generation Iron* is thought to be something of a sequel to George Butler's 1977 film as both were produced by Jerome Gary and both tracked participants preparing for the Mr. Olympia competition. In the nearly 40 years between the two films, the sport of bodybuilding has moved from a unique subculture of the fitness craze of the 1970s and 80s to a high-profile sport whose top competitors can earn prize money and endorsement deals rivaling those of athletes in any sport. In 1975, the year that Butler documented Mr. Olympia, total award money doled out was $2,500. By 2012, the year being documented by Yudin for *Generation Iron*, the total award money was $650,000, with $250,000 going to the winner. Although only true fans of the sport will likely recognize all the names, Yudin follows seven of the top competitors as they train and provide a tiny insight into their lives: Phil Heath, the reigning title holder, Kai Greene, Victor Martinez, Branch Warren, Roelly Winklaar, Dennis Wolf, and Hidetada Yamagishi.

Perhaps the most interesting person profiled in the film was not one of the seven competitors, it was Sibil Peters, a Dutch former female bodybuilder who now trains others and is known affectionately as "Grandma" by the competitors. Peters is training Winklaar and even those who know nothing about the particulars of this sport can see how helpful her insight is. Also interesting is Greene, who had a troubled childhood and was raised in foster care, but now is an accomplished artist as well as a bodybuilder. The majority of Yudin's focus, however, seems to be on Heath, and for good reason. A former college basketball standout, he is smart and charming, but also the one with the largest bullseye due to his status as the reigning Mr. Olympia. Distinctively narrated by actor Mickey Rourke, the film does not shy away from the elephant in the gym, as a few of the bodybuilders, trainers, and medical professionals openly speak about steroid usage in their sport. Getting a fairly wide theatrical release, the film was one of the most successful documentaries of 2013 and was released in DVD format in 2014 following several major festival screenings.

Awards: 2013 Accolade Competition: Feature Documentary Award of Excellence, Voice-Over Talent Award of Merit (Rourke); 2013 Nevada International Film Festival: Documentary Film Competition Gold Reel Award, Documentary Film Competition Platinum Reel Award; 2014 Buffalo Niagara Film Festival: Audience Choice Award; 2014 Rincon International Film Festival: Documentary Excellence Award; 2013 Copenhagen International Documentary Festival (CPH:DOX): Audience Award (nominated).

Gleason, 2016

Director: J. Clay Tweel; Running Time: 111 minutes; U.S.

In earning a reputation as a hard-nosed player with extraordinary courage, Steve Gleason carved out a seven-year NFL career as a special teams ace for the New Orleans Saints. As is the case with many defensive collegiate stars, Gleason was too small to play linebacker in the NFL (his position in college) and not fast enough to play defensive back, so in order to make a career out of professional football he needed to earn his keep as one of the few players kept on a team's roster solely for his contributions on special teams. In a play so historic that it inspired a statue outside of the New Orleans Superdome; Gleason blocked a punt that was recovered for a touchdown in the 2006 "homecoming" game for the Saints after the team had been displaced due to Hurricane Katrina and forced to play elsewhere the previous season. Airing on *Monday Night Football*, the play had such resonance because of the emotional nature of the game taking place in the very stadium which had served as a makeshift shelter amid the disaster taking place in the city 13 months before. Although Gleason was already a fan favorite due to his style of play on kick coverage, the free-spirited, atypical NFL player became a cult hero in New Orleans and symbolic of the city's resiliency after one of the worst natural disasters in American history. Sparked by his blocked punt in the third game of the season, the 2006 Saints went on to register the best season in the franchise's 40-year history.

The 2016 film *Gleason*, by director J. Clay Tweel, is not necessarily about the titular character's football career though. It is almost solely about his life after football, including the birth of his first child, Rivers, and his experiences dealing with amyotrophic lateral sclerosis (ALS), or Lou Gehrig's disease. Although the film largely neglects the football aspect of Gleason's life in order to focus on his battle with ALS, its production is inexplicably linked to the game and to the National Football League. Soon after being diagnosed with ALS in 2011, Gleason and his wife Michel also learned that they were expecting their first child, and Gleason in turn begins creating a video diary for his son in order to, as he puts it, "share with you who I am and give you as much of myself as I possibly can, while I can." Similarly, after the diagnosis, Gleason and filmmaker Sean Pamphilon begin work on the film that would eventually become *Gleason*, documenting his life with the incurable disease. According to journalist Michael Mooney, the Saints welcomed Gleason back into the fold following his diagnosis, which meant access to team facilities and meetings. At one of those meetings prior to a 2012 playoff game, Pamphilon seemingly filmed defensive coordinator Greg Williams instructing his players to injure their opponents and even speaking about bounties for doing so. Against Gleason's wishes, Pamphilon made the controversial tape public and it not only destroyed the relationship between filmmaker and subject, but it also led to the so-called "bountygate" scandal that rocked professional sports.

Despite the controversial production aspect of *Gleason*, it is a fascinating piece of filmmaking by Tweel (who took over directing and editing duties) and Gleason himself as they document the shockingly rapid decline in motor skills associated with ALS, beginning with slightly slurred speech and mobility problems to the eventual inability to walk or communicate without assistive technology. Even within the genre, *Gleason* is far more intimate, fearless, raw, and real than most documentaries ever get. Tweel edited over 1,300 hours of footage shot by videographers David Lee and Ty Minton-Small capturing Steve, Michel, and eventually Rivers, Gleason as they adapt to their new lives and establish Team Gleason, their foundation set up to help others living with ALS. As the film's original intent was for the sake of posterity, because he would soon appear very differently to his unborn son, the theme of father/son relationships is overarching and that is reinforced with the examination of Gleason's relationship with his own father, who views issues of religion, faith-healing, and the hereafter much differently than his son. Former Saints teammates Scott Fujita and Drew Brees appear in the film and served as producers, as do Eddy Vedder and Mike McCready of the rock band Pearl Jam, who also contribute musically. Shortlisted for the Documentary Feature Academy

Award, *Gleason* premiered at the 2016 Sundance Film Festival and was purchased by Amazon Studios for distribution. It is available in streaming or DVD format.

Awards: 2016 Critics Choice Documentary Awards: Most Compelling Living Subject of a Documentary (Gleason), Best Director (Tweel, nominated), Best Song in a Documentary ("Hoping and Healing," Mike McCready, nominated), Best Documentary Feature (nominated), Best Sports Documentary (nominated); 2016 Full Frame Documentary Film Festival: Reva and David Logan Grand Jury Award (Tweel); 2016 Montclair Film Festival: Junior Jury (Tweel); 2016 National Board of Review: Top Five Documentaries; 2016 Phoenix Film Critics Society Awards: Best Documentary; 2016 Seattle International Film Festival: Best Documentary; 2016 South by South West (SXSW) Film Festival: Festival Favorite Audience Award (Tweel); 2017 Cinema Eye Honors Awards: Cinema Eye Audience Choice Prize (Tweel), The Unforgettables (Gleason, Michel Varisco-Gleason), Outstanding Achievement in Editing (Tweel, nominated); 2017 Alliance of Women Film Journalists: Best Documentary EDA Award (Tweel, nominated); 2017 North Texas Film Critics Association: Best Documentary; 2017 Cinema Audio Society: Outstanding Achievement in Sound Mixing for Motion Pictures, Documentary (Mark Rozett, James Scullion, nominated); 2016 Dallas-Fort Worth Film Critics Association Awards: Best Documentary (3rd Place); 2017 Denver Film Critics Society: Best Documentary Film (nominated); 2016 Detroit Film Critics Society Best Documentary (nominated); 2017 Georgia Film Critics Association: Best Documentary Film (nominated); 2017 Guild of Music Supervisors Awards: Best Music Supervision for a Documentary (Dan Wilcox, nominated); Hot Docs Canadian International Documentary Festival: Audience Award (Tweel, nominated, 7th Place); 2016 Phoenix Critics Circle: Best Documentary Film (nominated); San Diego Film Critics Society Awards: Best Documentary (2nd Place); 2016 Satellite Awards: Best Motion Picture, Documentary (nominated); St Louis Film Critics Association: Best Documentary Film (nominated); 2016 Sundance Film Festival: Documentary Grand Jury Prize (Tweel, nominated); 2016 Washington, D.C. Area Film Critics Association Awards: Best Documentary (nominated).

Glena, 2014

Director: Allan Luebke; Running Time: 85 minutes; U.S.

Glena Avila is a single mother of two in Oregon facing the economic realities of balancing her home life and her career. Because her desired occupation is far more unconventional than most, the task of heading a family and succeeding in a career is indeed a great one. Glena is a mixed martial arts fighter who is making the leap from part-time amateur fighter to full-time professional fighter. For several reasons, this is a much bigger deal than when more typical combat athletes make a decision to pursue professional cage fighting: Avila is in her mid–30s, well past the years that are considered to be a fighter's prime; she has a good job at the Oregon Veterans Home, which she will almost certainly have to quit; her ex-husband is challenging her for custody of their daughter and using her fighting career as a reason why; she is behind in her mortgage payments and in jeopardy of losing her home; and perhaps most importantly, her two children must also make great sacrifices in order for her to follow her dream. In the 2014 film *Glena*, first-time feature filmmaker Allan Luebke follows Avila as she attempts to build on her 4–0 amateur record and follow her dream of earning a living through professional cage fighting.

The reason why Glena's story is so important is primarily because of her economic situation, and staking everything on her ability to continue winning, but she also reveals that it is far more than that. In fact, it is a very personal quest for her because of the times in her life that she did not follow her dreams due to fear of failure. Those themes of perseverance and dedication are overarching, but the themes of family and relationships are certainly present as well. Avila's relationship with her teenaged son is strained, as is her relationship with her boyfriend of six years, and both almost certainly because of her commitment to becoming a professional fighter. Luebke's film is more an examination of an atypical, charismatic athlete and the dedication required to be successful than it is about the actual sport of MMA, but it reveals the ever-popular sport as one to be taken seriously. Despite all the over-the-top machismo, raspy-voiced broadcasters, and apocalyptic-looking T-shirts, the sport is in fact serious business for top-notch athletes. The fact that Luebke bypasses the opportunity to examine gender as a major theme in the film is a testament to how far the combat sport has come since the 1990s, when Senator John McCain referred to it as "human cockfighting" and legislators were scrambling to have in banned (Bledsoe, 325). *Glena* premiered at the Slamdance Film Festival in early 2014 and was broadcast on Showtime later in the year. It is widely available for streaming online.

Awards: 2014 Arizona International Film Festival: Special Jury Award for Inspirational Filmmaking; 2014 Indie Memphis Film Festival: Special Jury Award; 2014 Women + Film VOICES Film Festival: Best Documentary

Audience Award; 2014 Slamdance Film Festival: Best Documentary Feature (nominated).

Go Tigers!, 2001
Director: Kenneth Carlson; Running Time: 103 minutes; U.S.

Massillon, Ohio, a rust-belt town of roughly 32,000, is often credited as being the birthplace of professional football. While there is some debate about that claim, surely no other city in America is as supportive of its high school team as is this place which was once dubbed "Touchdown Town" in a 1951 newsreel story. Football here is a lifelong obsession, where newborn boys are all given toy footballs and a local funeral parlor provides caskets in the team colors. Despite the fanatical support of the community and a bevy of talented players, all is not well as the school's 106th football season is set to open. A rival school has alleged that Massillon recruited a star player away, some faculty members have spoken out about the practice of redshirting (repeating grades) for the sole purpose of later athletic advantage, and students who are not athletes feel ostracized. But most of all, and perhaps as a result of misplaced priorities like the bloated football budget, the school is short of funding for much-needed repairs, textbooks, and even buses. A voter-approved tax levy would solve the problem, but it has already been defeated twice. The team posted an uncharacteristic 4–6 record the previous season, but the boosters, coaches, and players believe that a stellar 1999 season would assure the levy's passage the next time around. As the season unfolds and it becomes clear that winning and support for the levy are indeed linked together, the events fit together perfectly for an observational documentary.

Go Tigers! is a behind the scenes chronicle of the team's 1999 season, culminating with the annual Canton McKinley game, one of the most bitter rivalries in the country. Three players are specifically profiled in the film: Ellery Moore, a defensive end with a college career ahead despite a criminal past, Dave Irwin, the quarterback, and Danny Studer, a linebacker whose father and uncle are legendary past players. Filmmaker Kenneth A. Carlson's high definition filming captures unbridled teenage machismo, both in the locker room and away from the field, where binge drinking and vomiting seem ritualistic. His interview subjects provide a range of opinions, from the mayor who sees nothing wrong with the importance placed on football to a select few citizens who are willing to question those priorities. Carlson, a Massillon native and former Brown University football player, examines the over-the-top fanaticism and controversial issues fairly, but also the dichotomy that football can indeed bring good to the community and the players. Ultimately it is an interesting, but at times, disturbing look at a football-obsessed town. After premiering at the 2001 Sundance Film Festival, *Go Tigers!* was picked up for distribution by IFC Films. The Docurama DVD is loaded with special features, including the full 1951 newsreel story and tracks of the original songs for the film, performed by recording artist Katrina Carlson, the director's wife.

Awards: 2002 Golden Trailer Awards: Best Documentary; 2001 Sundance Film Festival: Documentary Grand Jury Prize (nominated); 2002 Chicago Film Critics Association Awards: Best Documentary (nominated); 2002 Independent Spirit Awards: Best Documentary (nominated).

Goal! The World Cup, 1966

Director: Abidin Dino, Ross Devenish; Running Time: 100 minutes; U.K.

Like the Olympic Games, each of the 15 FIFA World Cup Tournaments since 1954 have had an officially-sanctioned documentary film to detail the competition. This film covering the first World Cup held in England, the modern game's birthplace, is the first colorized version and widely considered to be one of the better films of the series. While World Cup matches had been televised since 1954, it was not until 1966 that the transmission went around the world, making it only the second truly global sporting event, following the 1964 Summer Olympics in Tokyo. The exciting final match gave many viewers in the United States their first taste of international football, and U.S. theatrical releases of *Goal!* the following year helped to foster the development of the newly-formed North American Soccer League in 1968. Following the script of longtime football writer Brian Glanville and the narration of actor Nigel Patrick, *Goal!* provides a glimpse of Great Britain in the mid–1960s amid the growing popularity and globalization of the event. Noting that the first World Cup in Uruguay in 1930 was reached by European teams after weeks of sea travel, the 1966 teams are filmed arriving by plane and given brief commentary about their history and expectations. Like the other official FIFA films, it is largely a straightforward account of the action on the pitch, but the few divergences are well-timed and meaningful: a curious look at Speaker's Corner in London's Hyde Park, the bustling football-watching pubs, and the many international supporters flocking back to where the game grew from England's industrialization.

The tournament itself featured several controversies involving rough play, the sending off of several players, and a forever-infamous questionable goal—all of which the film examines. Controversy surrounded the play and officiating of key Argentinian matches against West Germany, in group play, and in the quarterfinals against England (which would be the starting point for their fierce rivalry in years to come). Aside from the surprising early exit of the Brazilians, the two-time defending champions who had not lost a World Cup match since 1954, the early storyline was the shocking upset of North Korea over Cup favorite Italy. The mysterious North Korean team became the first Asian team to reach the quarterfinals and was the subject of Daniel Gordon's acclaimed 2002 film *The Game of Their Lives*. Only an amazing rally on four goals by Portugal star Eusebio kept North Korea from advancing to the semifinals. The semifinals paired England with Portugal and West Germany against the Soviet Union, with England and West Germany advancing to the final. Perhaps the most exciting and controversial of all World Cup moments came in the closing minutes of the final. The West Germans evened the score 2–2 in the 89th minute in order to send the match to extra time. Eleven minutes into extra time, England's Geoff Hurst sent a shot high into the cross bar, which then sent the ball deflecting straight down onto the goal line. Despite 50 years of reviews and arguments, it is still nearly impossible to determine whether the ball fully crossed the line. The film is easily available in VHS format, and with a proper internet search, can be found on DVD.

Awards: 1967 BAFTA Awards: Best Documentary, Robert Flaherty Award.

Gored, 2015

Director: Ido Mizrahy; Running Time: 85 minutes; U.S.

The centuries-old spectacle of bullfighting, with all of its flamboyance and pageantry, is on full display in Ido Mizrahy's 2015 feature *Gored*. The title comes from the fact that Spanish bullfighter Antonio Barrera, the film's subject, happens to hold the record for having been gored more times than any matador in history. Whether or not such a fact is actually an accomplishment to be honored, or even an actual bullfighting statistic at all, is never really clear. One thing that the film does make clear, however, is that the 23 times Barrera has been gored does not necessarily indicate that he is untalented. Instead, it indicates that he has been far more daring than most toreros, and perhaps also that the time has come for him to step away from the sport that he was raised to be a part of. Barrera has never found the glory that he desired in his native Spain, but his riskier style has been especially appreciated in Mexico. Mizrahy's film is a documentation of Barrera stepping away from the sport, but also a solid biographical portrait of a man whose purpose in life has been to achieve glory in the bullring.

The sport itself is still loved in certain parts of the world as a tradition steeped in art and culture, but is widely considered barbaric as well. One fan interviewed in the film describes the best bullfights as being a "tragic ballet of exceptional beauty." On the other hand, many see it as a brutal ritual, perhaps even choreographed torture of an animal, usually with the bull being stabbed to death, but sometimes with the matador being gored or even killed. This fact is presented fairly in the film, along with the accompanying voice of protest that is often seen at the events. While the film's focus is clearly on Barrera and his long-suffering wife, who has seen 19 of his 23 impalements, there is just enough information about the sport's history to spark interest for the unacquainted, but more would be useful. Also useful would be more examination of the tradition versus modernity theme as it relates to how bullfighting is thought of today. Similarly, the fact that Barrera was able to stand out in Mexico but not Spain raises plenty of unanswered questions as well. Following a successful festival run, *Gored* was acquired by FilmRise for distribution. DVD and streaming options both offer English subtitles.

Awards: 2015 Hot Springs Documentary Film Festival: Best Sports Documentary; 2015 Raindance Film Festival: Best Documentary Jury Prize; 2015 Tribeca Film Festival: Documentary Audience Award (nominated).

The Grand Olympics (*La grande olimpiade*), 1961

Director: Romolo Marcellini; Running Time: 142 minutes; Italy.

Italian Romolo Marcellini was selected to direct the official film of the 1960 Summer Olympics in Rome, and he does so with a much more stylized version than the Olympic films of the 1948, 1952, or 1956 Summer Games. The film begins in fantastic color with sweeping shots from a helicopter, in which the copter can be heard and seen via shadow. Following scenes of Pope John XXIII welcoming the athletes and the lighting of the Olympic Cauldron, the film gets to the actual competition and does a good job of detailing the games, which were dominated by the Soviet Union. Highlights from the events include Ethiopian Abebe Bikila winning the marathon bare-footed, American sprinter Wilma Rudolph winning three gold medals, American Rafer Johnson capturing gold in a thrilling Decathlon, and German sprinter Armin Hary setting a new Olympic record in the 100 meters. Locating the film in DVD or VHS format is possible, but difficult. The film, however, can be found online for streaming, but without subtitles and the narration mysteriously switches from Italian to English multiple times. According to *New York Times* film reviewer Howard Thompson, who described the film as an "absolute knockout" in 1964, when *The Grand Olympics* finally made it to theaters in the USA three years after its initial release, it was shown with the informative English narration track.

Awards: 1962 Academy Awards: Best Documentary Feature (nominated).

The Great Alone, 2015

Director: Greg Kohs; Running Time: 80 minutes; U.S.

With his 2015 film about four-time Iditarod champion Lance Mackey, filmmaker Greg Kohs has created a film that may have been overlooked among the many recent sports-themed documentaries gaining worldwide attention. Indeed, *The Great Alone* is partly a chronicle of the 2013 Iditarod Trail Sled Dog Race and partly a biographical movie about Mackey, perhaps one of the most charismatic and unique individuals that could be profiled from any sport. The scruffy look of Mackey certainly doesn't conjure up the idea of athleticism, but his warts and all candor about himself and the problems that he has overcome seem to be distinctively Alaskan and perfectly fitting of the rugged sport that he has so masterfully became a household name in. The sport is sled dog racing and its Iditarod is not only the most well-known race, but also may be the most grueling endurance competition on the planet. Taking place every March since 1973, the event is 1,409 miles across the arctic wilderness of Alaska, beginning in Anchorage and ending in Nome. Nowadays, the winning musher and dog team conquer the course in eight or nine days, but many competitors are still out on the trail for two weeks. An intertitle used early in the film sums up just how extreme and demanding the race is, reading that more people have summited Mount Everest than have successfully completed the Iditarod.

As interesting as the history of sled dogs in Alaska is, and as captivating as the cinematography of the Alaskan landscape is, Kohs film is first and foremost about Lance Mackey. He jokes that he was racing even before he was born, which is actually true considering that his mother was racing when she was seven months pregnant with him. His father was the co-founder of the Iditarod and its winner in 1978, but was soon estranged from the family. Admitting that he always wanted to make his father proud, and that for most of his life he had done just the opposite, the younger Mackey clearly harbors resentment for the years of a missing father. He was in and out of jail and forced to enter drug rehabilitation as a youth, but eventually found his way, and that may be thanks to the group of misfit dogs that he cared for and first began to race seriously with. Despite his new direction in life, Mackey was faced with an even tougher obstacle when he was diagnosed with throat cancer and told that continuing to race could kill him. Mackey's life is truly an inspirational one and Kohs uses his story of redemption to explore the overarching theme of growth. The fascinating aspect of *The Great Alone* is that the 2013 Iditarod, which is being followed in the film and which Mackey fails to be competitive in, takes a nearly-forgotten backseat to the biographical documentary unfolding at the same time. The DVD special features include several featurettes and behind-the-scenes footage.

Awards: 2015 Banff Mountain Film Festival: Grand Prize, Best Film—Exploration and Adventure; 2015 Homer Documentary Film Festival: Audience Award; 2015 Hot Springs Documentary Film Festival: Best Sports Documentary; 2015 La Costa Film Festival: Best Sports Documentary; 2015 Seattle International Film Festival: Grand Jury Award, Best Documentary (nominated).

The Great American Cowboy, **1973**

Director: Kieth Merrill; Running Time: 89 minutes; U.S.

Winner of the Academy Award for Best Documentary Feature of 1973, *The Great American Cowboy* details the competition between two stars of professional rodeo: Larry Mahan, a five-time champion, and Phil Lyne, a newcomer to the professional circuit. Before any real competition begins, director Kieth Merrill provides a fascinating overview of the sport, highlighted by slow-motion cinematography and narration by longtime Hollywood actor Joel McCrea. Everything from the personalities of the animals to chuck wagon racing to the annual suicide race at the Omak Stampede is covered. The competition between the two rodeo stars does not unfold in the observational way, where the viewer is taken along on the circuit stops, but rather in expository documentary fashion, where the film's narration and photography combine to educate viewers. In the same way that narrative "disaster movies" became a sort of popular genre within a genre during the 1970s, documentaries focusing on under-appreciated sports such as rodeo, motorcycle racing (*On Any Sunday*,

1971), roller derby (*Derby*, 1971), and bodybuilding (*Pumping Iron*, 1977) also became popular with moviegoers during the 1970s and spawned many narrative feature films on their topic. Thanks to its engaging and informative nature, Merrill's *The Great American Cowboy* may be the best of the bunch. This Oscar winner never made it to DVD, but can be found online for stream viewing.

Awards: 1974 Academy Awards: Best Documentary Feature; 1974 Western Heritage Awards: Western Documentary.

Hands on a Hard Body: The Documentary, 1997
Director: S.R. Bindler; Running Time: 98 minutes; U.S.

One five-minute break every hour; one 15-minute break every six hours, no sitting, no leaning, no squatting, and no sleeping during breaks: thus are the rules for the annual Hands on a Hard Body contest at Jack Long Nissan in Longview, Texas. The unique endurance contest offered a brand new Nissan pickup truck to the contestant who could remain with a continuous hand on the prize for the longest time. The 1995 edition of the contest, which seemed to be something of an annual summertime ritual for citizens of Longview until 2005, was the subject matter for S.R. Bindler's fascinating hit film of 1997, *Hands on a Hard Body: The Documentary*. Bindler, a native of Longview, takes a participatory approach as he films and continually probes the contestants about their physical and mental states as one day turns into the next. Bindler's final product, which probably had a shooting budget far lower than the actual $15,000 1995 value of the truck, is the rare example of a documentary film that has achieved cult status simply because it documents very ordinary people doing something very extraordinary. True to the documentary tradition of fly-on-the-wall evidence, the low-budget film is about engagement and participation, with an overarching theme of chasing the American dream emerging once the unique characters become more well-known. Themes of class and kinship can also be noticed as contestants seem to form a bond that replaces background and competitiveness.

Adding to the unfolding drama and reinforcing the theme of the American dream, Bindler is cautious not to exploit the characters despite their quirks and eccentricities that can be downright funny at times. A visit to central casting likely could not have yielded a better cross-section of Texans to document, but this mixture of ages, races, and personalities truly represent the diverse American populace and democratic ideals of fairness and equality. The one challenge to the idea of equal opportunity may be that of Benny Perkins, a cowboy-philosopher type of contestant, who is back in the contest despite winning it three years earlier (some of the other contestants think that he should be ineligible). Delivering some of the most memorable lines of the film ("it's a human drama kind of thing"), Perkins makes for an excellent interview subject throughout the film because of his previous experience. Another fantastic character among the 24 is Norma, a charismatic evangelical Christian convinced that winning is God's will. As some of her fellow church members show up to support her, she certainly seems to be imbued by something, perhaps the prayer chain of her friends or the gospel music coming from her headphones. Janis, a contestant that could have easily been exploited due to her missing teeth, storms off angry that the judges failed to expel a rulebreaker. Ronald seems strong and confident, but is done in by the countless candy bars consumed during breaks. Angie, Kelli, and Kerri, three of the younger contestants, all acknowledge that winning would help them financially. And finally, J.D., who smokes unfiltered cigarettes during breaks, is not very compelling, but he seems to be the most unfazed when others are becoming weak and delirious after two days.

Perhaps the most fascinating aspect of *Hands on a Hard Body* is that it predates the plethora of competition-based reality television shows such as *Survivor*, *Big Brother*, and *The Bachelor* that became staples of American culture during the 2000s. Likewise, the film also predates the concepts of "going viral" and famous for being famous, but get rich quick schemes may be more appropriate comparisons since the payoff is more tangible than fame. In a sociological context, *Hands on a Hard Body* offers examinations into the lengths that ordinary people will go to for a valuable prize, and also the introspective qualities that lead a person to believe that they can excel at this particular competition. Although Bindler never focuses on these sorts of questions, one has to wonder how the 24 contestants would have differed with a different type of contest. Along with other deep philosophical thoughts, Perkins points out that the contest is more about sanity than stamina. That issue became all too real during the 2005 edition of the contest when a contestant dropped out after 48 hours and immediately committed suicide. While that tragedy marked the final Hands on a Hard Body contest, the film's legend has continued to grow over the years, perhaps aided by the fact that the film was not available in DVD format until the digitally-remastered special edition was released in 2013. At the time of his death in 2006, director Robert Altman was adapting the story into a narrative feature and would have included Hillary Swank, Meryl Streep, Chris Rock, and Billy Bob Thornton in the cast. The

Hollywood adaptation may have not been made, but it did successfully make it to Broadway after being adapted into a musical, *Hands on a Hard Body: The Musical*.

Awards: 1997 AFI Fest: Best Documentary Film Audience Award; 1997 Austin Film Festival: Audience Award; 1997 Florida Film Festival: Special Jury Award; 1997 Gen Art Film Festival: Audience Award; 1999 Boston Society of Film Critics Awards: Best Documentary.

Hank Aaron: Chasing the Dream, 1995
Director: Mike Tollin; Running Time: 95 minutes; U.S.

In April of 1995, twenty-one years after Hank Aaron became baseball's home run king and just ten days after the nearly year-long Major League Baseball strike ended, the Turner Broadcasting System aired *Hank Aaron: Chasing the Dream*. Fittingly, the film was televised on the cable channel that had telecasted games of the Atlanta Braves (Aaron's former team) since 1973, about the same time that Aaron's chase for the record gained nationwide attention. Also fitting was the fact that the film came at the same time that the sport's popularity was at an all-time low, perhaps reminding angry fans of the national pastime's importance to American history and culture. While the crowning achievement of Aaron's long career is the chase and ultimate breaking of Babe Ruth's home run record, he has largely been underappreciated, both as a ballplayer and an important figure in the Civil Rights Movement. While maintaining a lifetime .305 batting average, Aaron hit 30 or more home runs in 15 of his 23 seasons and was a member of 21 consecutive All Star teams. Playing his entire career in Milwaukee and Atlanta, however, he never received the national exposure of contemporary players such as Willie Mays or Mickey Mantle. That is, until it became clear that Aaron could surpass Ruth's 714 career home runs, and then the attention of the nation was locked on him. As the pressure became more intense, some attention was supportive, but much was full of racial hatred. Aaron received so many scathing letters and death threats the FBI assigned him a personal bodyguard.

Writer and director Mike Tollin (*Radio*, 2003) tells the story of Aaron's life and playing career in a narrative fashion, but succeeds most when he focuses in on the chase of the hallowed record and allows his interview subjects, particularly Aaron's family, to tell wonderful stories. Tollin steps away from the cinéma vérité, or fly on the wall, filming tradition of most documentaries and instead creates a partial docudrama, using reenactments of Aaron's early life and a first-person narration which purports to be supplied by Aaron himself, but is actually actor Dorian Harewood. While based in fact, almost the entire first half of the film is an even mix of these reenactments from Aaron's youth and teen years and present-day interviews with family members, friends, and fellow ballplayers, but never Aaron himself. The story that emerges in the second half of the film, now relying on actual archival footage, photos, and interviews to document Aaron's big league career from Milwaukee in 1954 to the pressure-filled chase for the home run record in 1973 and '74, is baseball history at its best and a new examination of what Aaron meant to a culminating Civil Rights Movement. Tollin's film was never released on DVD, but can be found in VHS format or streaming online.

Awards: 1995 Heartland Film Festival: Crystal Heart Award; 1996 Peabody Award (Tollin/Robbins Productions); 1995 Emmy Awards: Outstanding Information Special (nominated); 1996 Academy Awards, Best Documentary Feature (nominated).

Happy Valley, 2014

Director: Amir Bar-Lev; Running Time: 98 minutes; U.S.

Across the United States, several areas treat college football as a near religious experience, taking ordinary fandom to the next level of fanaticism. One such place where support for the home team is a near religion is in State College, Pennsylvania, home of Penn State University. The general region of Central Pennsylvania surrounding the university is known as Happy Valley, and the type of fandom that exists there for the university's football program is much different from other areas that may support their teams just as strongly. The primary difference is that the local support for Penn State football, for more than 40 years, was a sort of loyalty and devotion to the team's coach that was simply unheard of in modern times. Joe Paterno had been the head coach at Penn State since 1966 and accumulated 409 wins, more than any other coach in major college football history. Because of his emphasis on academics, teamwork, and citizenship over athletic ability, he was thought of as a "beacon of integrity" across the college football landscape. Nine games into the 2011 season, Paterno was fired due to a child sex abuse scandal involving Jerry Sandusky, one of his former assistant coaches and the team's defensive coordinator from 1977 to 1999.

In his 2014 documentary *Happy Valley*, filmmaker Amir Bar-Lev examines the fallout from the 2011 scandal that shook college athletics and the Penn State football program. The film begins with ritualistic scenes of tailgating outside Beaver Stadium juxtaposed with the following scene of news crews and an assembled crowd outside of a courthouse awaiting the June 22, 2012, verdict of Sandusky. The crowd rightfully cheers the news that Sandusky had been found guilty on 45 counts of sexual abuse dating back to the time that he was the team's defensive coordinator in the 1990s. Clearly, Sandusky was a hated man in the community not only because of his horrific crimes, but also because of the damage that he had done to the way of life that surrounds the football program. Regardless of how the community now felt about Sandusky, it wasn't quite as simple as punishing the guilty man and saying a prayer for his victims. Questions soon began to arise about how it could have not been known, and when news broke that an incident had been witnessed and reported to Paterno in 2001, it started to become clear that other reputations were going to be seriously tarnished as well. Paterno reported the witness's 2001 allegation to his supervisor, what he was legally obligated to do, but was heavily criticized for not doing more and not cutting off Sandusky's access to athletic facilities (the reported incident had occurred at an athletic facility despite the fact Sandusky had retired two years earlier).

Within days of Sandusky's arrest, it became clear that Paterno may be fired, which triggered an outpouring of support for the coach in the community. After the firing became official, it triggered violence as thousands of students and fans rioted in the streets and made threats toward media members. Bar-Lev captures this pandemonium, which goes a long way in reinforcing the opinion that college football fandom may not be healthy when it reaches the level of insular nativism. Whether or not Sandusky operated as a citizen above suspicion because of the culture of football at Penn State is debatable, but the NCAA determined as much when it imposed severe sanctions against the school. Bar-Lev's film is much more about fandom and tarnished legacies than it is about the actual crimes of Sandusky and inaction of those who knew of his awful sins. He treats the topic of Paterno's ultimate culpability fairly by fully examining the issue and allowing voices of support to have their say, but the film's primary target seems to be the concept of hero-worship and big-time college athletics anyway. Instead of questioning how this could have happened, the obvious questions arising from *Happy Valley* are more along the lines of why we deem a living person such a hero to deserve a bronzed statue, and what happens if the already anointed hero makes a very bad mistake. Following a wide festival run in 2014, including Sundance and Full Frame, the film was released on DVD in 2015.

Awards: 2014 Sarasota Film Festival: Best Documentary Feature Jury

Prize; 2014 AFI Fest: American Independents Audience Award (nominated); 2014 Nashville Film Festival: Best Documentary Feature (Honorable Mention).

Harry and Snowman, 2015
Director: Ron Davis; Running Time: 84 minutes; U.S.

Still riding at 86 years old, Harry De Leyer is a Dutch immigrant and world-class horseman, who was known in the equestrian world as "the galloping grandfather" when he was winning Grand Prix events back in the 1970s. After being active in the Dutch resistance underground, a group of citizens who provided information to the Allies during World War II, De Leyer came to the United States at the bequest of the parents of a fallen American soldier whom he had helped in Holland. He later taught riding at an elite girl's school in New York, where his dream of becoming a professional horseman came true. On a trip to New Holland, Pennsylvania, in 1956 to procure cheap horses for the school's riding program, De Leyer arrived late to the auction but saw something in one of the horses that had been loaded onto a truck destined for the slaughterhouse. The gray Amish plow horse, which was named Snowman by De Leyer's children, became a champion show-jumper and earned the moniker "Cinderella Horse" due to its dominance over more typical and seasoned thoroughbreds in the high-society, high-profile sport of the 1950s. In his award-winning film, *Harry and Snowman,* filmmaker Ron Davis (*Pageant,* 2008) details the beautiful story of friendship and love that grew out of the $80 purchase.

Snowman became famous enough from his jumping ability to have his own fan club and travel the world for guest appearances, but it was his backstory and calm demeanor with children that truly made him one of the most legendary horses ever. Not yet realizing Snowman's gift, De Leyer sold him to a neighbor not long after the original purchase, but the large gray horse kept jumping his fence and traveling six miles back to De Leyer's farm (the last time dragging a tire and fence post in tow). He was what De Leyer calls a "family horse" and the archival footage of all four De Leyer children riding him at once, and even using him as a diving board while partially submerged in water, proves that to be very true. Davis mixes quite a bit of archival footage of competitions to his present-day interviews for the well-rounded story focusing both on the legendary horse and his timeless trainer. De Leyer's children add spark to the story, but also reveal that their lives were not exactly perfect because horses always seemed to be their father's top priority. Pre-occupied or absent fathers is probably a common theme with children of top athletes, but the fact that the family's living was made by virtue of horses being top priority in their lives creates a unique, matter-of-fact reality. After numerous festival circuit awards and a limited theatrical release, the film was released in DVD format in 2015. A narrative feature film about the story is apparently in the works as well.

Awards: 2015 Equus Film Festival: Best Feature People's Choice Award; 2015 Hot Springs Documentary Film Festival: Best Documentary Feature Audience Award; 2015 Malibu Film Festival: Audience Choice Award, Grand Jury Prize Award; 2015 Middleburg Film Festival: Best Documentary Audience Award; 2015 Nantucket Film Festival: Best Documentary Feature Audience Award; 2015 New Hampshire Film Festival: Audience Choice Documentary; 2015 New Orleans Film Festival: Documentary Feature Audience Award; 2015 Prescott Film Festival: Best Documentary Feature Audience Choice Award; 2015 Woods Hole Film Festival: Best of the Fest Audience Award.

Harvard Beats Yale 29–29, 2008
Director: Kevin Rafferty; Running Time: 105 minutes; U.S.

Referred to simply as "The Game," the annual Harvard–Yale football rivalry game has been played 133 times since 1875, the third most between any two schools in NCAA history. None of those games has been more thrilling and none hold a greater historical significance than the 1968 edition, a game which ended in a 29–29 tie. Despite the scoreboard revealing a tie as time expired, many at Harvard considered the outcome something of a moral victory due to the fact that Yale was heavily favored and ranked number 16 nationally. Just to provide an idea of how powerful the Yale team of 1968 was thought to be, only once since that time has any Ivy League team finished a season nationally ranked in the Associated Press poll (Dartmouth in 1970), and the last time an Ivy League team was ranked at any point in the season was Yale at number 20 on November 7, 1972, the same day that Richard Nixon carried 49 states in the presidential election (Bernstein, 238). The outcome of the game not only meant that the teams would share the Ivy League championship, both with 8–0–1 records; it also spawned one of the great newspaper headlines in American history: "Harvard Beats Yale 29–29," scrawled across the following day's issue of the *Harvard Crimson*, the school's student newspaper.

Filmmaker Kevin Rafferty (*The Atomic Cafe*, 1982, *Blood in the Face*,

1991), a Harvard student at the time, uses this fantastic piece of college football lore and memorable newspaper headline to put together a fascinating feature documentary that goes behind the scenes of the game and allows the many involved in it to speak about it. Taking place on the afternoon of November 23, 1968, at Harvard Stadium in Boston, the game represented the first time in nearly 60 years that both Harvard and Yale entered their year-end clash with undefeated records. Despite what might have looked like an even matchup due to their identical records, it really was not expected to be as such. Yale featured a stout defense and a spectacular offense led by halfback Calvin Hill and quarterback Brian Dowling. Hill was drafted by the Dallas Cowboys in the first round of the 1969 NFL Draft, twice rushed for more than 1,000 yards in the NFL, and was selected to play in four Pro Bowls during his 12-year NFL career. Dowling finished ninth in the 1969 Heisman Trophy balloting and later become immortalized as the basis for the "B.D." character in the comic strip *Doonesbury* by Gary Trudeau (a Yale graduate). While the Harvard defense was the team's strength, leading the league in most statistical categories, the Crimson offense had a major star as well, only not really a football star: offensive lineman Tom Jones, later known as Tommy Lee Jones, the Academy Award–winning actor.

Just as most expected, Yale jumped out to a 22–0 lead thanks to three first half turnovers by Harvard. After a quarterback change, Harvard gets on the scoreboard just before the half and gets an early second half touchdown to inch closer. As the fourth quarter draws down to the one minute mark, the Yale lead stands 29–13 and looks certain to hold. Sixteen points in the final 42 seconds seems unthinkable—a dream for Harvard and a nightmare for Yale—but it happened. Drawing from interviews with more than 40 players from the game, Rafferty cuts between the interviews and the actual game telecast and play-by-play. As remarkable as the game was, part of its lore clearly comes from unique connections to history that many on the field had and the unique time and place that an Ivy League campus was in 1968, eight months after the assassination of Martin Luther King, Jr., six months after the assassination of Robert F. Kennedy, and student activism against the Vietnam War raging. In addition to Hill, Dowling, and Jones (who was a roommate of future Vice President Al Gore at Harvard), one Yale player was a roommate of future President George W. Bush, another Yale player was dating future movie star Meryl Streep, another Yale player went on to a six-year Major League Baseball career, and one Harvard player was a Vietnam War combat veteran who had been at the siege of Khe Sanh only months before. *Harvard Beats Yale 29–29* was released theatrically on the 40th anniversary of the game and is available in both streaming and DVD format.

Awards: 2008 Toronto International Film Festival: Film Presented; 2008 Hamptons International Film Festival: Film Presented.

Hitman Hart: Wrestling with Shadows, 1998
Director: Paul Jay; Running Time: 93 minutes; Canada/U.S.

Since the very early days of televised professional wrestling, the manufactured storylines of heroes and villains have essentially been modern-day morality plays that mirror society as a whole. During the late 1990s, when the two major American promotions, the World Wrestling Federation (WWF, now WWE) and World Championship Wrestling (WCW), were competing for ratings and fans, the roles of heroes and villains within the former promotion became almost unrecognizable as the company's chairman, Vince McMahon, re-branded his product with themes focusing on sex, violence, and nationalism. Central to this shift from traditional storylines to ones of a more adult nature was the role played by Bret "The Hitman" Hart, a top draw in the WWF at the time who was offered a huge contract to jump to the rival WCW in 1997. In wrestling jargon, Hart was a "face," a fan favorite or a "good guy," as opposed to a "heel," or a "bad guy." Sensing that his audience was changing and embracing his edgier storylines, and even now cheering his supposed "heel" wrestlers such as "Stone Cold" Steve Austin, McMahon asked Hart to forego his hero persona and turn heel. The transformation of the WWF as a whole, the transformation of Hart's heroic character, and Hart's controversial departure from the WWF are the subjects of Paul Jay's 1998 documentary *Hitman Hart: Wrestling with Shadows*. Produced by the National Film Board of Canada, the film provides a unique look at the business of professional wrestling during its most profitable period while also examining the concept of what is reality in a completely artificial world.

Despite his supposed concerns over the WWF's raunchier new direction, Hart remains loyal to the company and rejects the WCW offer. Soon however, McMahon changes his mind about renewing an expensive contract with Hart and implores him to accept the WCW offer. McMahon asks Hart to lose the WWF championship to his new star, Shawn Michaels, before his departure, but instead agrees to allow Hart to win the title match and then relinquish the championship belt voluntarily. Debate still surrounds what happened at the Hart-Michaels championship match in Montreal in late 1997, but it most certainly did not turn out the way that

Hart had been promised it would. Now referred to as the "Montreal Screwjob," McMahon had the referee call the match early, claiming that Hart had submitted, and thus had Michaels winning the belt outright instead of it being voluntarily relinquished. Supposedly, the double-cross was a "work" (a scripted happening) orchestrated only by McMahon and the referee, whereas the outcome was a "shoot" (an un-scripted happening) to everyone else. In his 2005 book "Steel Chair to the Head: The Pleasure and Pain of Professional Wrestling," author Nicholas Sammond argues that Jay's film "problematizes the relationship between acting out and ascension in the class system, simultaneously blurring the boundaries between the performed self and the private citizen, and between wrestling artifice and reality" (218). Indeed, rather than providing insight into how real McMahon's betrayal actually was to Hart, Jay instead creates a participatory mode film that plays along with the perceived reality while giving no illusions that this world is not entirely contrived. The film was released as a special edition DVD in 2008 and can be found for online streaming at the NFB website.

Awards: 1998 Worldfest International Film and Video Festival: Gold Award; 1999 Banff Television Festival: Best Sports Program Rockie Award; 1999 Canadian Society of Cinematographers Awards: Best Cinematography in Documentary (Joan Hutton); 1999 Columbus International Film and Video Festival: Entertainment Bronze Plaque Award, Humanities Chris Award; 1999 Gemini Awards: Best History/Biography Documentary Program, Best Picture Editing in a Documentary Program or Series (Manfred Becker), Best Direction in a Documentary Program or Series (Jay, nominated); 1999 Hot Docs Canadian International Documentary Festival: Best Feature, Best Independent Canadian Film; 1999 Nashville Film Festival: Best Long Form Documentary; 1999 U.S. International Film and Video Festival: Gold Camera Award; 1999 Sidewalk Moving Picture Festival: Best Documentary (nominated).

Hoop Dreams, 1994

Director: Steve James; Running Time: 170 minutes; U.S.

Hailed as one of the greatest documentaries ever made, *Hoop Dreams* is the six-year chronicle of budding Chicago-area basketball players Arthur Agee and William Gates in the early 1990s. Filmmaker Steve James documents the personal lives of the two youths as well as their respective basketball careers at inner-city John Marshall High School and suburban St. Joseph High School. Both student-athletes were recruited by a local scout and enrolled at predominantly-white St. Joseph despite the long commute from their homes. Whiles Gates has a sponsor-family to pay the tuition cost of St. Joseph's, Agee does not and is forced to transfer back to his original public school. The theme of socioeconomic class as it relates to educational opportunity and the disparity in various school systems is a theme that James is attentive to, but not one that is overarching throughout the film. Athletics versus academics within the American education system is a theme that is much more obvious, and perhaps the most obvious theme is divulged within the film's title: basketball success as a means to life success and a certain way out of poverty. The issue of race is an undeniable reality of the film, but it really comes into focus only through the experiences of Agee and Gates at the predominantly-white private school. The myriad of issues in the film that are often grouped within the theme of race—crime, drugs, teen pregnancy, and unemployment—are more appropriately grouped within the issue of poverty.

Early in the film James focuses more intently on Agee, perhaps because his recruitment to St. Joseph is not as solidified as Gates. Agee is driven to a camp at St Joseph by Earl Smith, the scout that is recruiting him, which immediately raises questions about exploitation and the entire concept of who is really helping who. Smith is working as a scout for St. Joseph's head coach Gene Pingatore, who would eventually become the state's winningest coach, but at the time is most noted for having coached NBA All Star Isiah Thomas—who was recruited away from inner-city Chicago schools in the same fashion that Agee and Gates are. While Agee begins playing for the freshman team, Gates's talent level warrants playing time for the varsity during their respective first seasons. Both players have partial scholarships, meaning that their tuition must be partially paid by their family. Although both families live well below the poverty level, and both players seem to be struggling academically at their new school, one player (Gates) continues on at St. Joseph while the other is forced to leave the school. Because a benefactor (the president of Encyclopædia Britannica) came forward to pay Gates's remaining tuition, this may not be as shady as it seems, but it does somewhat expose the system for what it is— one in which athletic talent benefits the school as much as vice versa. The fact that a benefactor came forward for Gates may or may not have been because he was seen as the better prospect, but it certainly raises questions.

As the documentation of James and writer/producer Frederick Marx progresses to sophomore year, it is interesting to see how the respective families are brought into the film. Agee's father, Bo, and Gates's brother, Curtis, who was a talented player at the junior college level, serve as the basketball mentors for the young players and both seem to be investing hope in the kids while at the same time attempting to serve as role models. While Agee transfers to the public school after missing three months, his mother loses her job and his father leaves the family and begins using drugs. Gates, on the other hand, is thriving at St. Joseph, receiving letters of interest from major universities, and is offered a summer job at Encyclopædia Britannica. As junior year commences, the comparisons to Isiah Thomas begin for Gates, but he soon suffers a nagging knee injury and things begin to reverse for the players. The season may be lost for Gates, but Agee begins playing well and is noticeably bigger than the previous season. A large chunk of the film comes from the eventful junior years of the players, and the families again begin to take on a bigger role. Agee's father returns to the family after a year away and becomes active in their church. Meanwhile, Gates must undergo a knee operation and viewers learn for the first time that he and his longtime girlfriend recently became parents.

Prior to his senior year, Gates plays at the prestigious Nike All Star camp, where many of the top collegiate coaches are seen scouting for talent. Despite another knee flare-up and the camp being unsuccessful for Gates, his being there is juxtaposed with scenes of Arthur at the same time working at Pizza Hut and living a more carefree life typical of an American teenager. With the exception of Marquette University, a number of schools have slowed on recruiting Gates after his injury during senior year, but Agee is now getting interest from junior colleges. Once again, the contrast in how the two are seen within the system is evident—neither has yet qualified academically and one had a stellar senior year while the other struggled, yet the latter is moving on to major college basketball while the former is likely to be forced to go the junior college route, if at all. *Hoop Dreams* is a fair assessment of a system that seems rigged to favor the most athletically-gifted and the most educationally-benefited. The legacy of the film has changed not only many facets of high school and collegiate basketball, but also the filmmaking community and the way that documentary films are seen, distributed, and handled at the most prestigious awards ceremonies. James and Marx intended to make a 30-minute short film for PBS about street basketball in Chicago, but their story grew and developed into a film that has widely come to be regarded as one of the greatest American documentaries. The accolades for the film are almost too numerous to list, but in 2005 it received perhaps its greatest honor in that it was selected for preservation by the National Film Registry at the Library of Congress.

Awards: 1994 Amiens International Film Festival: Best Documentary; 1994 Boston Society of Film Critics Awards: Best Documentary; 1994 International Documentary Association: Feature Documentary IDA Award; 1994 Kansas City Film Critics Circle Awards: Best Documentary; 1994 Los Angeles Film Critics Association Awards: Best Documentary/Nonfiction Film; 1994 National Board of Review: Best Documentary; 1994 New York Film Critics Circle Awards: Best Nonfiction film; 1994 Society of Texas Film Critics Awards: Best Documentary; 1994 Sundance Film Festival: Documentary Audience Award, Documentary Grand Jury Prize (nominated); 1995 American Cinema Editors: Best Edited Documentary (James, Mark, William Haugse); 1995 Chicago Film Critics Association Awards: Best Picture, Best Director (James, nominated); 1995 Directors Guild of America: Outstanding Directorial Achievement in Documentary/Actuality (James); 1995 Independent Spirit Awards: Special Distinction Award; 1995 MTV Movie Awards: Best New Filmmaker (James); 1995 National Society of Film Critics Awards: Best Documentary, Best Film (3rd Place); 1995 Prix Italia: Best Documentary; 1996 Peabody Awards: Peabody Award; 2005 USA National Film Preservation Board: Selected for the National Film Registry; 1995 Academy Awards: Best Film Editing (James, Marx, Haugse, nominated); 1995 Dallas-Fort Worth Film Critics Association Awards: Best Picture (nominated); 1995 Southeastern Film Critics Association Awards: Best Picture (4th Place); 1995 Yamagata International Documentary Film Festival: Robert and Frances Flaherty Prize (nominated); 1996 Image Awards: Outstanding News, Talk or Information Special" Image Award (nominated).

The Hopeful, 2011

Director: Brendan Kirsch; Running Time: 90 minutes; U.S.

In his 2011 film *The Hopeful*, filmmaker Brendan Kirsch explores the ethical issues of young athletes transferring schools for the sole purpose of athletic benefit and the heavy involvement of parents in high school sports. With the story of Cody Keith, a quarterback from Charlotte and his journey to three high schools and a college prep academy over a four-year period in hopes of landing a major college scholarship, Kirsch's likely intention was to examine Keith's dreams of playing college football and chronicle his progress through his final two prep seasons. A different examination emerges, however, when one fully knows the story of the Keith family and their relocations in search of football success. Beginning the film with an intertitle acknowledging how common that transferring for athletic purposes has become and that none has been more publicized ("or criticized," according to the film) than that of Cody Keith, Kirsch largely presents the Keiths as sympathetic figures who have been unfairly scrutinized. While it is no doubt true that parents Greg and India Keith, a very wealthy and very influential North Carolina couple, simply want what's best for their children and want to afford them the best opportunity to follow their dreams, their story goes a little deeper than *The Hopeful* acknowledges because of the extraordinary lengths that they have gone to in order to aid their son's dream of playing quarterback at the NCAA Division I level. Those lengths include pricey quarterback camps, expensive evaluations with famous quarterbacking experts, a relocation of only a few miles to a new school district, then relocating across the country to another school, and a final transfer back across the country to a prep academy.

The criticism spoken about by the Keiths at the beginning of the film refers to a 2008 *Charlotte Observer* article about Cody and his parents. It details how Cody began his high school years at Myers Park High in Charlotte, but transferred to South Mecklenburg High for his junior year due to his inability to win the starting quarterback job at the former school. The article also suggests that the Keiths attempted to influence coaches through their generous donations to the athletic program and that Greg Keith came into conflict with other parents and coaches by openly pushing for playing time (Frazier and Gordon). Greg Keith denies this, but does talk candidly about the transfers and expensive private coaching as simply being a decision that was in the best interest of his son. They found a starting quarterback job for Cody at South Meck, where he impressed and led the team deep into the 2008 NCHSAA playoffs, but transferred again for his senior season—this time to California—because of the lack of passing in the offensive playbook at South Mecklenburg. At his new school in California, Maranatha High in Pasadena, Cody was the starting quarterback, but the Division I scholarship offers did not come. Yet another move was in store, as he moved back to the East Coast and played a postgraduate season at Cheshire Academy, a college prep school in Connecticut. After setting numerous passing records at Cheshire, Cody did gain the attention of major colleges and ended up deciding on East Carolina University. The majority of the film is a chronicle of Cody's senior and postgraduate seasons at Maranatha and Cheshire.

The high school years of Tim Tebow, the 2007 Heisman Trophy-winning quarterback, are not specifically mentioned as a comparison to Keith, but they are probably inevitable. As part of the Evangelical homeschooling movement, the Tebows rejected public education largely because of its constitutionally-mandated secular nature and then sought to use public education's extracurricular activities for their benefit, as did many other homeschooling families, citing that their tax dollars gave them that right. Tebow began playing at the school whose Florida district he lived in, but his parents rented an apartment in a neighboring district so that he could play quarterback at a new school the following season. The ethical questions in the cases of Keith and Tebow differ somewhat, but the examination more needed in both cases might be why their respective sons had to be a quarterback rather than just a football player. Widely available in streaming format, *The Hopeful* is a well-made film addressing an important issue, but Kirsch may miss a major point in just chronicling Cody Keith's success in chasing his dreams. It would have been interesting to know if Greg and India Keith would have been receptive to Cody helping any of his teams by playing a position other than quarterback. It would also have been interesting to understand more fully why the film strikes such a sympathetic tone with the Keiths rather than being more investigative into their insistence that Cody be a starting quarterback. Following some injury-plagued seasons at East Carolina, Cody transferred to UNC Charlotte and then later to Division II New Mexico Highlands University.

Awards: 2011 All Sports Los Angeles Film Festival: Documentary Audience Award, Best Documentary (second place); 2011 Fort Collins Tri-Media Festival: Best of the Festival, Director's Award (Kirsch); 2011 Ft. Lauderdale International Film Festival: Documentary Spirit of the Independent Award (Kirsch, SportsArc); 2011 Las Vegas International Film Festival: Documentary Silver Ace Award; 2011 Mexico International Film Festival: Documentary Silver Palm Award; 2011 Orlando Film Festival: Most Inspirational Film; 2012 Charlotte Film Festival: Best Documentary Festival Prize (nominated).

The Horse with the Flying Tail, 1960

Director: Larry Lansburgh; Running Time: 48 minutes; U.S.

Winner of the Academy Award for Best Documentary Feature, *The Horse with the Flying Tail* is a Walt Disney Productions film that severely stretches the classical notion of documentary filmmaking, but may be of interest to children or those concentrating on equestrianism or show jumping. The film is about a palomino horse named Nautical (though originally named "Injun Joe") and the long road of many different owners on its way to winning jumping fame in the King George V Cup competition in 1959. Although nearly the entire first half of the film features scenes that are clearly staged, including one with actor Slim Pickens for some reason, it does lay out Nautical's personality and the bumpy road that the horse traveled before finally falling under the ownership of Hugh Wiley and the U.S. Equestrian Team. Thankfully, the final segment of the film consists of actual footage from the King George V Cup, in which viewers can get a good look at Nautical's jumping ability and signature waving tail signaling that a jump was coming. The film can be found online for streaming and was also released in DVD format recently.

Awards: 1961 Academy Awards: Best Documentary Feature.

Ice Guardians, 2016

Director: Brett Harvey; Running Time: 108 minutes; Canada/U.S.

In the 2008 film *Pond Hockey,* filmmaker Tommy Haines explores the changing culture of recreational ice hockey in that the pure outdoor game has nearly disappeared. The 2016 film *Ice Guardians,* by filmmaker Brett Harvey (*The Union: The Business Behind Getting High,* 2007), explores a changing element of professional North American ice hockey—the diminishing role and continued existence of the "enforcer." Often referred to as a "goons," the role of the enforcer in ice hockey is slightly more complex than being a team's designated fighter. They are largely the protectors of the team's star players and the administrators of justice on the ice when opponents step out of line. Using a lengthy buildup to the film's central thesis, the enforcer role and fighting in hockey are necessary evils; Harvey throws lots of information at viewers, but covers it meticulously. Broken down into a number of titled segments such as "History," "The Power of Intimidation," and even "Etiquette," the film mixes talking head-style interviews with tons of video footage. The interview subjects represent a veritable who's who of the NHL's toughest brawlers of the post-expansion era: Dave Schultz, Nick Fotiu, Clark Gillies, Dave Semenko, Brian McGrattan, Kevin Westgarth, Gino Odjick, Riley Cote, Kelly Chase, Scott Parker, Todd Fedoruk, Luke Gazdik, and George Parros, to name a few.

Aside from toughness, perhaps a little craziness, and a general lack of handsomeness among the many enforcers featured in *Ice Guardians,* the one most common trait they share is that they were adored by their teammates. With the adoration and respect of their teammates comes a deeper cultural and sociological understanding of the role. Harvey succeeds in this as well, bringing in expert interview subjects from the academic world such as Dr. Victoria Silverwood, a lecturer and criminologist in the United Kingdom specializing in violence in hockey, Howard Bloom, an author and specialist in mass behavior and human evolution, and Dr. Charles Tator, a physician specializing in concussions. The film makes the case that fighting has been a part of hockey since the beginning of the sport more than a century ago, but most experts acknowledge that it was pretty rare up until NHL expansion in the late 1960s led to a dilution of talent and players needed to become specialists in order to stick in the league. Throughout the 1970s and 1980s, most teams had more than one enforcer, but they have become increasingly fewer in number nowadays, as have the fights since the league has made a concerted effort to scale back the violence. Likewise, the enforcer role has also become more specialized than ever before as those common to today's game are typically not as skilled in other areas as those were from past decades.

In a 2016 *Sports Illustrated* article in which *Ice Guardians* was named one of the magazine's "Best of Film" selections for 2016, Jeremy Fuchs summarizes that the enforcer role is being phased out of the game as teams attempt to get faster. Fuchs argues that the film allows older players "who made a living with their fists reminisce about the halcyon days of the goon." It seems more that enforcers are being phased out because of rules implemented to curb fighting, but they are certainly fewer in number regardless, and many in the film acknowledge that their careers have ended not exactly by their own volition. One glaring statistic glossed over in the film is that 98 percent of current NHLers do not want fighting removed from the game, and considering that only a small percentage of players are known to regularly drop the gloves, it speaks to the recognized and respected role that enforcers play. As concussions and head trauma continue to be a serious issue in all contact sports, the debate concerning the necessity of fighting in hockey will surely rage on, but those who choose to be enforcers in order to live out a dream of playing professional hockey seem only to want their role to be more fully understood by the public. Many documentaries take a stance on a controversial issue and present compelling arguments to justify that stance, but very few have the ability to change opinions of viewers that have already formed an opinion. *Ice Guardians* may be one of those films. It is available in streaming and DVD format.

Awards: 2016 Calgary Film Festival: Audience Favorite (Top 10); 2016 Newsweek Magazine: Favorite Documentaries of 2016; 2017 Alberta Media Production Industries Association Awards: Best Documentary Over 30 Minutes (nominated), Best Music Score (nominated—Alec Harrison), Best Screenwriter Nonfiction (nominated—Scott Dodds); 2017 Leo

Awards: Best Documentary (nominated), Best Direction in a Documentary Program (nominated—Harvey).

In Football We Trust, 2015

Director: Tony Vainuku, Erika Cohn; Running Time: 87 minutes; U.S.

There are only 240,000 Samoans and Tongans living in the United States, but they are 28 times more likely to play football in the NFL than any other ethnic group. This is the intertitle that begins *In Football We Trust*, the 2015 film by directors Tony Vainuku and Erika Cohn. Former NFL All Pro safety, Troy Polamalu, explains that Polynesians come from a line of warriors, adding that their culture "embodies what football is." Whether or not this is the reason for the remarkable success that this small ethnic group (less than one percent of the U.S. population) has had in producing professional football players is debatable, but the fact that football is ingrained within the culture of Pacific Islander Americans is certain. The reason why is more likely related to culture and socialization and the tendency for young athletes with Polynesian ancestry to drift toward football more than other sports. Culture and socialization are also likely the explanation for another question that arises from the film: why is it that the state of Utah, as the film puts it, is the center of this Polynesian football pipeline? Vainuku and Cohn do not overtly state or examine the connection of Pacific Islander Americans to Mormonism, which comes

One of the primary subjects of *In Football We Trust* (2015), Harvey Langi (21), takes part in a traditional pregame haka.

primarily from extensive missionary efforts in Polynesia between the mid–1800s and mid–1900s, but that connection explains how the nexus of football, Polynesians, and the state of Utah came to be. Rather, in chronicle fashion, the filmmakers explore the lives of four young NFL hopefuls as they deal with the mounting pressure of their high school football careers and their potential athletic success at the next level of play.

Fihi Kaufusi, a defensive lineman at Highland High School in Salt Lake City, is potentially the first member of his family to go to college. His parents in Tonga sent him to live with relatives in the U.S., where he has become active in his church and hopes that football can lead to a better life. Harvey Langi is a heavily recruited running back from Bingham High School in South Jordan, Utah. He is one of nine children with supportive parents and lives in a more affluent area. Brothers Vita and Leva Bloomfield are backfield mates at Hunter High School in West Valley City, Utah. They share a more tumultuous family life and have to deal with their father's football legacy as well as his checkered past, which includes gang affiliations. The theme of family is felt throughout the film. Fihi's tearful confession that he lacks respect for his Tongan father because of his way of life is juxtaposed with his strong relationships at church. Harvey's supportive family, which includes the mother who takes cheerleading to a whole new level at his games, seems to bond together when some of their white neighbors are suspicious of them. The Bloomfield brothers admit that their whole family has been involved in drugs and gangs, but Vita has decided to change that trend. Leva, however, may waste his natural talent of running the football if he cannot break away from the cycle of bad decisions and jail time that has surrounded him. The well-made film concludes with updates on the players four years later. Widely available for streaming, the film premiered at the Sundance Film Festival and was aired on the PBS film series *Independent Lens* in January 2016.

Awards: 2015 Logan Film Festival: Best of Festival Award; 2015 Spotlight Documentary Film Awards: Gold Award; 2015 Hawaii International Film Festival: Best Documentary Feature Halekulani Golden Orchid Award; Milano International FICTS Fest: Sport and Society Award (nominated); 2015 Milano International Film Festival: Leonardo Da Vinci's Horse Award (nominated).

Jose Canseco: The Truth Hurts, 2016

Director: Bill McAdams, Jr.; Running Time: 64 minutes; U.S.

In the latter half of the 1980s, Jose Canseco became perhaps the best power-hitting baseball player in the world. He was voted the *Baseball*

America Minor League Player of the Year in 1985 and the American League Rookie of the Year the following season. Over his first three full seasons, he hit 106 home runs and drove in 354 runs, and in 1988 he became the first player in Major League history to steal 40 or more bases and hit 40 or more home runs in the same season. Powered by Canseco's meteoric rise, the Oakland Athletics also won three consecutive AL pennants from 1988-to-1990. He had made good on a promise that he made to become the best player in the world after his mother's death in 1984. It might have been arrogant when Canseco frequently touted himself as the best player in the game in those days, but it was true—at least from a power-hitting perspective. Fast forward 20 years and Canseco was speaking some truth again, even though it was equally controversial and peppered with dubious assertions. In his 2005 book "Juiced: Wild Times, Rampant 'Roids, Smash Hits & How Baseball Got Big," Canseco admitted to having used anabolic steroids throughout his career. He also made the claims that up to 85 percent of major leaguers used steroids and that he had once been clocked at 3.9 seconds in the 40-yard dash. Those claims were almost certainly bullshit, so it was probably easy for MLB stars implicated in Canseco's book for steroid usage to deny it, but as the congressional investigation into MLB's steroid issue and the ensuing scandal unfolded later that year, Canseco slowly began to be vindicated.

Produced in 2013 and released via streaming and DVD format in 2016, *Jose Canseco: The Truth Hurts* is a documentary film directed by Bill McAdams Jr., that examines Canseco's career, his controversial role as whistleblower in the secretive world of MLB clubhouses, and his subsequent and alleged blacklisting by Major League Baseball. Mixing archival footage with a present-day question and answer style interview, Canseco speaks frankly about his decision to name names and clearly regrets doing so in terms of the damage it did to the reputations of some of his past teammates, but seems to have few regrets in terms of the damage it did to baseball. In fact, he seems to feel entirely justified, but perhaps more so because of what he saw as MLB's hypocritical black-balling of his career rather than the integrity of the game. He very well may be correct in that baseball wanted his career over, but it may also be true that clubs simply did not want the baggage that he brought. In his early career, Canseco carried himself with a braggadocio and swagger that rubbed many the wrong way; he was immature and acted and spoke impulsively and had several brushes with the law, usually due to violent outbursts. Nowadays, those characteristics don't even disqualify American politicians from the highest offices, but athletes who act in such a manner are vilified (and usually by the same people who respect brash, self-aggrandizing politicians). Both before and after his tell-all book, Canseco was indeed hated by many fans and vilified by the press, but when he decided to speak out about how rampant performance-enhancing drugs were in America's pastime, he was simply telling the truth.

Awards: 2013 Hot Springs Documentary Festival: Spa City Moxie Award; 2014 Boston International Film Festival: Best Documentary Feature; 2014 San Antonio Film Festival: Best Documentary Feature Audience Choice Award, Best Feature Narrative.

Keepers of the Game, 2016
Director: Judd Ehrlich; Running Time: 82 minutes; U.S.

Few places in the United States are as passionate about the sport of lacrosse as Upstate New York. In fact, the game originated with the native peoples in the St. Lawrence Valley, and at one time 90 percent of the lacrosse sticks in the world were produced on the Mohawk Territory of Akwesasne, New York, on the Canadian border. The sacred nature and tradition of the game is not lost on the residents there; they refer to it as a gift from their creator, which was once considered a medicine game and played to heal members of the tribe. Lying just off the reservation, Salmon River Central School in Fort Covington, New York, has a student body that is nearly 70 percent Native American, the highest population of native students attending any public school in the state of New York. In 2011, the Salmon River Shamrocks girls' varsity lacrosse team played its first season, but pretty much funded itself through its booster club. That has remained the case through its first four seasons, but the team members face another obstacle in that some feel that girls should not be playing the sacred game. The 2016 film, *Keepers of the Game,* by filmmaker Judd Ehrlich, profiles the all-native girls lacrosse team at Salmon River as they fight for funding, fight for the right to play the sport thought to be reserved for boys only, and fight to bring home a sectional title. In his beautifully-shot and edited film, Ehrlich effectively explores the legacy of colonization on a culture that struggles to balance tradition with modernity.

As male callers to a radio program and some of the boys in the school express their opinions about girls playing lacrosse, the theme of gender roles within the community takes shape, but a secondary theme of culture arises as well. Two players who viewers are first introduced to are sisters Mimi and Jacelyn Lazore, who recently transferred to Salmon River and attend Catholic Church services. They describe themselves as native but not traditional, and because of that non-traditional upbringing, they learned the sport at a young age. Team captain Tsieboo Herne serves as a stark contrast to the Lazore sisters. As the daughter of the Clan Mother, Tsieboo was raised very traditionally and struggled with depression from the pressure of two different worlds as she grew older. The fact that she is playing lacrosse while her mother is tasked with upholding the very traditions that disallow female participation makes their lives even more difficult. While at the same time describing the difficulty of growth and change within traditional ideas, the Clan Mother finally gives her blessing for the team to tear down the walls of a cultural norm and even invites them to prepare for their season with a sweat lodge ceremony. Perhaps as a sad example of "winning cures all," gender roles begin to be questioned less and funding becomes available when the team advances to the championship game. The Shamrocks will face its bitter rival, the Massena Central Red Raiders, where the theme of culture is reinforced simply by their opponent's mascot—an Indian in a headdress. Following a premiere at the Tribeca Film Festival, Keepers of the Game was aired on ABC and ESPN in 2016.

Awards: 2016 Red Nation Film Festival: Courage Award, Best Documentary (nominated); 2016 Critics Choice Documentary Awards: Best Sports Documentary (nominated).

The King of Kong: A Fistful of Quarters, 2007

Director: Seth Gordon; Running Time: 79 minutes; U.S.

The sporting aspect of *The King of Kong: A Fistful of Quarters* might be debatable, but the competition is not. Nor is the bitter rivalry that has developed because of this quirky hit film which was considered one of the best documentaries of 2007. And, don't confuse quirkiness with a tongue-in-cheek, or non-serious, examination of competitive gamers. These aren't the computer gamers of the 21st century, though, they are ones who love the 1980s and stay fiercely loyal to the classic arcade games that swept the nation three decades ago. The game at the center of the storm here is Donkey Kong, one of the most difficult games of its era. The two main characters, Billy Mitchell and Steve Wiebe, fit so perfectly into the villain and hero roles they could be sporting respective black and white cowboy hats. Wiebe is a talented musician, former athlete, and middle school teacher who has often came up short in life despite tons of potential. He is the perfect contrast to Mitchell, a confident hot sauce entrepreneur, self-proclaimed consummate winner, and widely regarded as the best classic arcade gamer of all time.

The King of Kong, 2007 89

In *The King of Kong: A Fistful of Quarters* (2007), rivals Billy Mitchell (left) and Steve Wiebe fit perfectly into hero and villain roles.

Another primary character in this story of games and antagonism is Twin Galaxies, an organization formed in 1982 by Walter Day to record and track world record high scores and organize gaming contests. When Wiebe sets out to break Mitchell's 20-year-old Donkey Kong record, he follows the typical Twin Galaxies procedure and videotapes his game to send in for verification. Because no one is this tight-knit community of gamers has ever heard of Wiebe, it is viewed skeptically and even leads to strangers paying him a visit to inspect his arcade cabinet. Not only that, the calculating Mitchell (whose influence in this community is even greater than his reputation) now stresses the importance of live records. Wiebe then travels cross-country to the famous Fun Spot Arcade in New Hampshire and breaks the record live, but only moments later Mitchell has a video tape delivered with him posting an even higher score. To this point, it appears that Wiebe truly embodies the cliché about nice guys finishing last, but it isn't quite over yet. When the Guinness Book of World Records contacts Day about using Twin Galaxies' scores for their upcoming edition, he announces a tournament and the competing starts again. The pressure is now on Mitchell to play live.

Gordon uniquely avoids exploiting this odd cast of characters while crafting the story into one about competition, fame, and community. While those respective themes are overarching throughout the film, it also zeroes in on the concepts of rivalry, obsession, and success. Whereas Mitchell is immensely confident and success is a given for him in seemingly all facets of life, that is not the case with Wiebe, who more resembles a naturally talented athlete that lacks focus and confidence. Sometimes, however, natural talent, obsession, and preparation can lead to a breakthrough for even the most unlucky among us. Despite a limited theatrical release in 2007, the film grossed nearly $1 million and has since spawned a number of similar gaming documentaries focusing on the aspect of competition. *The King of Kong* was the debut feature for filmmaker Seth Gordon (*Four Christmases*, 2008, *Horrible Bosses*, 2011), who has since gone on to direct several major narrative comedy feature films and hit television shows. Following the film's festival success and DVD release, it was rumored that New Line Cinema would adapt the story into a narrative feature film.

Awards: 2007 Austin Film Critics Association: Best Documentary; 2007 Dallas-Fort Worth Film Critics Association Awards: Best Documentary; 2007 North Texas Film Critics Association: Best Documentary; 2007 Oklahoma Film Critics Circle Awards: Best Documentary Feature, Best Film (nominated); 2007 Utah Film Critics Association Awards: Best Documentary Feature Film; 2008 Central Ohio Film Critics Association: Best Documentary; 2008 Cinema Eye Honors Awards: Audience Choice Prize; 2008 Houston Film Critics Society Awards: Best Documentary Feature; 2008 Online Film Critics Society Awards: Best Documentary; 2007 Boston Society of Film Critics Awards: Best Documentary (2nd place); 2007 Chicago Film Critics Association Awards: 2007 Indiewire Critics' Poll: Best Documentary (3rd place); 2007 Satellite Awards: Best Motion Picture, Documentary (nominated); 2007 St Louis Film Critics Association: Best Documentary Feature Film (nominated); 2008 Broadcast Film Critics Association Awards: Best Documentary (nominated); 2008 Chlotrudis Awards: Best Documentary (nominated); 2008 Gold Derby Awards: Documentary Feature (nominated); 2008 International Cinephile Society Awards: Best Documentary (2nd place).

Legendary Champions, 1968
Director: Harry Chapin; Running Time: 77 minutes; U.S.

Approximately six years before singer-songwriter Harry Chapin was nominated for a Grammy Award for his 1974 number one hit song "Cat's in the Cradle," he was nominated for the Best Documentary Feature Academy Award for his 1968 film *Legendary Champions*. Although severely dated now, the film is an absolute goldmine of rare archival photos and moving images. It tracks the succession of the heavyweight boxing championship from 1882 (John L. Sullivan, the last bare-knuckle champ) to 1929 (Gene Tunney). The dated film does not treat controversial African-American champion Jack Johnson as sympathetically as more recent retrospective films do, but his reign, 1908–1915, is given considerable attention. Just as he did with song lyrics in his later career as a popular folksinger, writer and director Chapin molds the grainy black and white footage into a story of American history, connecting boxing to such figures as Jesse James, Wyatt Earp, Thomas Edison, Theodore Roosevelt, Charlie Chaplin, and Charles Lindbergh. Options for viewing this title are either dusting off the old VHS player or online streaming.

Awards: 1969 Academy Awards: Best Documentary Feature (nominated).

The Life and Times of Hank Greenberg, 1998
Director: Aviva Kempner; Running Time: 90 minutes; U.S.

Although Major League Baseball had a number of Jewish players dating back all the way to the dead ball era of the 1910s, most of those players changed their names to better blend in with the American pastime. Hank Greenberg, the first great Jewish sports superstar, never changed his name. He proudly acknowledged his roots, dispelled the stereotypes that came along with it, and became a hero to American Jews of the 1930s in a way that is almost unimaginable today. With the publication of Henry Ford's *The International Jew* and the anti–Semitic preaching of radio evangelist Father Charles Coughlin, Detroit had become a center of American bigotry toward Jews by the 1930s. It was in the face of this bigotry that Greenberg excelled with the Detroit Tigers, becoming one of the most feared power hitters in baseball history. Greenberg won two World Series titles, was a five-time All Star, became the first player to win two MVP awards while playing two different positions, and in 1938 he nearly broke Babe Ruth's single season home run record. Following America's entry into World War II, Greenberg was the first major leaguer to volunteer for service in the military, and ultimately served longer than any other pro player—missing almost four full seasons.

Filmmaker Aviva Kempner draws from a wealth of archival material, over 40 interview subjects, and oral testimony Greenberg himself provided for his biography in the 1980s to paint a stirring portrait of the man who became such an icon. From the Yiddish version of "Take Me Out to the Ballgame" that opens the film to the final anecdote explaining how Greenberg was one of the few players to embrace Jackie Robinson when their career paths crossed in 1947 (Greenberg's final season and Robinson's first), it is a loving tribute to the man and a nostalgic look at America in the 1930s and 1940s. Along with family members and former players, the interview subjects largely represent second-generation Jewish Americans who found in Hammerin' Hank a hero that made them feel proud and truly American. Among these are writers Ira Berkow and Dick Schaap, attorney Alan Dershowitz, Senator Carl Levin, and actor Walter Matthau, who humorously explains that even though he didn't play tennis, he joined the Beverly Hills Tennis Club in hopes that he could lunch with Greenberg, his idol. Kempner spent more than a decade making the film, which has grossed over $1.7 million and won numerous awards. It is available in DVD format and the newly-released special edition offers a director commentary track and extra interviews.

Awards: 2000 National Board of Review: Best Documentary. 2002 Peabody Award. 2001 Broadcast Film Critics Association: Best Feature Documentary. 2001 Chicago Film Critics Association: Best Documentary. 1998 Hamptons International Film Festival: Audience Award, Most Popular Documentary. 2001 Columbus International Film & Video Festival: Silver Chris Award, Religion. 2001 Florida Film Critics Circle Awards: Best Documentary. 2001 National Society of Film Critics: Best Documentary. 2000 Kansas City Film Critics Circle Awards: Best Documentary. 2000 Las Vegas Film Critics Society: Sierra Award, Best Documentary. 2000 New York Film Critics Circle: Best Nonfiction Film.

Mad Hot Ballroom, 2005

Director: Marilyn Agrelo; Running Time: 105 minutes; U.S.

Earning more than $9 million at the box office, *Mad Hot Ballroom* is the highest-grossing documentary film that deals with sports or competition and one of the most successful nonfiction films of all time, regardless of subject matter. Filmmaker Marilyn Agrelo examines New York City fifth graders participating in a ballroom dance program, culminating with a citywide competition to determine the winning school. The program was introduced in 1994 with only two schools participating, but a decade later the program had grown to include over 6,000 kids from 60 schools in Manhattan, the Bronx, Brooklyn, and Queens. Public School 115, in the Washington Heights neighborhood of Uptown Manhattan, Public School 150, in the Tribeca neighborhood of Downtown Manhattan, and Public School 112, in the Bensonhurst neighborhood of Brooklyn, are three schools which Agrelo focuses on. At the participating schools, the ten-week course is required and the children are provided with dance instructors to teach them the basics of ballroom dancing, including specific dances such as the foxtrot, the merengue, the swing, the rumba, and the tango. In her debut feature film, Agrelo follows in the footsteps of *Spellbound*, the highly-successful Oscar-nominated film from a few years earlier following kids at the Scripps National Spelling Bee, to look in on children as they develop, improve, and compete. The themes of competition and teamwork are obvious, but the film can also be seen as an examination of race, class, and diversity. Likewise, the cruel reality and life lessons that come from losing play a central role in the film as two of the schools are eliminated.

The kids at PS 115 in Washington Heights are primarily Dominican, and the school has a 97 percent poverty rate. The principal there stresses the program's value in that it is free and allowing them to master something important that other kids might take for granted. PS 150 in Tribeca is more affluent and its kids seem to be more confident. The principal at PS 112 in Brooklyn argues that the program is more than simply learning dance steps or a branch of physical education; it's about etiquette, knowledge of other cultures, and learning about life. The diversity at the three schools is largely representative of the melting pot that New York City is. Similarly, the teamwork that begins to develop among the children is reminiscent of the unity that took place in the city only a few years earlier after the 9/11 terrorist attack. Stepping away from the pure vérité observational mode of filmmaking, Agrelo conducts some quirky interview segments with the kids away from class in which they speak about life in general in a candid, matter of fact way that older kids likely would not. Another aspect at play in *Mad Hot Ballroom*, and probably the one that makes the film so charming, is that the children are mostly 11 years old, which happens to be the stage of development that serves as something of a dividing line between the outright rejection of the opposite sex and when interest guided by puberty starts to take over. Based on a 2003 feature article written by Amy Sewell (who also co-produced) for *The Tribeca Trib* newspaper, the film had a remarkable theatrical run of six months in 2005. It is available in DVD and streaming format.

Awards: 2005 Gotham Awards: Celebrate New York Award (Agrelo, Amy Sewell); 2005 Karlovy Vary International Film Festival: Best Documentary Special Mention; 2005 National Board of Review: NBR Award, Top Five Documentaries; 2005 Philadelphia Film Festival: Best Documentary Audience Award; 2005 Satellite Awards: Outstanding Motion Picture—Documentary, Outstanding Documentary DVD; 2006 Christopher

Awards: Christopher Award; 2006 Young Artist Awards: Jackie Coogan Award, Outstanding Youth Feature Documentary; 2005 Dallas-Fort Worth Film Critics Association Awards: Best Documentary (nominated); 2005 International Documentary Association: IDA Award, Feature Documentaries (nominated); 2005 St. Louis Film Critics Association: Best Documentary Feature Film (nominated); 2006 Broadcast Film Critics Association Awards: Best Documentary (nominated); 2006 Chicago Film Critics Association Awards: Best Documentary (nominated); 2006 Gold Derby Awards: Documentary Feature (nominated); 2006 Golden Trailer Awards: Best Documentary (nominated); 2006 Image Awards: Outstanding Independent or Foreign Film (nominated); 2006 Online Film and Television Association: Best Documentary Picture (nominated).

Maidentrip, 2013

Director: Jillian Schlesinger; Running Time: 82 minutes; U.S.

Laura Dekker, a 14-year-old Dutch girl, became an international news item in 2009 when she announced that she planned to become the youngest sailor to solo circumnavigate the globe. Her plans sparked international outrage because of her age and the inherent danger involved, and a court battle lasting almost a year ensued when the Dutch government intervened to prevent her from setting sail. The government prevented her departure by taking sole custody of her away from her approving father (also an accomplished sailor) and placing her in shared custody with the Council for Child Care. The custody decision was eventually overruled and the decision was left up to her divorced parents concerning her safety. With supreme confidence in her sailing ability, Dekker's father (whom she lives with) points out in the film that there was no law to prevent it, so the government's efforts were "really weird." The media circus and court battle in Holland take a clear backseat to Dekker's personality and record-breaking circumnavigation in filmmaker Jillian Schlesinger's 2013 film *Maidentrip*, which documents the entire 518-day voyage that began with her departure from Gibraltar in late August 2010.

Wanting to focus narrowly on the voyage itself while exploring themes relating to isolation, self-confidence, and personal autonomy, Schlesinger steers away from the subject of the 2009 controversy surrounding Dekker. In her debut documentary, the filmmaking employed by Schlesinger is atypical to most documentaries because it is a very subjective story told only from the subject's point of view. Dekker even serves as something of a co-director, filming herself at sea in a similar fashion to what was employed by legendary filmmaker Werner Herzog in his 2005 film *Grizzly Man*, which features his subject filming himself among the bears in Alaska. Schlesinger makes great use of graphics and beautifully-animated map sequences to show Dekker's route and progress. While the risk for such a trip was not lessened, it should be explained that Dekker's voyage was not planned to be a non-stop circumnavigation, similar to those explored in the 2006 film *Deep Water*, about the 1968 *Sunday Times* Golden Globe Race. Dekker would be atop the high seas for weeks at a time, but also had planned to make numerous stops along the way, where she would be met by Schlesinger for filming and a support team or family members. In addition, she spent several weeks on land in the Canary Islands in October 2010 waiting out hurricane season and flew home to the Netherlands for two weeks the following March for media appearances.

Through the self-filmed footage of Dekker aboard her 38-foot ketch named "Guppy," a portrait of a very typical teenager emerges, one who puts off cleaning and school work (which she was doing via distance learning) in order to dye her hair and enjoy her recreational sailing. At the same time, however, that portrait also reveals one who is disciplined on her own terms, supremely confident, and an expert sailor who is completely at peace in her isolation. Certain moments in her filming also reveal a teenager who is clearly now harboring a grudge against her homeland for its objections to her plans and the media attention that she received. For example, when a Dutch reporter boards the Guppy to interview her, Dekker is not only aloof, but downright nasty. The age-old questions about government control versus personal freedom come into play when one considers Dekker's story, but as is typically the case with such arguments, the viewpoints are rarely consistent and change often depending on circumstances and especially on who is being controlled. Similarly, the theme of gender empowerment arises in *Maidentrip*, as does the extra question concerning whether or not the government objections and media storm were based on gender. The questions about personal autonomy and gender bias are fair, but may not be relevant since Schlesinger chooses to focus almost entirely on the accomplishment and journey rather than the controversy. The film won the prestigious Visions Audience Award at the 2013 South by South West (SXSW) Film Festival and was released on DVD the following year.

Awards: 2013 Camden International Film Festival: Audience Award; 2013 Flagstaff Mountain Film Festival: Best Feature; 2013 Port Townsend Film Festival: Special Jury Prize for First Time Director; 2013 South by

South West (SXSW) Film Festival: Visions Audience Award; 2013 MountainFilm in Telluride Festival: Festival Director's Award; 2014 Annapolis Film Festival: Best Documentary Feature.

The Man Who Skied Down Everest, 1975

Director: Bruce Nyznik, Lawrence Schiller; Running Time: 86 minutes; Canada/Nepal/Japan.

What is known today as big mountain skiing, freeskiing, or collectively as extreme skiing, was in its infancy during the 1960s. One of the adventuring pioneers of the sport was Yuichiro Miura, a Japanese alpinist and world class skier who, in Italy in 1964, set a world speed record of almost 108 miles per hour. Two years later, he became the first person to ski down Japan's Mount Fuji, where he developed an innovative safety system of deploying a parachute to slow his descent. By the close of the 1960s, Miura had skied down the highest peaks in North America and Australia. The daring adventure that lied ahead would be the subject for only the third sports-related film to win the Best Documentary Feature Academy Award. As the majority of the film is a documentation of the 22-day expedition of getting to the base camp and the scaling of Everest, *The Man Who Skied Down Everest* deals as much with alpinism, or mountaineering, as skiing. The film was recently restored for a DVD release and in 2010 it was selected for preservation by the Academy of Motion Picture Arts and Sciences Film Archive.

The 185-mile expedition began in Katmandu on March 6, 1970, using 800 porters and Sherpas to carry 27 tons of equipment, with the remaining team consisting of a Japanese ski team, scientists, and a film crew. Throughout the long journey, Miura narrates (via dubbed voice-over) from his own personal diary in a most reflective and introspective tone. His mood of narration only slightly changes when a cave in kills six of the Sherpas and he considers aborting his mission. The viewer is left wondering even more than Miura if one man's quest for adventure is worth it all. Ultimately, on May 6, Miura made the famous descent on Everest's South Col in which he would be traveling roughly 4,000 vertical feet at a 40–45 degree angle. Despite the questions about Miura's motivation and whether or not the loss of life and tremendous cost would ever be worth one man's daredevil adventure, filmmakers Bruce Nyznik and Lawrence Schiller's observational documentary will have viewers gripped to a true life and death situation. With an almost perfect fit, as the crisp cinematography becomes downright spooky during the surreal climax, Miura's voice-over narration is provided by Canadian actor Douglas Rain, the voice of HAL 9000 in Stanley Kubrick's *2001: A Space Odyssey.*

Awards: 1975 Academy Awards: Best Documentary Feature; 1975 Telluride Film Festival: Film Presented.

Meru, 2015
Director: Jimmy Chin, Elizabeth Chai Vasarhelyi; Running Time: 90 minutes; India/USA.

The multi-award-winning 2015 film *Meru* tells the story of the first successful ascent of the Central Meru Peak via the "shark's fin" route. Lying within the Himalayan Region of India above the Ganges River, Meru's Central Peak is considered one of the most difficult climbs in the world primarily because it requires excellence in all mountain climbing disciplines—ice climbing, rock climbing, and big wall climbing. John Krakauer, an experienced mountaineer and author of the bestselling books *Into the Wild* and *Into Thin Air*, describes Meru as the "anti–Everest" because it is a solitary endeavor—there are no Sherpas there to carry equipment, fix ropes, and take risks. Working as something of a narrator in the film's beginning; Krakauer adds that the shark's fin route on Meru Central has seen more attempts and more failures than any route in the Himalayas. The three American alpinists who first set out to conquer Meru in 2008 were Conrad Anker, Jimmy Chin, and Renan Ozturk. Anker, the lone member of the trio who has attempted Meru previously, is one of the best climbers in the world, but may be best known for locating the body of famed mountaineer George Mallory 75 years after his Mount Everest disappearance. Chin, who directs the film with his wife Elizabeth Chai Vasarhelyi, is known for his photography and big mountain skiing as much as climbing. Ozturk, who seems to be the least experienced of the trio, came to the attention of the others from his free solo climbing.

One of the elements that immediately sets *Meru* apart from other documentaries chronicling mountain-climbing expeditions is the fact that it is really a film in two major parts: the 2008 attempted ascent by the trio and their ultimately successful ascent three years later. This sort of organization fits the story perfectly because of circumstances that all three climbers are forced to deal with after their 2008 attempt falls short by only 100 meters. Faced with bad luck, unimaginable weather, and a lack of fuel and food, the decision to turn back despite being so close in 2008 was clearly taxing, but one gets the impression that the story of these three men would be much different had it not been made. Chin and Ozturk begin working together in the ensuing year and both have life-changing experiences. While skiing on assignment, Chin is swept up in a disastrous avalanche, but amazingly walks away. Ozturk, on the other hand, is not so lucky when he suffers a severe head injury and broken neck while skiing. His injuries are so serious that friends in the climbing community are aghast when they learn that Anker and Chin are allowing Ozturk to climb with them when they return to Meru in 2011. Therein lays the film's major themes: trust and loyalty. Although Anker suffers no life-changing experiences after their first attempt, his resolution to conquer Meru seems to be driven by the loss of a past partner and the family he is now responsible for.

Another element that sets *Meru* apart is Chin's participatory-mode filmmaking. With Anker typically being in the lead-climber role and Ozturk being Chin's secondary cinematographer, viewers get a bird's eye view of both the 2008 failed attempt and the 2011 successful ascent. In both cases, the cinematography is astonishing given the fact that it is taking place while scaling perhaps the world's most unclimbable peak. Scenes of the trio preparing to sleep via portaledge tent while dangling at nearly 20,000-feet really drive home the idea that shooting a film under these conditions is about as unique as filmmaking can possibly get. The two expeditions bookend the meaningful middle segment of the film which primarily details Ozturk's injury and rehabilitation, but also provides quite

Featured in *Meru* (2015) and known as one of the most difficult in the world, the Shark's Fin route on the central Meru Peak requires skill in all disciplines of climbing.

a bit of background information on all three men. In addition to Ozturk's injury, the film's themes of trust and loyalty are explored through Anker's decision to return and his unique personal story. In 1999, while on a skiing expedition in the Himalayas, Anker was seriously injured in an avalanche that killed his longtime climbing partner, Alex Lowe. Anker later married Lowe's widow and adopted his three children. His decision to return is obviously weighed against the commitment that he has made to his new family and the way he wants to honor the memory of his friend. Following a world premiere at the 2015 Sundance Film Festival, *Meru* had a fairly wide theatrical release and was shortlisted for the Documentary Feature Academy Award. It is widely available in streaming and DVD format.

Awards: Film Club's The Lost Weekend, 2015: Lost Weekend Award Best Documentary; 2015 Sundance Film Festival: Documentary Audience Award, Documentary Grand Jury Prize (nominated); 2015 Telluride Mountain Film Festival: Charlie Fowler Award; 2016 Cinema Eye Honors Awards: Audience Choice Prize, Outstanding Achievement in Cinematography (Chin, Ozturk), Outstanding Achievement in Production (nominated—Chin, Vasarhelyi, Shannon Ethridge), Outstanding Achievement in Original Music Score (nominated—J. Ralph); 2015 Amsterdam International Documentary Film Festival: IDFA Audience Award (nominated); 2015 Indiana Film Journalists Association: Best Documentary (nominated); 2015 Nashville Film Festival: Documentary Grand Jury Prize (nominated); 2015 San Diego Film Critics Society Awards: Best Documentary (nominated); 2015 San Francisco Film Critics Circle: Best Documentary (nominated); 2015 Shanghai International Film Festival: Best Documentary Golden Goblet (nominated); 2016 Director's Guild of America: Outstanding Directorial Achievement in Documentary (nominated); 2016 Film Independent Spirit Awards: Best Documentary (nominated); 2016 Guild of Music Supervisors Awards: Best Song/Recording Created for a Film (nominated—Adrian Gurvitz, Andra Day, Lauren Christy, Tracy McKnight); 2016 Producer's Guild of America Awards: Outstanding Producer of Documentary Theatrical Motion Pictures (nominated—Chin, Vasarhelyi).

Mighty Jerome, 2010

Director: Charles Officer; Running Time: 84 minutes; Canada.

Produced by the National Film Board of Canada and directed by filmmaker Charles Officer, *Mighty Jerome* revisits the life and career of track and field athlete Harry Jerome, who represented Canada in three consecutive Olympic Games during the 1960s and held several world records. Jerome was born in Prince Albert, Saskatchewan in 1940 and later moved with his family to North Vancouver where he first started competing in track and field. Along with Valerie, his equally-athletic sister who also competed in the 1960 Summer Games, Jerome was one of only three black kids in his high school and fully aware that his family was not welcomed in the area. At the 1959 Vancouver District Track Meet, Jerome shattered the Canadian record for the 220-yard sprint that was held by Percy Williams, the Canadian hero who had won two gold medals in the 1928 Summer Olympics. The record thrust Jerome into the spotlight and he was now considered one of the favorites for the 100 meter gold medal at the 1960 Summer Games in Rome. Despite growing up amid racial tension in an overwhelmingly white area, Jerome was quiet and unaccustomed to the attention and pressure that would soon come his way only one year after his high school graduation. Officer delivers the story in artistic fashion, opting for black and white photography, archival footage, and dramatic reenactments transporting the viewer back to the 1950s and early 1960s. Officer also conducts interviews with moody shading in a sporting museum atmosphere and uses intertitles similar to William Klein's 1974 artistic film *Muhammad Ali, the Greatest: 1964–1974.*

Jerome was heavily criticized by the Canadian press for his performance in the Rome Olympics, in which he failed to complete the race due to a pulled muscle. Only a few months prior to the games, he had tied the world record 100 meter time of 10.0 and as a result unfair expectations were placed on him to bring the gold back to Canada. Officer next takes the film to Jerome's years as a student-athlete at the University of Oregon, where he met his future wife, Wendy, and dealt with the backlash of an interracial marriage in the United States. Competing in the 1962 British Empire and Commonwealth Games in Perth, Australia, Jerome once again performed poorly and the media was even more scathing, referring to him as a "quitter," but his injury this time around was so severe that doctors thought he would never run again. Following a year of rehabilitation, Jerome returned to compete in the 1964 Tokyo Olympics, taking bronze in the 100 behind his close friend, co-world record holder, and American rival Bob Hayes. Bill Bowerman, the legendary track coach at the University of Oregon, called Jerome's return to the top of world class sprinting "the greatest comeback in track and field history." The comeback continued with gold medals at the 1966 British Commonwealth Games and the 1967 Pan-American Games. While not too uncommon today, it was virtually unheard of for a sprinter to compete in three Olympics during the 1960s, but Jerome did that when he returned to compete in the 1968 Mexico City Olympics. The film is available in DVD format from the NFB website and available for streaming elsewhere.

Awards: 2011 Leo Awards: Best Feature Length Documentary Program, Best Picture Editing in a Documentary Program or Series (Jesse James Miller), Best Overall Sound in a Documentary Program or Series (Jon Ritchie, Eric Harwood Davies), Best Musical Score in a Documentary Program or Series (Schaun Tozer); 2012 Northwest Regional Emmy Awards: Best Historical Documentary; 2011 Vancouver Film Critics Circle: Best British Columbia Film (nominated); 2012 Hot Docs: Don Haig Award (Honorable Mention).

More Than a Game, 2008
Director: Kristopher Belman; Running Time: 105 minutes; U.S.

Sian Cotton, Dru Joyce III, Willie McGee, and Romeo Travis: these were the four childhood friends and high school basketball teammates of LeBron James—collectively known as Akron's Fab Five. Filmmaker Kristopher Belman, an Akron, Ohio, native himself, spent seven years following this group of friends for his film *More Than a Game*. Belman found their friendship to be inspiring and unique, and his film certainly captures that strong bond. Long before any of the group was dunking, the earliest footage of the group comes from their days in youth AAU basketball. Their coach, Dru Joyce II, knew that the team could be something special because his "neighborhood team" was dominating all-star teams from entire geographic regions. The group of James, Cotton, Joyce III, and McGee all attended St. Vincent-St. Mary High School in Akron, where Travis would later join and have a difficult time embracing the already tight-knit group.

When the team's coach moves on to the collegiate level, the group's former AAU coach, Joyce II, takes over. Aside from the meteoric rise of James as a high school phenom, the most interesting aspect of the film may be the coach-player, father-son dynamic of Coach Joyce and his diminutive son, the team's point guard and emotional leader. Despite the team's swagger and the media circus that their national exposure brings, the team still consists of ordinary high school students who often faced not so ordinary circumstances in life. The themes of friendship and unity are thoroughly explored, but like some other films about high school basketball, it may miss a golden opportunity to explore the growing commercialism of the sport at what should be its most purely amateur level. The

DVD special features include a look at the film's music and a featurette about sports psychology.

Awards: 2008 Toronto International Film Festival: People's Choice Award (2nd place); 2010 Black Reel Awards: Best Documentary (nominated); 2010 Image Awards: Outstanding Documentary (nominated); 2010 Independent Spirit Awards: Best Documentary (nominated).

Muhammad Ali, the Greatest: 1964–1974, 1974

Director: William Klein; Running Time: 110 minutes; France.

William Klein, an American expatriate turned French artist, fashion photographer, and occasional filmmaker, provides the definitive cinéma vérité account of Muhammad Ali's rise to stardom and controversy during the 1960s. Following a 1969 release under the title *Float Like a Butterfly, Sting Like a Bee*, Klein added a second half to his film when he documented Ali and then-champion George Foreman in Zaire as they prepare for their 1974 title bout. Unlike the many other films which take a retrospective look at young Cassius Clay, Klein allows viewers a more intimate, fly on the wall glimpse of the events as they happen. Shot in black and white with the use of tight shots and artistic divergences into American culture of the time, the first half of the film is a documentation of Ali's first year in the public eye—his upset of champion Sonny Liston, in Miami in 1964, his conversion to Islam, and his rematch with Liston the following year in Maine. While the film defers to an examination of Ali as a cultural icon and polarizing figure instead of more technical examinations of boxing, it includes several rare pieces of footage which might make it the most important film on the subject of Ali.

Among these rare gems, an interview with the Louisville Syndicate, a group of older, wealthy Southern businessmen who had financed Ali in his early career is both fascinating and revealing. Likewise, a candid interview with Malcolm X only two weeks before his assassination, footage of the Beatles visiting with Ali, a young Angelo Dundee haggling with boxing officials, dramatic interpretations of Ali by students in Harlem, and the crowd's suspicious reaction to Ali's knockout of Liston in their 1965 rematch highlight the first half of Klein's work. As the film takes on the additional subject of the 1974 match against Foreman in Zaire, it is connected by a series of intertitles which fill the viewer in to what has transpired since 1965, specifically Ali's controversial stance on the Vietnam War and subsequent banning from the sport. It also appropriately switches from Klein's shaky black and white 1960s photography to pristine color and a more technical approach. Klein remains preoccupied with the persona of Ali in the film's second half, but reverts back to his artistic style of photography, taking in advertisements and public reactions along the way to a final collage of symbolic American images.

As it is really a compilation of films and often mislabeled among internet sources, beware the confusion of this title amid the many other documentary films, feature films, and videos about Ali. Klein's artistic *Muhammad Ali, The Greatest* is really a film of two parts edited from three different productions: his 1964 award-winning short film for French television *Cassius le Grand*, his 1969 American theatrical release *Float Like a Butterfly, Sting Like a Bee*, and this 1974 version which added the chapter of Ali regaining the world title in Zaire. Perhaps because the full 110-minute version was not remastered and released on DVD until 2003, this brilliant film has not been given the same attention as others covering the same subject. Similarly, Klein's low-budget films have usually screened in the United States only as part of museum retrospectives or special presentation film series. Part one of the film was screened in New York in 1969, but the full version did not find U.S. theaters again until 2003. Also covering the 1974 fight with Foreman in Zaire, comparisons to Leon Gast's 1996 Academy Award-winning *When We Were Kings* are inevitable, but Klein's film deserves similar attention due to his poetic and artistic approach. The Facets DVD release features an interesting commentary track with the director for select scenes.

Awards: *Cassius le Grand*: 1970 Oscar of the Havana Festival (Cuba); 1965 Grand Prix of the Tours Festival (France); 1965 Festival of the People of Firenze (France); *Muhammad Ali, The Greatest*: 2007 Thessaloniki International Film Festival (selection); 2009 Buenos Aires International Festival of Independent Cinema (selection).

Murderball, 2005

Director: Henry Alex Rubin, Dana Adam Shapiro; Running Time: 88 minutes; U.S.

While basketball and racing may be the most well-known wheelchair sports, rugby is easily the most physical. The sport is often called "murderball" because of its physical nature, or quad rugby because it was designed for athletes with function loss in the upper body as well as lower body. In other words, the sport is limited to those with quadriplegia or amputations rather than paraplegia. The sport itself is unique because of the physical contact it requires. Players use their specially-designed wheelchairs to ram others in order to stop advances, and often end up on the floor. In their Oscar-nominated film, directors Henry Alex Rubin and Dana Adam Shapiro venture into this world to document the lives of members of the United States National Wheelchair Rugby Team and their quest to remain at the top of international competition leading up to the 2004 Paralympic Games. The focus of Rubin and Shapiro is not limited strictly to the U.S. team though; they also spend quite a bit of time with Joe Soares, an American who is coaching Canada's team. Soares, perhaps the sport's most decorated player ever, indicates that he is coaching Team Canada because he still wants to be involved in the sport, but some of the American players and personnel argue that it's sour grapes because Soares had been cut from Team USA after their gold medal run in 1996 due to age and diminishing skills. Naturally, the rivalry between the two countries has intensified because of this, and when you learn that Soares sued Team USA before heading north to coach with the American playbook, the rivalry is ratcheted up even more.

Aside from a brief explanation of the point system relating to players' disability classification levels, in which players can be deemed a 1, 2, or 3 depending on how much upper body function they have (no team can have more than eight points on the court at a time), not much of an introduction to the sport is provided. Because the film develops in such a character-driven way with the supplemental conflict of the USA/Canada rivalry unfolding in participatory documentary fashion, not much information about the rules and history of the sport is needed. We do find out, however, that Team USA has dominated the sport, winning all 11 international competitions since its worldwide acceptance in the mid–1990s. The next international competition, the 2002 Wheelchair Rugby World Championships, involves 12 nations and is where Rubin and Shapiro begin their documentation. The central focus remains on the rivalry between Team Canada and Team USA while the 2002 tournament and 2004 Paralympic Games in Athens take place, but the film also explores the private lives of a few American players. This examination is critical to understanding the dynamic of team, community, and interaction among a previously marginalized group. Likewise, *Murderball* also clearly explores the theme of masculinity in that the idea or notion of masculinity is sometimes an internal perception rather than an outward projection. Distributed by ThinkFilm, the relatively low-budget film was incredibly successful, collecting numerous awards and earning more than $1.5 million.

Awards: 2005 Boston Society of Film Critics Awards: Best Documentary; 2005 Dallas-Fort Worth Film Critics Association Awards: Best

Documentary; 2005 Full Frame Documentary Film Festival: Audience Award, Jury Award; 2005 Gotham Awards: Best Documentary; 2005 Indianapolis International Film Festival: Best Feature Audience Award; 2005 Jackson Hole Film Festival: Best Documentary, Best Sports Action; 2005 Kansas City Film Critics Circle Awards: Best Documentary; 2005 National Board of Review: Top Five Documentaries; 2005 Seattle International Film Festival: Best Documentary; 2005 Sundance Film Festival: Documentary Audience Award, Documentary Special Jury Prize; Documentary Grand Jury Prize (nominated); 2005 Utah Film Critics Association Awards: Best Documentary Feature Film; 2006 Austin Film Critics Association Best Documentary; 2006 Chlotrudis Awards: Best Documentary; 2005 British Film Institute Awards: Sutherland Trophy (Special Mention); 2005 International Documentary Association: Feature Documentaries (nominated); 2005 Satellite Awards: Outstanding Motion Picture, Documentary (nominated), Outstanding Documentary DVD (nominated); 2005 St Louis Film Critics Association: Best Documentary Feature Film (nominated); 2006 Academy Awards: Best Documentary Feature (nominated); 2006 Broadcast Film Critics Association Awards: Best Documentary (nominated); 2006 Central Ohio Film Critics Association: Best Picture (6th place); 2006 Chicago Film Critics Association Awards: Best Documentary (nominated); 2006 Gold Derby Awards: Documentary Feature (nominated); 2006 International Documentary Film Festival of Navarra Punto de Vista: Grand Prize (nominated); 2006 Online Film & Television Association: Best Documentary Feature (nominated); 2006 Online Film Critics Society Awards: Best Documentary (nominated).

My Run, 2009

Director: Tim VandeSteeg; Running Time: 85 minutes; U.S.

In the months leading up to the 1996 Summer Olympics, Terry Hitchcock ran 2,100 miles from St. Paul, Minnesota, to Atlanta, and he did it in marathon-sized chunks every single day. To be exact, he ran a little more than the 26.2-mile marathon distance for 75 consecutive days. This alone is a monumental accomplishment for even the most seasoned, highly-trained, and conditioned athlete, but when one considers that Hitchcock did this at 57 years old with virtually no distance running experience, it stands out as remarkable even more. When one factors in that Hitchcock accomplished this feat after suffering a heart attack when his training first began and that he finished the 75 marathons with bone fractures in both ankles, it is downright amazing. Both of the obvious questions that come to mind—what motivated Hitchcock to do this and how on earth did he accomplish it—are explored in the 2009 film, *My Run*, by director Tim VandeSteeg. Rather than simple *Forrest Gump*–type therapeutic reasoning, Hitchcock ran for a very personal reason that he wanted to make public. Inspired by Terry Fox, the Canadian athlete who lost a leg to cancer and ran across Canada in 1980 to raise money and awareness for cancer research, Hitchcock ran in order to raise awareness for the issue of single-parent families. He had discovered that 35 million American families were just like his, children being raised by a single parent, and he hoped that his run would make people take notice of that number.

Roughly a decade before Hitchcock began his 2,100-mile run, his wife, Sue, was diagnosed with breast cancer and passed away not long afterward. On top of that blow, Hitchcock lost his job immediately after and he soon found himself as a single parent with no income. Within a matter of weeks, Hitchcock had gone from being the breadwinner of a family, with very little experience in day-to-day care for his three children, to doing everything alone. By the mid–1990s, when his children had become young adults and he had started multiple successful businesses, Hitchcock decided that he wanted to give something back to the millions of other single parents and children of single parents. His idea was simply to gain media exposure to their plight. His journey began with a full crew traveling with him, but it soon dwindled down to just one of his sons, which ended up being all the support he needed. In the modern age of fame-seeking and instant celebrity, it would be easy to misconstrue his efforts for media exposure, but Hitchcock's authenticity for his cause is obvious. VandeSteeg presents this heartwarming story with elements of an expository mode documentary, with narration by Oscar-winner Billy Bob Thornton, elements of the observational mode, in which we unobtrusively see the actual run, and elements of participatory mode, in which Hitchcock and others offer one-to-one testimonials to the filmmaker. With help from the 1990s archival footage of Hitchcock in various towns across the country, that unique filmmaking mixture comes together beautifully in this award-winning film about a not-so-exceptional athlete with tons of determination. The film is available for streaming of in DVD format.

Awards: 2009 Austin Film Festival: Best Documentary Audience Award; 2009 Mammoth Film Festival: Best Documentary; 2010 DocMiami International Film Festival: Audience Award; 2010 Las Vegas International Film Festival: Best Feature Film Grand Jury Prize; 2010 Newport Beach

Film Festival: Outstanding Achievement in Documentary Filmmaking; 2010 Visionfest (Domani Vision Film Society): Documentary Feature.

Next Goal Wins, 2013

Director: Mike Brett, Steve Jamison; Running Time: 97 minutes; U.K.

Next Goal Wins is a heartwarming story about the world's worst soccer team: the national team of American Samoa. The tiny island nation of just under 60,000 played its first FIFA-recognized international match in 1998 and by 2011 it had lost 24 matches in a row, surrendering 210 goals in those matches. This includes a 31–0 loss to Australia, which stands as the worst international defeat in history. The 2001 match versus Australia is where the film begins as viewers see an excruciating montage of all 31 goals. Comically bad and obviously inferior to every team they will face on the international stage, it becomes impossible not to cheer for this team when their dedication and unity are witnessed throughout the film. Filmmakers Mike Brett and Steve Jamison do far more with their 2013 film than the typical underdog story. The themes of unity and redemption are front and center, but the film also explores pride—both personal pride and pride in one's nation and heritage. The humiliating losses and notoriety of being the worst team in the world are not the only things serving as motivation: unlike many international footballers, the players of American Samoa hold regular jobs and train around their work schedules, while also attempting to rebuild from the devastating 2009 tsunami.

The story develops around the team's attempt to qualify for the 2014 World Cup and its relationship with their new coach, Thomas Rongen. Rongen is a fiery, Dutch-born American who was the only applicant for the job through the United States Soccer Federation's posting. Rongen's disciplinary approach at first clashes with the laid-back players, but he eventually wins them over with his softer side after revealing his deeply personal motivation for taking the job. In addition to the typical coaching and professionalism brought in by Rongen, the team also hopes to improve by adding a few American Samoan players living in the United States. Aside from Rongen, viewers are not intimately introduced to many of the players, with Nicky Salapu and Jaiyah Saelua being exceptions. Salapu is the team's former goalkeeper, who had left the sport to work in Seattle, but returns to attempt to expel the demons of past humiliating losses. Saelua is fa'afafine, which is the culturally-accepted third gender of Samoan people. In the 2011 qualifying matches, she not only became the first transgender player in FIFA history, but also started and played outstanding at

Next Goal Wins **(2014) explores the unique relationship between the national football team of American Samoa and its coach, Thomas Rongen (right).**

her defensive center back position. After premiering at the 2014 Tribeca Film Festival, *Next Goal Wins* was released theatrically in the United States, United Kingdom, France, Australia, Japan, and the Middle East. It is available in both streaming and DVD format.

Awards: 2014 British Independent Film Awards: Best Documentary; 2014 Abu Dhabi Film Festival: Documentary Special Jury Award; Best Documentary Feature Black Pearl Award (nominated); 2015 Sunscreen Film Festival: Best Documentary; 2015 Thinking Football Film Festival: Audience Award; 2015 London Critics' Circle Film Awards: Documentary of the Year (nominated).

No No: A Dockumentary, 2014

Director: Jeff Radice; Running Time: 100 minutes; U.S.

A treasure-trove of baseball nostalgia and archival footage, *No No: A Dockumentary* examines the colorful career of former Major League Baseball pitcher Dock Ellis. With his feature directorial debut, filmmaker Jeff Radice uses the most well-known anecdote about Ellis's career as the basis and the starting point for his film, but he dives far deeper into the pitcher's background and career in order to create a solid biographical documentary. Ellis's career statistics of a 138–119 win/loss record, 3.46 earned run average, and 1,136 strikeouts over 2,128 innings may only be slightly above average, but his on and off-field persona was Hall of Fame worthy. The most notable example of this comes from his lone no-hit game occurring in 1970, roughly two years after his MLB debut. Despite no-hitting the

Padres (a "no-no" in baseball jargon), Ellis was particularly wild in the outing, walking eight batters and hitting one, which he explained some 14 years later as a result of having been under the influence of LSD. Many former players and writers doubt that his claim is true, and offer his tendency to embellish, but others find it quite believable simply because his drug usage was so heavy. Regardless of *how* accurate the anecdote is and just *how* under the influence Ellis really was, his drug and alcohol usage, his outspokenness, his battles with management, and his overall flamboyant nature are primarily what Ellis became most known for.

While the majority of contemporary sports documentaries examine a specific issue or sport in the present, *No No* instead revisits the past and takes viewers back to the 1970s, when Baseball was still the number one sport in America and the changing culture clashed with it frequently. In participatory documentary fashion, with heavy use of archival footage and a 1970s soundtrack, stories about Ellis abound from former teammates with the Pittsburgh Pirates of the 1970s, a club that won five NL East titles in six years from 1970 to 1975. Ellis took to wearing curlers in his hair, which led to a battle with management, and he once began a game by beaning the first three batters of the arch-rival Cincinnati Reds, which led to a quick hook and one of the more interesting box score stat lines in baseball history. Radice treats the antics of Ellis with the humor that some of them deserve, but also doesn't shy away from offering the warts and all account of his troubles stemming from alcohol and drug dependency. Two of his former wives provide details of singular violent episodes that were likely the direct result of drugs or alcohol, but both interestingly seem to remember him fondly. Prior to passing away in 2008 from a liver ailment, Ellis had not only gotten clean, but also become a successful drug and alcohol counselor to inmates. Following a premiere at the 2014 Sundance Film Festival, the film was made available in both streaming and DVD format.

Awards: 2014 Boulder International Film Festival: Best Editing (Sam Wainwright Douglas); 2014 Sundance Film Festival: Documentary Grand Jury Prize (nominated); 2014 South by Southwest Film Festival (SXSW): Festival Favorites Audience Award (nominated); 2015 Houston Film Critics Society Awards: Texas Independent Film Award (nominated).

Okie Noodling, 2001

Director: Bradley Beesley; Running Time: 57 minutes; U.S.

In some areas of the Southern United States it is called grabbling or hogging, but in Oklahoma it is called noodling. Technically, its name is handfishing and it may be the purest and most primitive form of fishing. It involves catfish hunters submerging themselves to the bottom of lakes or rivers and finding holes, where the fish are enticed to bite the hunter's hand and then are pulled to the surface. A host of wet, usually-shirtless characters proudly display scarred forearms and offer tales of encounters with snapping turtles, snakes, and beavers. Filmmaker Bradley Beesley, an Oklahoma native whose relatives are noodlers, explores his personal fascination with this rural subculture adventure and takes viewers along in his participatory documentary. Beesley is even the catalyst for the first statewide noodling tournament, which unfolds at the film's conclusion and is still held annually. The film not only spawned the yearly noodling tournament, but also a sequel documentary (*Okie Noodling II*, 2008) and a television show (*Mudcats*). Indie rock band, and fellow Oklahomans, The Flaming Lips, provide the soundtrack. Okie Noodling is available in DVD or streaming format.

Awards: 2001 Great Plains Film Festival: Best Documentary; 2001 South by Southwest Film Festival (SXSW): Best Documentary Audience Award, Documentary Competition (2nd place).

Olympia, 1938

Director: Leni Riefenstahl; Running Time: 226 minutes; Germany.

A film of nearly four hours split into two parts. *Festival of the Nations* and *Festival of the Beauty*, *Olympia* is German filmmaker Leni Riefenstahl's documentation of the 1936 Summer Olympics in Berlin. Although a few attempts had been made of documenting previous summer and Winter Olympics via film, this was the first true feature-length documentary of the Olympic Games in the post-silent film era and post-documentary film movement in Great Britain. In what basically began the tradition of a filmmaker being commissioned and sanctioned to document each Olympic Games, Riefenstahl's account of the 1936 games is at once both brilliant and disturbing: brilliant in the innovative filmmaking techniques she used and disturbing in the relative proximity that Adolf Hitler had to the film. Riefenstahl first gained notoriety as an actress and dancer, but moved on to directing films in the 1930s. While her outright allegiance to Hitler and the Nazi Party has been debated for decades, she certainly brought her skillful filmmaking to the Nazi cause by directing *Der Sieg des Glaubens* (*The Victory of Faith*, 1933), and *Triumph des Willens* (*Triumph of the Will*, 1935), two of the most notorious examples of Nazi propaganda films. Questions still linger about Riefenstahl's true intent of

Olympia and to what degree that her original film even exists, but its importance to Olympic history and the history of documentary film is clear.

In his book *Olympia*, first published in 1993, historian Taylor Downing examines both of these lingering questions, pointing out that although it was received with great acclaim throughout Europe, "the war transformed the history of the film." What Downing is probably referring to is that different language versions of the film were seized by different military authorities during the war and were likely censored and altered from Riefenstahl's original version. In addition, Riefenstahl was imprisoned by Allied authorities after the war and investigated as a war criminal, subsequently cutting and re-editing the film herself as part of her "de-Nazification." Downing argues that possibly none of the versions in existences in archives around the world are the "same as that first shown in Berlin in April 1938 at the gala premiere on Hitler's birthday" (11). With that in mind, one might have a hard time detecting overt Nazi propaganda elements in the film as it exists now, but it seems to be clearer that a nationalistic element is evident when Riefenstahl fixates her camera on Hitler as a spectator numerous times in *Festival of the Nations*. Although Riefenstahl was never convicted as a war criminal and only deemed to be guilty of Nazi sympathies, the brilliance of her filmmaking in the case of *Olympia* has taken a back seat to the controversy of her horrific ideology of the time.

As for the film itself, Part One, *Festival of the Nations*, is a fairly straightforward account of the games, but focuses almost entirely on the track and field events and is far more artistic than the official Olympic films that would follow. It begins with a clear poetic mode bent as Riefenstahl dreamily views Greek architecture and a statue of a Greek athlete that transforms into a real athlete. An artistic segment with similarly nude female dancers follows before the scene of ancient Greece morphs into the torch lighting and eventually into the parade of nations inside Olympic Stadium in Berlin. It is here that disturbing images of Hitler emerge and Nazi salutes are common among both the spectators and many of the parading athletes, and presumably not just German athletes. Most notably in Part One, however, is the men's 100 meter event, won by American Jesse Owens—one of his four gold medals in 1936. The topic of Owens, a black man, winning in the face of Hitler's Aryan superiority beliefs has been covered plenty and even became a legendary sports moment, but one has to wonder if this part of the film was one that Riefenstahl heavily edited because Hitler is missing altogether. The announcer and subtitles for the men's 110 meter hurdles, on the other hand, continually refer to bronze medal winner Fritz Pollard, Jr. (son of the Pro Football Hall of Famer) as "the black American."

Part Two, *Festival of the Beauty*, is more of a pure poetic mode documentary as it offers plenty of divergences into the artistic side of athletics and seems to be far less concerned with the actual outcomes or creating a statistical record of the events. Starting with another celebration of the human athletic body, Riefenstahl films male athletes as they jog, swim in a pre-dawn lake, and take a nude sauna break. Its most famous sequence is the artistic venture into male divers as Riefenstahl mixes unique camera angles, lighting, and underwater filming to transform the competition into more of a painting on canvas. Many other filmmaking techniques that Riefenstahl employed were used for the first time in nonfiction film, but became standard and common afterwards. These primarily include her usage of a motorized system for tracking shots and camera angles both from above below the athletes. While at the same time that *Olympia* and Riefenstahl could be admired as perhaps the most important sports film and sports filmmaker of all-time, it also can be seen as a mere tool for Nazi propaganda, ordered up by Hitler himself through his personal filmmaker. Fortunately, however, the version widely available for steam viewing or in DVD format in North America is clearly the later version edited by Riefenstahl to cut back on the Nazi propaganda elements.

Awards: 1938 Greek Sports Prize; 1938 Swedish Polar Prize; 1938 Venice Film Festival: Best Foreign Film Mussolini Cup; 1941 Kinema Junpo Awards: Best Foreign Language Film; 1948 International Lausanne Film Festival: Olympic Diploma.

The Olympics in Mexico (*Olimpiada en Mexico*), 1969

Director: Alberto Isaac; Running Time: 120 minutes; Mexico.

This official film of the 1968 Summer Olympics in Mexico City may be the most underrated among all of the Olympic films. Its director was Alberto Isaac, a Mexican athlete-turned-filmmaker who himself had competed in the 1948 and 1952 Summer Olympics as a swimmer. With heavy use of narration, Isaac takes a straightforward expository approach of recounting the different events, but also creates an artistic picture through a mixture of outstanding cinematography, music, and slow-motion detail. Isaac also provides viewers with an interesting look at the concurrent 1968 Cultural Olympiad, a festival to celebrate international excellence in the arts. The film steers very clear, however, of any mention of the two major political controversies surrounding the Olympics: the threat of a boycott by several nations and athletes if the apartheid nation of South Africa was represented and the Tlatelolco massacre, in which hundreds of protesting students were killed during a military suppression attempt only ten days before the games were set to begin.

The most controversial aspect of the actual competition, and one of the most memorable Olympic moments of all-time, was also avoided by the film's narration, but Isaac treats the now-famous black power salute of American 200-meter sprinters Tommie Smith and John Carlos by silently zeroing in on the raised back-gloved fists of the athletes on the medal podium. The third medalist on the podium after the 200 was Australian Peter Norman, who strongly supported Smith and Carlos's political statement, and whose nephew, Matt, explored the famous moment in his own 2008 documentary film *Salute*. Other historically-important Olympic moments covered in the film include American discus champion Al Oerter becoming the first track and field athlete to win four consecutive golds in the same event, American high-jumper Dick Fosbury capturing gold while introducing his now-standard leap and backward flop technique, and American long-jumper Bob Beamon's 29.2-feet jump, which shattered the world record by nearly two feet.

Awards: 1970 Academy Awards: Best Documentary Feature (nominated).

On Any Sunday, 1971

Director: Bruce Brown; Running Time: 96 minutes; U.S.

In the 1960s, documentary filmmaker Bruce Brown explored the growing pastime of surfing in *The Endless Summer*. In 1971, he did the same thing with the sport of motorcycle racing in his Oscar-nominated film *On Any Sunday*. In both cases, Brown explored the subjects in such a way that appealed to those already involved and those who were just curious. Just as *The Endless Summer* sent people deep into surfing and beach culture, *On Any Sunday* surely had an enormous impact on the unprecedented interest in motorcycle racing in the United States during the 1970s, and especially with the off-road variety of motocross. Brown touches on obscure and extremely specialized forms of motorcycle sport such as the very unique sidecar racing, ice racing, hill climbs, and land speed racing to the more common forms like endurance racing, drag racing, road racing, and dirt track racing.

A number of the greatest motorcycle racers in the world are briefly profiled in the film, but the most time is spent with prolific champion Malcolm Smith, Mert Lawwill, and actor Steve McQueen, who had competed in many events and who was a chief financer of the film. An interesting aspect of *On Any Sunday* is the fact that the film sets out to welcome viewers and introduce them to motorcycle sport. There is no secret society lingo or any sort of elitism that one may sense in films dealing with sports such as surfing or rock climbing. Aside from the quintessential early 1970s music by composer Dominic Frontiere (who would later marry LA Rams majority owner Georgia Frontiere), the film largely avoids being dated by technological advances and many changes in the sport. A far less successful sequel to the film, *On Any Sunday II* by directors Ed Forsyth and Don Shoemaker, was released in 1981. Brown's son, Dana, directed *On Any Sunday: The Next Chapter* in 2014.

Awards: 1972 Academy Awards: Best Documentary Feature (nominated).

On the Ropes, 1999

Director: Nanette Burstein, Brett Morgen; Running Time: 94 minutes; U.S.

In their Oscar-nominated 1999 film *On the Ropes*, co-directors Nanette Burstein and Brett Morgen (*The Kid Stays in the Picture*, 2002) follow three young amateur boxers and their inspirational trainer as they train for the 1997 New York Golden Gloves Tournament. Having once served as the home gym for champions such as Riddick Bowe and Mark Breland, the New Bed-Stuy Boxing Center in the Bedford-Stuyvesant neighborhood of Brooklyn is the central location for the film and where all three boxers train under Harry Keitt. Keitt is a middle-aged man who was once a promising boxer in his own right, but wound up in prison for attempted murder and was homeless for a period after his release. Keitt credits boxing with saving his life and he seems intent on not just training young boxers in the ring, but also being an inspirational force to keep them from making the same mistakes out of the ring. In addition to Keitt's story of redemption, Burstein and Morgen explore a number of overlapping themes through the respective stories of the three boxers: confidence and discipline with Noel Santiago, a high school dropout from a troubled home, loyalty and betrayal with George Walton, already a Golden Gloves champion on the cusp of becoming a professional, and dignity and self-respect with Tyrene Manson, a silver-medalist from the previous year who is now facing incredible difficulties in her personal life.

Keitt's life lessons could be most easily applied to Santiago, a teenager who grew up without a father and a mother addicted to crack. Despite not showing much promise, Keitt continues to push Santiago in the ring and keep him focused on the straight and narrow out of it. Walton, the middleweight Golden Gloves champion from 1996, clearly has a bright future ahead; the only questions are when he will move on to the pro ranks and with whom. Walton's segments are particularly interesting as they provide a close look at the business side of the sport and the trail of animosity that those business decisions often leave behind. When boxing promoters come calling on Walton, he is forced to make a decision that tests his loyalty to Keitt. Perhaps the most heartbreaking and inspiring character is Manson, who showed lots of potential in winning the silver medal in 1996, but is now facing a long prison sentence. Raising two young cousins as her own children in a house with her drug-addicted uncle, Manson is guilty only of association, but the police and court system seem uninterested in the facts. Manson's story could actually become a separate film entirely, providing both a tale of caution and an examination of an unfair justice system. With this being Morgen's second feature film (*Ollie's Army*, 1996) and Burstein's first, the filmmakers capture the lives of the three boxers in perfect cinéma vérité fashion, using low-budget approaches and intimate participation. After a premiere at the 1999 Sundance Film Festival, *On the Ropes* was released theatrically and had a DVD release the following year.

Awards: 1999 International Documentary Association: IDA Award, Feature Documentary; 1999 San Francisco International Film Festival: Film & Video—Society & Culture Silver Spire Award; 1999 Sundance Film Festival: Documentary Special Jury Prize, Documentary Grand Jury Prize (nominated); 1999 Urbanworld Film Festival: Best Documentary Jury Prize; 2000 Director's Guild of America: Outstanding Directorial Achievement in Documentary; 2000 Santa Fe Film Critics Circle Awards: Best Documentary; 1999 Taos Talking Picture Festival: Taos Land Grant Award (nominated); 2000 Academy Awards: Best Feature Documentary (nominated); 2000 Independent Spirit Awards: Truer Than Fiction Award (nominated).

Once in a Lifetime: The Extraordinary Story of the New York Cosmos, 2006

Director: Paul Crowder, John Dower; Running Time: 97 minutes; U.S.

Filmmakers Paul Crowder (*Amazing Journey: The Story of the Who*, 2007) and John Dower (*Thrilla in Manilla*, 2008) provide a needed documentary film treatment to the history of professional soccer in the United States with their 2006 film *Once in a Lifetime: The Extraordinary Story of the New York Cosmos*. While their ambitious treatment is certainly entertaining, its focus is almost singularly upon the one most notorious and most famous franchise rather than its league or sport as a whole—just as the film's title indicates. The sport of soccer was virtually non-existent in the United States in the 1950s and 1960s, but after the 1966 World Cup in England received high television ratings across America, investors became convinced that professional soccer could be successful in the U.S. Two leagues sprung up in 1967 and merged into one a year later, calling itself the North American Soccer League. The league was failing badly in the early years, but when Warner Communications president Steve Ross decided to get involved by establishing a team in New York in 1971, the league's fortunes would soon change.

That change, however, would not come until Ross was able to sign legendary Brazilian player Pelé in 1975. Well past his prime but still a great scorer, Pelé immediately paid dividends by nearly tripling the team's average attendance. The attendance continued to rise over the next three seasons as Ross continued to add some of the greatest players in the world to the Cosmos lineup: Giorgio Chinaglia, Franz Beckenbauer, and Carlos Alberto. Not only did the Cosmos feature the World's greatest players, their celebrity fandom and decadent lifestyle in 1970s New York City became legendary as well. With their added star power and now playing in the new Giants Stadium, the Cosmos went from averaging just over 3,500 fans per game in 1974 to over 10,000 in 1975 and to nearly 50,000 in 1978. As an example of a rising tide lifting all boats, the Cosmos largely made the league successful in terms of attendance and a much-needed television contract and their blueprint of opening the bank to pay older international stars was being copied by other teams.

The NASL became so successful in the late 1970s that it made the fatal error of over-expanding and diluting the talent level. Add to that the fact that Pelé retired and the enthusiastic attendance numbers did not carry over to television viewership and the league was again in trouble by the early 1980s. Crowder and Dower do a fantastic job of documenting the rise of the Cosmos and the personality clashes that existed within their rise (specifically Chinaglia versus everyone else), but they fail to add much examination into the league's lack of television success and eventual folding in 1984. Likewise, the cultural impact of the 1970s soccer boom on youth programs across America is touched upon, but could stand a deeper examination. The summer of 1977 in New York City is remembered for the "Son of Sam" serial killer, blackouts and looting, the New York Yankees first World Series title since 1962, but perhaps mostly as the year that professional Soccer gained footing in the United States. It only took the deep pockets of a media-titan as owner and the greatest players in the world to make it happen. Narrated by Academy Award nominated actor Matt Dillon and featuring a great 1970s soundtrack, *Once in a Lifetime* was distributed by Miramax Films and released in DVD format in 2006.

Awards: 2006 Hot Docs Canadian International Documentary Festival: Top Ten Audience Favorite (5th Place); 2007 Writers Guild of America: Documentary Screenplay Award (Dower, Mark Monroe, nominated).

The Other Dream Team, 2012

Director: Marius Markevicius; Running Time: 89 minutes; U.S./Lithuania.

During World War II, the tiny European nation of Lithuania was invaded and annexed by the Soviet Union. That remained the case until 1990, when it declared itself independent a little more than a year before the Soviet Union was formally dissolved. During the half-century that Lithuania was a Soviet Republic, its athletes were forced to compete for the USSR. This became especially significant in the late 1980s when the Soviet Union men's national basketball team won gold at the 1988 Summer Olympics in Seoul, South Korea with a starting lineup consisting of four Lithuanian players: Arvydas Sabonis, Šarūnas Marčiulionis, Rimas Kurtinaitis, and Valdemaras Chomičius. Team USA in 1988 was a heavy favorite and stocked with collegiate stars such as David Robinson and Mitch Richmond, but lost to the USSR in the semifinals. Team Yugoslavia, the silver medal winners, was similarly stocked with future NBA players such as Dražen Petrović and Toni Kukoč, and like the USSR, many were professionals in various non–NBA leagues. Largely as a response to Team USA's loss in 1988, only its second loss in Olympic history, the International Basketball Federation declared that current NBA players were no longer barred from competing in the Olympics due to their status as professionals. This, of course, led to the formation of "The Dream Team," the squad of NBA legends assembled to compete in the 1992 Barcelona Summer Games that is widely considered the greatest collection of talent in any sport's history. *The Other Dream Team*, by first-time feature filmmaker and Lithuanian-American Marius Markevičius, examines another team at the '92 games that was just as worthy of that label.

While Sabonis had actually been drafted by the Portland Trailblazers in the first round of the 1986 NBA Draft, Soviet policies concerning their players' availability and later injuries delayed his NBA debut for nearly a decade during his prime years. Marčiulionis, however, became the first "Soviet" player to debut in the NBA when he did so with the Golden State Warriors in 1989. Precisely as the four Lithuanians had felt after their 1988 gold medal-winning exploits for the USSR, Marčiulionis was quick to get the message across that he was Lithuanian and not Russian. Soviet-era Russia was simply an occupying force in their homeland and an oppressor of Lithuanians for nearly 50 years. The opportunity to get that message across loud and clear came in the 1992 Olympics; two years after Lithuania had declared its independence from the USSR and almost a year after Soviet tanks rolled into Lithuania in a bloody attempt to restore Soviet rule. Lithuania would finally gain its independence for good and in 1992 its athletes would finally be competing for their country. With the exception of sorely-needed funding, the Lithuanian basketball team was talented, motivated, and ready to serve as a symbol of national pride and an embodiment of freedom. On the way to a bronze medal and a symbolic win against the Unified Team (post–Soviet Russia), the team certainly looked the part of free citizens in their tie-dye attire donated by artist Greg Speirs. The tie-dye uniforms were inspired by the skeleton logo of the rock band The Grateful Dead, who collectively were basketball fans and inspired enough by their struggle to fund the team.

Markevičius takes the story of a group of talented players from a basketball-loving nation and mixes their on-court success with the eventual success of a nation fighting for freedom and independence to create a truly inspiring film that explores the Cold War, political ideology, and sports history. Although inspirational and entertaining, Markevičius questionably veers away from his successful participatory mode historical documentary to sprinkle in a modern example of Lithuanian basketball as he semi-follows 20-year-old Jonas Valančiūnas preparing for the 2011 NBA Draft. Valančiūnas was selected fifth overall by the Toronto Raptors and is currently in his fifth season. The connection that Valančiūnas has to the broader story may be that he was born in 1992, or he could simply be there as a reminder of Lithuania's basketball legacy. Hall of Famer Bill Walton, a sincere activist and longtime fan of The Grateful Dead, serves as a great talking head interview subject as he is able to colorfully explain the struggle of a top athlete forced to comply with oppressors. Donnie Nelson, an NBA general manager and a pioneer in bringing European players to the NBA, provides keen insight into the hardships for the players brought about by restrictive Soviet policies. Sportscaster Jim Lampley, however, is even more effective as he tearfully sums up the film's thesis:

"the dream of freedom, the dream of independence, the dream of being able to chart your own destiny—that was the bigger dream." *The Other Dream Team* is available in streaming or DVD format.

Awards: 2012 Seattle International Film Festival: Best Documentary Golden Space Needle Award (First Runner-Up); 2012 Sheffield International Documentary Festival: Special Jury Prize (nominated); 2012 Sundance Film Festival: Documentary Grand Jury Prize (nominated); 2013 Producers Guild of America Awards: Outstanding Producer of Documentary Theatrical Motion Pictures (nominated—Markevicius, Jon Weinbach).

Palio, 2015

Director: Cosima Spender; Running Time: 91 minutes; U.K./Italy.

Dating back to the Medieval Period, the city of Siena, Italy has been divided into a number of largely-independent districts, or contrade. Each of its 17 contrade carries its own unique culture, history, mascot, and colors. The tribalism inherit in this system is on full display twice each year when the Palio di Siena takes place in the city's historic Piazza del Campo. It is the oldest bareback horse race in the world still being contested and it is the subject for filmmaker Cosima Spender in her visually-stunning 2015 film *Palio*. The race itself lasts about 90 furious seconds and usually attracts 70,000–80,000 spectators, but it is very obvious that there is more going on in Spender's examination than just a centuries-old horse race. Spender, who grew in Siena, clearly has a familiarity with the Palio and that shines through most in how she frames the race as more than just a fascinating sporting event, but rather as a story about love and pride for one's home and heritage. This is most evident during the Corteo Storico, a Medieval-looking parade for each contrade that takes place before the races in July and August. Along with Spender's focus on tribalism, she also touches upon themes of generational conflict between jockeys and the concept of purity versus corruption within those generations.

As exciting as the spectacle of the Palio di Siena is, it does nothing to dispel the notion that Italy is one of the most politically and socially corrupt nations in the world. Bribery and pre-race secret deals between jockeys in order to aid themselves or hinder a rival are commonplace, as is the sight of one jockey using his crop (made out of a stretched and dried ox penis) on a competitor just as much as his own horse. Interviewed in the film, the city's official Palio archivist goes as far as to describe the race as "a game of legitimate corruption," while a former jockey explains that "cunning" is just as important as skill. Perhaps the most fascinating aspect of this is that it truly is legitimate. It is in no way hidden from the public that some jockeys take money to prevent a rival contrade from winning, while others take money to aid an allied contrade in winning. The fact that the jockeys are professionals who are usually hired by the contrade rather than actual natives and that the horses are assigned by allotment only days before the race probably adds to the level of corruption, but it is still quite surprising to see an event that is taken so seriously be so easily manipulated.

In addition to the examination of the unique rules, history, and customs of the race, the film profiles two famous retired jockeys and two active jockeys preparing for the upcoming races. The retired jockeys include the primary commentator Silvano Vigni, who won five Palios and now trains upcoming jockeys, and the legendary Andrea Degortes, whose tongue-in-cheek arrogance is perfectly fitting of the man who owns the record for the most Palio wins (14). The active jockeys include Gigi Bruschelli, who has won 13 times in only 16 years and is widely thought of as a master manipulator of the Palio's unique fairness-stretching nuances, and Giovani Atenzi, an upstart jockey who was mentored by Bruschelli. Spender's theme of generational conflict is seen with Degortes, who has a genuine disdain for Bruschelli, the man who is challenging his record, and Atenzi, who is on his way to overtaking his mentor despite owing his success largely to him. As one commentator explains how the jockeys lack loyalty for the contrade and even compares them to prostitutes, the theme of corruption versus purity arises in that Atenzi is seemingly surpassing Bruschelli without the aid of the latter's Machiavellian

Palio (2015) tells the story of upstart jockey Giovani Atenzi and the oldest bareback horse race in the world.

advantages. *Palio* is not only an interesting story about corruption in a beloved sporting event, but its vibrant cinematography and top-notch editing of the exhilarating race sequences must be seen to be believed. Following a world premiere at the 2015 Tribeca Film Festival, the film was released via streaming and DVD format.

Awards: 2015 Tribeca Film Festival: Best Editing in a Documentary Feature Jury Award (Valerio Bonelli), Best Documentary Feature Jury Award (nominated; 2015 British Independent Film Awards: Best Documentary (nominated); 2015 Karlovy Vary International Film Festival: Best Documentary (nominated); 2015 Melbourne International Film Festival: Best Documentary People's Choice Award (3rd runner-up); 2015 Stockholm Film Festival: Best Documentary (nominated); 2016 London Critics Circle Film Awards: Documentary of the Year Award (nominated).

Pin Gods, 1996
Director: Larry Locke; Running Time: 82 minutes; U.S.

When Walter Ray Williams won seven tournaments during the 1993 professional bowling season he became the most dominant pro that the sport had seen in years. Williams was effectively in route to legendary status at that time, and has only cemented that status in the years since. Despite his 1993 accomplishments, Williams was barely mentioned in sports pages across the country. This is how the quirky and entertaining film *Pin Gods* introduces itself: assuring the viewer that pro bowling does indeed still exist, just like its heyday of the 1960s. Hundreds of bowlers who think that they have the talent try to make the television cut at every PBA Tour stop, but it is a long road from event-to-event and the competition is fierce. The bowlers who fail to qualify for the few slots on the televised events also fail to win prize money, and depending upon expenses and sponsorships, can end up losing lots of money. Filmmaker Larry Locke follows three young bowlers during the 1994 season, each of whom is convinced that they have the talent, if not the finances, to keep chasing their dreams. While Locke's focus is the three newcomers, updates on the success of Williams (the PBA's reigning Player of the Year, and incidentally the world champion of horseshoes as well) are never far away to serve as lofty goals.

Tony Rosamilia, a 21-year-old from New Jersey, is not a picturesque athlete, but easily the most likable of the three. His expenses are paid by his supportive family, but they seem to be going to waste as he struggles to even come close to qualifying for the first several events. Ultimately,

Tony has a breakthrough and is on the verge of living his lifelong dream, but is done in by a cruel twist of fate. Sonny Pavelchak is a cocky second generation bowler from New York who seems to feel more pressure from his domineering father than from the tour itself. Sonny's fate on the tour becomes predictable when his self-confidence begins to match his father's indignation. Bob Vesi, a Florida bowler who fancies himself as a *GQ* model, is different from his counterparts in that he has already found success on the PBA Tour, winning $30,000 in prize money during the previous season. Even with the early self-bravado, it is painful to watch Vesi self-implode later in the season like a pitcher who suddenly cannot find the plate. The respective stories of the three young bowlers are supplemented by colorful, periodic insights about professional bowling by Hall-of-Fame member Carmen Salvino. Despite some indie film festival success, *Pin Gods* has not been released for home video. However, DVD copies can be purchased by contacting the production team and the full film can be found for online streaming with a proper search.

Awards: 1997 Cinequest San Jose Film Festival: Special Jury Artistic Merit Award, Best Documentary (nominated); 1996 International Documentary Festival Amsterdam (IDFA): Film Selected.

Pond Hockey, 2008

Director: Tommy Haines; Running Time: 82 minutes; U.S.

Those who grew up in areas where the ponds don't freeze may not even be aware of pond hockey as a recreational sport. A comparison could be made to playground basketball or backyard football. It is a pure, but less formal, form of ice hockey played exactly where the purists would like for all hockey to be played—outdoors on a frozen body of water. Also similar to playground basketball and backyard football, it isn't seen with the same regularity that it was decades ago. Shorter and warmer winters may have something to do with that, but more likely it's because the sport of ice hockey has moved away from its outdoor roots to indoor rinks. As for the sport itself, it differs from modern indoor hockey primarily in that the rinks and goals are much smaller and it emphasizes passing and skating prowess more than checking. With access to dozens of current and former NHL greats sharing their own outdoor hockey experiences and opinions about its ethos, filmmaker Tommy Haines examines the subject in his 2008 film *Pond Hockey.*

Along with the general examination of this stripped-down version of hockey that seems to have a very clear culture surrounding it, Haines also follows two teams as they compete in the 2006 U.S. Pond Hockey Championships. Although hockey on frozen water has a long history as the place where most players got started as children, the 2006 tournament would be the first of its kind. Including players ranging from ex-professionals and collegiate All-Americans to amateur recreationalists, it consisted of 116 teams and 25 rinks on Lake Calhoun in Minneapolis, Minnesota. While the unfolding U.S. Pond Hockey Championship tournament is entertaining to follow in the vein of so many other participatory mode sports documentaries, it is Haines's early divergences into the culture and history of outdoor hockey that is most interesting. Rather than just documenting this first of its kind tournament, which is plenty entertaining and still going strong in 2016, the film is also making a strong argument about a specific sporting culture that has almost been lost for one reason or another. The film is available in DVD format and can be found online for stream viewing.

Awards: 2008 Landlocked International Film Festival: Documentary Feature Audience Award; 2008 Minneapolis/St. Paul International Film Festival: Best of Fest Award.

Pulling John, 2009

Director: Vassiliki Khonsari, Sevan Matossain; Running Time: 73 minutes; U.S.

Pulling is the term often used by arm wrestlers when referring to their sport; the titular John is John Brzenk, widely considered to be the greatest arm wrestler in the young sport's history. Filmmakers Vassiliki Khonsari and Sevan Matossian examine Brzenk's career and legacy, while also documenting the fierce competition between the top challengers to replace the aging champion. When the directors approached Brzenk about their arm wrestling film, he was close to retirement, not only dealing with a nagging injury, but also knowing that losing to the younger and stronger challengers was inevitable. Rather than retiring and walking away with an unblemished legacy, Brzenk chooses to face the competition and either extend his already-remarkable dominance or pass the torch. What results is a combination of both—Brzenk proving that he is still the best, perhaps like no other in the history of any individual sport, yet he is clearly at the dusk of his career. *Pulling John* is a four-year chronicle, focusing equally on Brzenk and his two primary challengers: Travis Bagent, a second generation puller from West Virginia, whose persona and braggadocio is as

Pulling John, 2009

John Brzenk (left), the subject of *Pulling John* (2009), is widely considered the greatest arm-wrestler of all time.

big as his stature, and Alexey Voyevoda, a hulking Russian who harkens back to Soviet-era discipline and is quietly motivated to become champion.

Considering the short running time and multiple storylines, the film is able to maintain focus on its primary subjects while also delving deep into the culture, history, and technical aspects of the sport. The filmmakers use animated sequences to briefly describe arm wrestling's history, rules, and strategies. They also make great use of intertitles to relay information such as the fact that the sport receives government funding and is even taught in the schools of many nations. Therein lies the film's true appeal—a serious examination into the relatively-unknown, yet quite serious sport. Aside from the 1987 Sylvester Stallone motion picture *Over the Top* (the real competition and real prize which was the film's basis was won by Brzenk in 1986) and the popular televised competitions on ABC's *Wide World of Sports* during the 1970s and 1980s, arm wrestling is largely under recognized in the United States. The film's culminating event is the prestigious Zloty Tour Cup in Warsaw, Poland, where all three competitors will be together for the first time and where the excitement and suspense on the grand stage can rival any other individual sporting event. Following a world premiere at South by Southwest (SXSW) and other 2009 festival screenings, the *Pulling John* DVD was released by IndiePix Films. The DVD special features include a commentary track with Brzenk and Khonsari, deleted scenes and numerous segments profiling other arm wrestlers.

Awards: 2009 Mexico International Film Festival: Golden Palm Award. 2009 Lighthouse International Film Festival: Audience Award.

Pumping Iron, 1977

Director: George Butler, Robert Fiore; Running Time: 85 minutes; U.S.

One of the most well-known sports documentaries of all-time; *Pumping Iron* is a look at the world of professional bodybuilding, and specifically the 1975 Mr. Universe and Mr. Olympia competitions in Pretoria, South Africa. The film's popularity and cult status primarily lays in the fact that it helped to launch the careers of movie star and future California governor Arnold Schwarzenegger and television star Lou Ferrigno, who went on to play *The Incredible Hulk* on the TV series. Like the 1974 George Butler and Charles Gaines book of the same title that it was based upon, the film is deemed as historically important among nonfiction sports films because it is often credited with introducing worldwide audiences to this relatively unknown sporting subculture and setting off a fitness craze throughout the 1980s. The film has also stirred controversy over the years, primarily because its status as a true documentary has been challenged, but also because of scenes in which Schwarzenegger smokes marijuana and compares his muscles being "pumped up" to ejaculation, neither of which was too controversial until he entered the political world with strong support from "family values" advocates. In terms of the staging of some of the film's scenes, directors George Butler and Robert Fiore have acknowledged as much, as has Schwarzenegger in regards to his treatment as the arrogant, reigning champ and villain to Ferrigno's treatment as the shy, unassuming challenger.

Subsequently, the film is often classified as a docudrama rather than a documentary because of some of the interactions being played up a bit for drama, but the athletic endeavors of training and competition are most certainly cinema vérité documentation. As the film begins, Schwarzenegger arrives at Gold's Gym in Venice, California, to begin training and soon is explaining to a reporter the sculpting concepts of bodybuilding and the difference between the Mr. Universe and Mr. Olympia competitions (essentially, the former is amateur and the latter is professional). Butler and Fiore spend quite a bit of time in the first half of the film on the Mr. Universe competition and specifically on Mike Katz, a former football player from Connecticut. One example of the dramatic license used by Butler and Fiore is when fellow contestant Ken Waller pranks Katz by hiding his lucky T-shirt, which in actuality was entirely staged to build up the competition aspect between competitors. When the film shifts to focus on the Mr. Olympia competition and the budding rivalry between Schwarzenegger and Ferrigno, the future movie star is very convincing as someone attempting to exude confidence and maintain dominance over inferior competitors. Perhaps if this persona was as contrived as Schwarzenegger now claims, it signals that his future Hollywood acting career was sure to be a success.

Butler, a British photographer who first met Schwarzenegger while on assignment covering the 1972 Mr. Universe competition in Baghdad, Iraq, conceived the film to be more of a whimsical Hollywood examination of bodybuilding. Butler cast actor Bud Cort of *Harold and Maude* (1971) fame to play himself being trained by Schwarzenegger, the champion bodybuilder-turned-actor who had appeared in the low-budget *Hercules in New York* (1970), Robert Altman's *The Long Goodbye* (1973), and the 1976 film *Stay Hungry*, which was also written by Gaines and for which Schwarzenegger had received critical praise. Cort's scenes were cut and the film's focus was changed, but Cort can still be heard narrating. The film led to an unprecedented interest into the culture of "working out" and maybe even new ideas of masculinity in feature films as well, as muscle gyms began springing up in towns across the globe and leading men of the meaningful Hollywood films of the 1970s gave way to chiseled action stars of the 1980s big-budget blockbusters. Butler even explored women's bodybuilding in his 1985 sequel, *Pumping Iron II: The Women*, but it was nowhere near the critical or commercial success. *Pumping Iron* was finally released on DVD in 2003 as a 25th anniversary special edition with tons of bonus features, including several featurettes and *Raw Iron*, a mini-documentary on the making of the film.

Awards: 1977 Kansas City Film Critics Circle Awards: Best Documentary.

Quantum Hoops, 2007

Director: Rick Greenwald; Running Time: 85 minutes; U.S.

The California Institute of Technology, or Caltech, counted 31 Nobel Prize winners among its faculty in 2006. The 2005–06 Caltech Beavers men's basketball team, on the other hand, had not won a conference game since the Reagan Administration (1985, to be exact). Indeed, academic prestige rather than athletics is why the university in Pasadena regularly ranks as one of the top science and engineering schools in the world. In addition to its 243-game conference losing streak, the team also had not won a game against an NCAA Division III opponent since 1996 and had not won a game even against non–NCAA teams its last 60 attempts. The putrid losing streak for the Beavers is not terribly surprising considering that there are more high school valedictorians (8) on its roster than there are players who even played high school basketball (6). Because Caltech's undergraduate enrollment is substantially smaller than most other Division III schools and its co-members of the Southern California Intercollegiate Athletic Conference (SCIAC), the rigorous academic standards are not the lone disadvantage they face. What is afoot when filmmaker Rick Greenwald chronicles the final week of the Beavers 2006 season for his film *Quantum Hoops* is that the team is slowly improving. What needs to be understood about their improvement, however, is that their average margin of defeat has dropped from 60 points over the last few years to only 23. Beginning with Greenwald's opening montage of on-court turnovers and miscues; the film takes a close look at the team of academic overachievers and their charismatic head coach, Roy Dow, now trying desperately to achieve any semblance of athletic success by virtue of a single win.

Before viewers learn about the study/play balancing act of the current players and their ultimate success or failure in getting that elusive win in the season's final game, Greenwald provides a great deal of history about Caltech. In fact, the lion's share of the story in *Quantum Hoops* is more about the school's unique athletic history than about the current team's ability to finally win a game. That history is not as bleak as one may think, or at least that was the case in the early days. Narrated by actor David Duchovny, the film blends elements of expository mode and observational mode documentaries as it traces the Beavers athletic history all the way back to the formation of the SCIAC in 1915. The football team often defeated crosstown rival UCLA in the 1920s and in 1944 it was the only undefeated and unscored upon team in the nation. Aside from its lone conference championship in 1954, however, the basketball team has historically been nearly as bad as they currently are. Greenwald's lengthy historical overview fits nicely into the contemporary narrative because he features scores of past players who have been in the exact same situation that the current players are—trying to salvage an entire season by getting just a single win or two. Checking in with players from select squads from the 1950s to the 1990s, the most interesting aspect of the film might be witnessing some of the most successful scientists and engineers in the world reminisce so fondly about their woeful intercollegiate athletic careers rather than their academic and professional achievements. The film is available in both streaming and DVD format and was reportedly purchased by Disney for a feature adaptation, but production details are scarce.

Awards: 2007 Santa Barbara International Film Festival: Top Ten Audience Choice Award; 2007 Video Librarian Magazine: Best Documentaries List; 2008 Booklist Magazine: Editor's Choice List, Media; 2010 American Library Association: Fabulous Films for Young Adults.

Racing Dreams, 2009

Director: Marshall Curry; Running Time: 93 minutes; U.S.

Of the many minor leagues and training grounds for professional athletes, the ones that most sports fans and media know the least about are those which produce the professional race car drivers of tomorrow. Those motorsports stars of tomorrow start early and might be every bit as competitive, and probably much more dedicated, as any little league baseball player. For most, they start in the WKA, the World Karting Association, an organization formed in the early 1970s to regulate and promote the sport of competitive kart racing. In fact, most of today's NASCAR drivers honed their skills on the very same tracks in these karts that travel up to 70 miles-per-hour with only an inch of ground clearance. *Racing Dreams* introduces viewers to this unofficial little league while also examining what it takes to succeed and taking an observational look at the private lives of three young racers making their way from event to event. Winning several awards along the way, *Racing Dreams* proved to be a major festival hit, from New York and Chicago to the racing hotbeds of Indianapolis and Florida. Following its 2010 theatrical release, the film was reportedly optioned to be adapted into a narrative feature film. Available in both streaming and DVD formats, the film was broadcast in early 2012 as part of the POV film series on PBS.

Two-time Oscar-nominated filmmaker Marshall Curry (*Street Fight*, 2005, *If A Tree Falls: A Story of the Earth Liberation Front*, 2011) takes a participatory documentary approach as he follows three young racers and their families during a WKA season crucial to determining whether their dreams of moving to the next level can come true. Stock car racing is the next level, but skill alone doesn't get these young racers there. As one event alone can cost up to $5,000, it takes either deep pockets or sponsorships. Josh Hobson, a 12-year-old from Michigan with perfect manners and a 4.0 grade point average, seems like a NASCAR pro already: he knows

Filmmaker Marshall Curry explores the World Karting Association, the unofficial minor league of NASCAR, in *Racing Dreams* (2009).

how to shill for sponsors, graciously congratulate opponents, and even hold fundraising events for himself. Brandon Warren, a 13-year-old from rural North Carolina with a temper and a tumultuous family life, is just the opposite. Warren, who has been in trouble for rough driving on the track and fighting off of it, is currently living with his grandparents due to his parents incarceration and drug problems. Annabeth Barnes, 11, also from North Carolina, comes from a family "addicted to racing" and hopes to benefit from NASCAR's Drive for Diversity program, which sponsors select minority and female drivers. While she clearly loves the sport, by film's end the viewer is left wondering if Annabeth's racing dreams are actually the dreams of her parents.

Awards: 2009 Chicago International Film Festival: Best Documentary, Silver Hugo Award; 2009 Jacksonville Film Festival: Best Documentary Feature; 2009 Tribeca Film Festival: Best Documentary Feature; 2010 Florida Film Festival: Audience Award Best Documentary; 2010 Indianapolis International Film Festival: Audience Award Feature Documentary; 2010 Nashville Film Festival: Best Documentary Feature.

Red Army, 2014

Director: Gabe Polsky; Running Time: 84 minutes; U.S/Russia.

During the 1970s and 1980s, as the nuclear arms race symbolized the military Cold War battle between the United States and the Soviet Union, another battle going on between the Soviets and the West was more symbolic of their competing ideologies. As one interview subject in Gabe Polsky's 2014 film *Red Army* explains, "sports were, in a way, a kind of warfare for the Soviets." Founded under Joseph Stalin to show superiority over the West, the Soviet Union had a well-organized system of youth ice hockey that produced medal-winning teams in every Winter Olympics from 1956 to 1988, and all but two of those were golds. Despite the stunning "Miracle on Ice" upset loss to Team USA in 1980, the Soviet teams of the 1980s were especially powerful. The core unit of those teams, known as "The Russian Five" and consisting of Slava Fetisov, Alexei Kasatonov, Vladimir Krutov, Igor Larionov, and Sergei Makarov, left a lasting legacy on both hockey and international relations. Polsky, who was a hockey player at Yale and the son on Soviet immigrants, focuses on the compelling story of Fetisov and the political barriers that prevented Soviet players from entering the National Hockey League up until the 1990s.

Fetisov, one of the most decorated and honored players in world hockey history, is clearly something of an unwilling subject for Polsky. His cantankerousness may be because some of the Cold War nerves are still raw, but more likely it is because he is a Russian politician nowadays. Retelling some of the tactics employed by the communist regime in order to keep players loyal to their homeland 30 years ago isn't exactly an indication that their ideological fight was the right one. Polsky spends quite a bit of

Red Army (2014) examines Cold War politics and the dominant Soviet Union hockey teams of the 1970s and 1980s (from left, Boris Mikhailov, Vladimir Petrov, and Valeri Kharlamov).

time exploring the system of Red Army hockey, and specifically on the contrasting styles of the team's two main head coaches during its heyday: Antoli Tarasov and Viktor Tikhonov. Whereas Tarasov was nurturing and beloved by his players, Tikhonov was despised and more emblematic of the country that sent KGB agents with the team to prevent "escapes" and confiscated their passports upon return. The bitterness that developed between player and coach when Fetisov quit the team altogether instead of defecting was really the starting point for the mass exodus of Russian players to the West. Fetisov was clearly instrumental in that regard, but the harsh economic reality of the failing communist state was equally to blame.

In a 2015 interview with National Public Radio, Polsky explains that during Mikhail Gorbachev's Perestroika period, the government could no longer afford to fund the sports program so they would sell older players to NHL clubs, and then "basically take all that money for the government. So the players would make, let's say, $1,000 a month and then the rest of that money would go to the government." Despite this, and additionally not being welcomed too well in the U.S. and Canada, most players were accepting of this arrangement in order to play in the NHL. Fetisov, however, was not and had his life turned upside down by the communist government before finally winning the battle of wills. As with a few other sports documentaries dealing with global politics of the Cold War, for example *The Game of Their Lives* (2003) and *Sons of Cuba* (2009), an interesting comparison of American training methods can be made to those employed by the communists. More importantly, though, is the obvious comparison of sports psychology and the dynamic of national ethos between American athletes during the Cold War and those of communist nations. American athletes have always rallied around the flag for Olympic competition, but it seems that athletes of nations such as Cuba, North Korea, and the USSR during the Cold War period were far more motivated by proving the virtues of communism as they related to sport. Polsky chose a great subject in order to explore the nexus of sports, politics, and patriotism, and he does so by covering every possible angle and point of view. Executive produced by legendary filmmaker Werner Herzog, *Red Army* won a number of awards worldwide and was released in DVD format in 2015.

Awards: 2014 AFI Fest: World Cinema Audience Award; 2014 Chicago International Film Festival: Audience Choice Award; 2014 Pacific Meridian International Film Festival of Asia Pacific Countries: Will-to-Win Spirit Award (Fetisov); 2014 Zurich Film Festival: International Documentary

Film Special Mention, Best International Documentary Film (nominated); Copenhagen International Documentary Festival (CPH: DOX): Politiken's Audience Award (nominated); Hollywood Music in Media Awards: Best Original Score, Documentary (Christophe Beck, Leo Birenberg, nominated); 2014 Satellite Awards: Best Motion Picture, Documentary (nominated); 2014 St. Louis Film Critics Association: Best Documentary Feature Film (nominated); 2015 Cinema Eye Honors Awards: Outstanding Achievement in Graphic Design or Animation (Philippe Gariepy, Benoit St-Jean, nominated); Dublin Film Critics Circle Awards: Best Documentary (3rd place); 2015 Writers Guild of America: Best Documentary Screenplay (Polsky, nominated); 2016 Chlotrudis Awards: Best Documentary (nominated).

Riding Giants, 2004

Director: Stacy Peralta; Running Time: 105 minutes; U.S.

A cinematic history lesson about the sport and culture of big wave surfing, *Riding Giants* was the first-ever documentary film to open the Sundance Film Festival when it did so in 2004. Director Stacy Peralta (*Dogtown and Z-Boys*) uses a trove of archival footage to document how surf culture grew on the California Coast and how the pioneers of the sport fostered its development on the beaches of Hawaii simply by doing what came natural to them—searching for bigger waves. Appropriately, the film provides a very brief historical look at the Polynesian roots of surfing before delving into the true birth of what began as a countercultural pastime on the California Coast in the early 1950s. After learning of surfers like George Downing and Buzzy Trent and the waves they were riding in Hawaii, a handful of Californians flocked there to live a bohemian lifestyle and revolutionize big wave surfing over the next decade. Soon, however, with the fictional character *Gidget* and a slew of beach films, surfing would explode in popular culture and those few pioneers of the sport were no longer alone. *Riding Giants* is a virtual who's who of big wave surfers throughout history, but it most prominently focuses on Greg Noll, Jeff Clark, and Laird Hamilton and the three eras of big wave riding that they represent

Noll, with his bullish personality and style, would become the first true celebrity of the sport while seeking out the biggest waves and most daring rides in the many Hawaiian locales. He rode that celebrity into legend and lifestyle, but also into a booming surfboard business. In the mid–1970s, Jeff Clark became a true pioneer in riding the huge waves near San

Francisco that no one thought possible and few even knew about. For 15 years, Clark surfed the dangerous rocky coast known as Mavericks completely alone. By the mid–90s, however, the area had become a world-class big wave destination, producing breaks just as big as those on Hawaii's North Shore. Laird Hamilton grew up around many big wave legends in Hawaii, but no one ever suspected that he would ultimately become the world's best known surfer and the one pioneer who would take the sport to the next levels—tow-in surfing, the shortboard revolution, and conquering waves of unimaginable size. The archival footage, coupled with the amazing contemporary cinematography, makes comparing the waves to mountains and the wipeouts to being in a washing machine very understandable for the non-surfer. As with Peralta's *Dogtown*, music is integral to the film and a soundtrack fitting perfectly with the spectacle of big wave surfing makes the film a true viewing experience. Riding Giants is available for streaming and in DVD format.

Awards: 2005 American Cinema Editors: Best Edited Documentary Film (Paul Crowder); 2004 Sundance Film Festival (Official Selection); 2005 Dallas-Fort Worth Film Critics Association Awards: Best Documentary (nominated).

Ring of Fire: The Emile Griffith Story, 2005
Director: Dan Klores, Ron Berger; Running Time: 87 minutes; U.S.

Boxing fans of a certain age likely saw the televised lightweight championship boxing match of November 13, 1982, when South Korean boxer Duk-Koo Kim fell into a coma following a brutal fight against Ray Mancini and died four days later. Slightly more than 20 years before Kim's death, boxing fans of a more advanced age might have seen a similar tragedy take place on March 24, 1962, when Emile Griffith squared off against Benny Paret for the world welterweight title in a televised fight from Madison Square Garden. In the 12th round of the third fight between the two boxers in less than a year, Griffith hit Paret with a flurry of punches that were shocking to those who witnessed it in person. Perhaps the best description comes from the great American writer and boxing fan Norman Mailer:

> Griffith was in like a cat ready to rip the life out of a huge boxed rat. He hit him eighteen right hands in a row, an act which took perhaps three or four seconds, Griffith making a pent-up whimpering sound all the while he attacked, the right hand whipping like a piston rod which has broken through the crankcase, or like a baseball bat demolishing a pumpkin. I was sitting in the second row of that corner—

they were not ten feet away from me, and like everybody else, I was hypnotized. I had never seen one man hit another so hard and so many times [244].

Paret died ten days later, but Mailer's disturbingly accurate description continues by making the case that "Paret died on his feet" that night in 1962 on ABC's popular *Fight of the Week* broadcast. What led up to the third Griffith–Paret title fight, the fallout that took place after it, and the fascinating story of Griffith's life are the subjects of the highly underrated 2005 documentary film *Ring of Fire: The Emile Griffith Story* by filmmakers Dan Klores (*Crazy Love*, 2007) and Ron Berger.

Griffith was born in the Virgin Islands, but immigrated to New York City, where he started working as a delivery boy at 15 years old and then as a designer of women's hats. From the hat factory he was recruited into boxing based on his chiseled physique, which led to Hall of Fame trainer Gil Clancy and eventually to world championship belts in three different weight classes for Griffith. As journalist Pete Hamill points out in the film, in the early 1960s New York was still the city that immigrants had built, but the Jews, the Italians, and the Irish had largely moved past boxing, which had become "a sport of the poor set up to entertain the middle class." Sensitive and likeable, Griffith had to be coaxed into the sport, but he was eager to please and the reluctant fighter with lightning fast hands quickly became Golden Gloves champion. With each early fight that he won in the pro ranks, it meant air fare for another family member from St. Thomas to New York. Klores and Berger masterfully build their nostalgic story by taking the time to describe its setting—New York City in the early 1960s, when boxing was extremely important because of the void left by the Dodgers and Giants departures to the West Coast and when television was becoming a major part of people's lives.

World welterweight champion Benny Paret was not a reluctant fighter. The Cuban immigrant was known as an especially tough fighter who could take extreme punishment. Griffith took the title from Paret on April 1, 1961, but lost it back to him in the return match only six months later. At the weigh-in for their second bout, bad blood between the fighters began to boil, but it went even further at the weigh-in for their third fight—both times because Paret called Griffith a maricón, the Spanish word for "faggot." It was no secret to some, but Griffith's sexuality was now being whispered about more loudly at a time when it was simply unthinkable that a professional athlete could be gay. Griffith continued to fight, but he was really never the same boxer. The referee of the match, Ruby Goldstein, who ironically had been criticized in the past for stopping fights too quickly, never refereed again. Paret's manager, Manuel Alfaro, also came under heavy criticism because he was seen as using his fighter as a cash cow, arranging matches as quickly as possible despite the beatings. In their story of both love and violence, Klores and Berger hone in on the sensitivity of Griffith in his three post-boxing decades, but never use his sexuality in a heavy-handed way. In the film's final scene, the sensitive and gentle nature of the fighter who once beat a man to death is on full display when he tearfully meets the man's son. The film was aired on the USA Network in 2005 and the DVD features an excellent commentary track with the filmmakers.

Awards: 2005 Sundance Film Festival: Documentary Grand Jury Prize (nominated); 2006 Black Reel Awards: Best Documentary (nominated).

Rising from Ashes, 2012

Director: T.C. Johnstone; Running Time: 82 minutes; U.S.

The tiny African nation of Rwanda is known as the Land of a Thousand Hills, but most people in the West know it only as the country in which one of modern day history's most devastating genocides took place. Most of the members of the national cycling team of Rwanda were only small children in 1994, but all of them have been haunted by the devastation of the genocide that killed nearly one million people. As a direct result from ethnic hostility brought on by European colonization in the early 20th century, the 100 straight days in 1994 in which an average of one person was killed every ten seconds is the backdrop for the story of Team Rwanda's formation and success. The moving story of the team and their coach, Jacques "Jock" Boyer, is told in the multi award-winning 2012 film *Rising from Ashes* by director T.C. Johnstone. The beautifully-shot film should immediately be set apart from many other contemporary sports documentaries not only because of its high production values, but also because Johnstone and narrator Forest Whitaker take the time to explore the horrific genocide from a generation ago, its root causes, its devastating legacy, and its personal effect on the inspiring members of Team Rwanda. Whereas other films might briefly explore that history and fail to tie together its legacy on the psyche of the next generation, or even avoid the ramifications altogether, Johnstone does the opposite and explains how Rwandans have coped with their history and how new positivity can come from its cycling team.

The story of how Team Rwanda came about dates back to 2005 when American mountain biking pioneer Tom Ritchey toured the country and discovered lots of talented riders on primitive bikes. As a result, Ritchey formed the nonprofit organization Project Rwanda with hopes of building a national cycling team, organized an annual event called the Wooden Bike Classic, and recruited his friend Boyer to participate and eventually coach the young riders. Boyer, who became the first American to race in the Tour de France back in 1981, was hesitant at first, but turned out to be the perfect coach for a group of young men who had all lost family members during the 1994 genocide. Boyer himself had experienced abandonment by his father and had spent time in jail for "overstepping his boundaries" with an underage girl. Although the redemption for Team Rwanda members come from an awful past that they had no fault in and Boyer's redemption comes from a past which includes his felony child molestation conviction, their stories become intertwined within the theme of outrunning the past. From their first race, the 2007 Cape Epic in South Africa, to their tour of the United States the next year, the team shows promise and begins to trust that Boyer will not leave them in the way that so many Westerners had in the past. One rider in particular, Adrien Niyonshuti, actually qualifies for the 2012 Summer Olympics, but Johnstone's focus is clearly more on the team unit. One curiously missing aspect, perhaps purposefully, is the ethnic makeup of the team (Hutu/Tutsi) and how the legacy of strife between these groups has been overcome by its members. Following a theatrical release in 2012, the film was released in DVD format in 2013.

Awards: 2012 Aspen Filmfest: Audience Favorite Documentary; 2012 Austin Film Festival: Audience Choice Award; Bahamas International Film Festival: Audience Choice Award; 2012 Denver International Film Festival: People's Choice Award—Documentary; 2012 Hamptons International Film Festival: Brizzolara Family Foundation Award for a Film of Conflict and Resolution, Documentary Feature Award (nominated); 2012 Heartland Film Festival: Best Documentary Feature; 2012 Napa Valley Film Festival: Best Documentary Audience Award; 2013 Albuquerque Film and Media Experience: Best Documentary Audience Choice Award; 2013 Boulder International Film Festival: Award of Excellence; 2013 Crested Butte Film Festival: Best Documentary Festival Award; 2013 River Run International Film Festival: Documentary Feature Audience Choice Award, 2013 San Luis Obispo International Film Festival: Best Sports Documentary; 2014 Motion Pictures Sound Editors: Best Sound Editing, Documentary Feature Film (nominated—David Barber, Ben Zarai, Michael Kreple, Sean Gray, Gonzalo Espinoza, David Kitchens).

Rocks with Wings, 2001
Director: Rick Derby; Running Time: 113 minutes; U.S.

In northwestern New Mexico, near the famous Four Corners area, stands a rock formation protruding up more than 1,500 feet from the flat landscape. White settlers named it Shiprock due to its resemblance to a ship's mast and sail, but the Navajo who inhabit the area call it Tsé Bit'a'í, meaning "rock with wings." Within this portion of the Navajo Nation, nearly 40 percent of the population currently lives below the poverty threshold, but that was closer to 50 percent in the late 1980s, when running water and telephones were also a rarity for families of the area. The community of Shiprock was severely divided and mired in desperation at that time, but a new sense of unity and hope began to take shape as the town's high school basketball team became a state powerhouse. Filmmaker Rick Derby spent more than a decade making his fascinating 2001 film *Rocks with Wings*, which explores an intersection of cultures and races by telling the story of the Shiprock High School Lady Chieftains basketball teams of 1987 and 1988. There has been no shortage of documentary films about high school basketball in the 21st century, but Derby's stands apart for a number of reasons. According to Derby, *Rocks with Wings* is not a sports film; it is first and foremost a film about healing. Derby argues that the sports aspect "was an ideal way to measure the degree of healing" (Derby).

In addition to the cultural aspect of the all-Navajo team, Derby also explores race and culture through the experiences of Jerry Richardson, the team's African-American head coach. Therefore, the examination of race relations within the team dynamic is not that of Native/Anglo as one may expect, but rather Native-American/African-American. Because Derby's documentation took place more than a decade before the film's actual release, the racial and cultural context concerning Richardson may be difficult for some viewers to grasp. Clearly, an African American head coach at any level was uncommon in the early to mid–1980s and that is delicately reflected in the film through the fact that Richardson had been unfairly held back because of race and his personal experiences led to a more demanding and less nurturing style that clashed with the girls and with Navajo culture. Having grown up in the segregated South, Richardson used athletics as a tool to achieve a college education. He took over the head coaching job in 1982 and quickly transformed the program from one that was used to failure into one that was competing for a state championship in 1987. During that championship run, however, the festering culture clash came to a head between coach and players as both sides aired their grievances that were rooted in issues of race, gender, and respect. Rather than tearing the team apart, the emotional outburst brought them together and ultimately led to three consecutive state titles beginning the next season.

An early segment in the film explains the meaning of the spirit line in Navajo art, suggesting that a woven pattern must allow the art to escape in order to be used again. This can be seen metaphorically as the film later examines how the airing of grievances relating to Richardson's coaching style allowed for free communication, unity, and most importantly, trust between the players and their coach. The filmmaking aspect that sets Derby's work apart is not only that it predates similar films about high school basketball (despite the 2001 release date, its documentation was from the late 1980s), but also that it features more detailed and extended game sequences. In comparison to similar films, it is extraordinarily unique to simply watch the thrilling championship games of 1987 and 1988 unfold, both against the rival Anglo-centric school from only miles away that had dominated the sport for years. Concerning these extended game sequences, Derby suggests that the importance of the game was evident to him and he needed to "set the stage" for a viewer to appreciate the game the same way that he had perceived it (Derby). *Rocks with Wings* aired on PBS in 2002, on the BBC Storyville film series in 2003, and on the CBC's Aboriginal Peoples Television Network in 2005. The film can be found online for streaming or in DVD format through the filmmaker's production company, Shiprock Productions.

Awards: 2002 Native American Film & Television Alliance Film Festival: Best Feature Film Jury Award, Visionary Award (Derby); 2002 Urbanworld Film Festival: HBO Documentary Feature Prize; 2004 Indian Summer Film Festival: Film & Video Image Award of Distinction; 2005 Durango Film Festival: Regional Audience Award; 2005 Winnipeg Aboriginal Film Festival: Best Feature Documentary; 2002 First Peoples Festival of Montreal: Rigoberta Menchú Tum Award (2nd Prize).

Running for Jim, 2013

Director: Robin Hauser, Dan Noyes; Running Time: 78 minutes; U.S.

In late 2010, the California State Girls Cross Country Championship became national news after a short video clip of a runner collapsing from dehydration and crawling the remaining few yards to the finish line went viral. The video showed junior Holland Reynolds of University High

School in San Francisco nearing the finish line, slowing to a very-labored walk, and finally collapsing. A race official appears to offer help, but Reynolds instead crawls across the finish line as a number of other runners pass by her. When it became known what the race official said to her and why she crawled to the finish, the story became even more inspiring. The video was likely used by coaches as an inspirational tool around the world, but none with greater results than Tom Coughlin and the New York Giants during their run to the Super Bowl the following season. The story behind that viral video is the subject for the multi award-winning 2013 film *Running for Jim*, but Reynolds herself plays only a tiny part despite the fact that her mother, Robin Hauser, along with Dan Noyes, are the filmmakers. The film is about the coach at University High School, Jim Tracy, who was already a local legend due to his seven state championships, but it was his eighth state title in 2010 and his battle against amyotrophic lateral sclerosis (ALS), or Lou Gehrig's disease, that made him legendary around the world. That 2010 title came only after Reynolds collapsed and was told by the official that if she received help she would be disqualified, but if she simply finished the race her team could win another championship by virtue of the points already secured by other runners.

While it may be the case that Reynolds would have chosen to crawl to the finish regardless of her team's title hopes or regardless of the team's pre-race meeting in which they declared that another state title would be for their beloved coach, those inspiring factors did indeed exist. Tracy, who himself was a decorated runner at Cal Berkley, had regularly trained with his runners since taking the coaching position in 1994, but began noticing the muscle deterioration common to ALS only a year or so before his diagnosis was made in 2010. Leading to the moving video captured at the 2010 championship, Tracy was reluctant to inform the team of his diagnosis, but did so only because of the rapid decline in motor skills that were becoming more and more noticeable. A slightly eccentric man who clearly has a natural ability to bring out the best in the athletes he trains, Tracy's life was so immersed in running and other philosophical pursuits that he really never had a home until the students and community pitched in to provide him one when his condition worsened. The film works largely as a biographical story about Tracy, but also as a story about the incurable disease that little is known about. In participatory mode, Hauser and Noyes present interviews with contemporary and past students, family members, friends, and people working to bring about awareness of the disease. From the film's genesis of Reynolds' desperation crawl in 2010 to the way that the students and community responded to the news of their coach's disease the following year, there is nothing contrived about this story. Following numerous film festival entries in 2013, *Running for Jim* was released in DVD format in 2014 and is also widely available for streaming.

Awards: 2013 All Sports Los Angeles Film Festival: Best Documentary Feature; 2013 Big Bear Lake Film Festival: Best Documentary Audience Choice Award; 2013 Central Florida Film Festival: Best Documentary Festival Prize; 2013 International Festival of Sports Films Krasnogorsky, Moscow: Best Film Character, Ministry of Culture Award; 2013 LA Indie Film Festival: Feature Film Best of the Fest Jury Award; 2013 Naples International Film Festival: Neapolitan Award; 2013 San Francisco Independent Documentary Festival: Best Documentary Audience Choice Award; 2013 SoHo International Film Festival: Best Documentary Festival Prize; 2013 Tiburon International Film Festival: Best Documentary Film Audience Choice Award; 2013 Tiger Paw International Sports Film Festival: Best Feature Film; 2013 White Sands International Film Festival: Best Documentary Audience Choice Award; 2014 Julien Dubuque International Film Festival: Best Documentary Silver Feather Award, Best Director (Hauser, Noyes).

Running on the Sun: The Badwater 135, 2000
Director: Mel Stuart; Running Time: 100 minutes; U.S.

Ultramarathons, ultra-running, or ultra-distance-running is any race or training that is longer than the 26.2 miles which make up traditional marathon distance. If the "runner's high" of these distance events, which often go to 100 miles, is not enough, some events take place in extreme conditions. One such event is the Badwater 135, which starts 282 feet below sea level in the Badwater Basin of Death Valley, California, and ends at an elevation of 8,300 feet in Whitney Portal, California. The event bills itself as the world's most grueling ultra-marathon, not only because of the changes in altitude or the fact that nearly the first third of the race takes place in a desert in mid–July where temperatures often reach 120 degrees, but also simply because of the distance—135 miles. Dr. Ben Jones, the race coordinator, who early on in the film admitted "I don't think there's a thing about this that's good for the body," also explains that usually two-thirds of the 40 entrants will finish the race within the 60-hour period required to earn the race's only prize: a belt buckle. The other third, he explains, will usually drop out of the race for any number of reasons. After reviewing the resumes of applicants from all over the world, only 40 are invited to participate and those entrants must provide their own support crews, typically consisting of a small group of family members or friends, or even with one runner the film focuses on, a hired hand whom she met just before the race.

Renowned director of feature films and documentaries, Mel Stuart (*Willie Wonka and the Chocolate Factory,* 1971, *Four Days in November* 1964), selected 13 entrants of the 1999 race to focus on. Stuart does a fine job of providing just enough of their biographical stories to interest the viewer in them, while still allowing the two days of the race itself to be the story. The 13 runners who are spotlighted represent a broad spectrum of unique athletes: two are amputees, three are women (including the previous year's female champion), a super-macho marine, the highly-likable returning champ and record-holder, the early leader and new favorite for the '99 race, a *New York Times* journalist, a race-walker and trumpeter from Miami, a 68-year-old retiree, a fiery New York truck driver, and a 64-year-old British runner who is enticed to finish via the carrot-and-stick trick, using a can of Murphy's Irish Stout attached to his crew's van. After being picked up for distribution by Galaxy entertainment, *Running on the Sun* was an official selection at a number of film festivals. The film is available on DVD and for online streaming.

Awards: 2000 Arizona International Film Festival: Best Documentary; 2001 Golden Trailer Awards: Best Documentary.

Salute, 2008

Director: Matt Norman; Running Time: 91 minutes; Australia.

At the 1968 Summer Olympics in Mexico City, Australian sprinter Peter Norman ran the race of his life in the 200-meter final. His time of 20 seconds flat equaled the previous world record, but he still finished behind American Tommie Smith. Also tying the previous world record was another American, John Carlos, who finished third. As the three competitors were receiving their respective gold, silver, and bronze medals at the medal ceremony after the event, Smith and Carlos provided one of the most iconic and controversial moments in Olympic history when each raised a single black-gloved fist during the playing of the "Star-Spangled Banner." Taking place during the height of the Civil Rights movement in the United States, their gesture was portrayed as a "black power" salute, but the athletes later indicated that it was more a human rights salute. Regardless, it was an overt act of political protest that made headlines around the world and led to great controversy in the United States. Largely an afterthought or just a footnote in history for decades, the third athlete on the podium was far more involved in Smith and Carlos's silent gesture than most knew about. Norman strongly supported Smith and Carlos and even wore an Olympic Project for Human Rights (OPHR) button on his track suit while being awarded the silver medal. In his award-winning 2008 documentary, *Salute*, filmmaker Matt Norman examines this powerful moment in time and specifically his uncle's role in it.

Rather than taking a narrow approach and focusing in on the single event at the games, Norman, the filmmaker, instead broadly examines the social and political climate worldwide during the late 1960s and how the winds of societal change swept into the Olympics. As much as the International Olympic Committee (IOC) would have liked to keep the games free of any sort of political statements, it seemed destined to not be the case as protests were taking shape across the globe for a number of different reasons in 1968. In addition to the American Civil Rights Movement, worldwide anti-war protests, student protests and labor strikes in France, and the Prague Spring reforms in Czechoslovakia, the very city which was set to host the Olympics was shaken when scores of protesting students and civilians were killed by government forces in the Tlatelolco area of Mexico City just days before the opening ceremony. In Australia, the native Aboriginals had been granted the right to vote a few years earlier, but were still forcibly segregated and the policy of taking Aboriginal children away from their families for purposes of assimilation into white society was still practiced. Likewise, the White Australia Policy, which prevented any person of color from gaining citizenship to Australia, was largely still practiced. Norman, the athlete, had been raised in a very religious family and was taught the values of compassion and the equality of all men by the Salvation Army Church. Because of his Salvation Army religious teachings, Norman rejected discrimination of any kind and opposed many of his own country's racial policies.

Salute equally explores the backgrounds of Smith and Carlos, both of whom had been student-athletes at San Jose State University. It was at SJSU where both became politically active and where the OPHR was formed by civil rights activist Dr. Harry Edwards in 1967. The seeds of the silent protest by Smith and Carlos were planted when the OPHR planned a boycott of the Olympics by African American athletes. Perhaps as a precursor to the outrage that would follow Smith and Carlos back to the U.S., the plan to boycott was highly controversial and never materialized, but it put the IOC on edge and gave warning to the political power structure in America that black athletes would no longer be silent concerning matters of inequality. In the moments before the medal ceremony, Norman asked to wear an OPHR badge in order to support Smith and Carlos, who had both received death threats from the fallout of the proposed boycott. American rower Paul Hoffman showed support as well by providing Norman with his badge. The role that both men played in helping to create one of the most powerful images of the 20th century has long been overlooked, but is brought to light in the film. With elements of both the expository and participatory documentary modes, the film appropriately builds up to the race and symbolic demonstration that would forever link the three men together, then explains the repercussions that all three faced. The repercussions faced by Smith and Carlos have been well known, but Norman arguably faced a backlash just as severe in Australia for his show of solidarity with the American Civil Rights Movement. The film is widely available for streaming and in region 2 DVD format.

Awards: 2008 Rhode Island International Film Festival: Best Documentary Audience Award; 2008 Sydney Film Festival: Best Australian Documentary Audience Award; 2009 Atlanta DocuFest: Best Social Documentary; 2009 Santa Cruz Film Festival: Best Documentary Feature Jury Award; 2009 Film Critics Circle of Australia Awards: Best Feature Documentary (nominated).

Senna, 2010

Director: Asif Kapadia; Running Time: 106 minutes; U.K.

During the 1950s, the first decade of competitive Formula One racing, 15 drivers were killed while competing in an F1 event. During the 1960s, the number of driver-fatalities decreased to 14, and during the 1970s it decreased to 12. As the sport grew in popularity during its first three decades, safety became more of a concern with numerous standards being put into place and by the 1980s new technology and safety-awareness had combined to dramatically decrease fatalities even further. Among the 51 total fatalities of F1, perhaps the most shocking was the death of three-time world champion Ayrton Senna at the 1994 San Marino Grand Prix in Imola, Italy. A true legend and cultural icon in his native Brazil, Senna won the Formula One world championship in 1988, 1990, and 1991, and is widely regarded as the greatest F1 driver of all-time. Oscar-winning filmmaker Asif Kapadia (*Amy,* 2015) creates a stirring portrait of Senna by almost strictly using archival racing and interview footage instead of typical commentary, narration, and retrospective interviews. In a 2011 interview with *The Guardian,* Kapadia explains that getting approval for the film from Senna's family and gaining access to the archival footage was vital for the film. Ultimately, 15,000 hours of archival footage came from F1 tycoon Bernie Ecclestone, which then was edited down to 90 minutes over four years (Jeffries, "The Saturday Interview").

Born into wealth, Senna was able to chase his dreams of racing by becoming competitive in the expensive sport of kart racing as a teenager. The film only briefly touches upon Senna's youth and instead jumps almost immediately into his 11-year career in Formula One racing, beginning with the 1984 Brazilian Grand Prix. While his time with Toleman Motorsport in 1984 and later with Team Lotus from 1985 to 1987 is examined, it was when Senna joined the McLaren Team in 1988 that his career became meteoric and also the point at which Kapadia really zeroes in on the personality of the charismatic racer. It was also in this period with McLaren that the fierce rivalry with four-time world champion Alain Prost developed. Prost and Senna were teammates with McLaren in 1988 and 1989, but tensions between the two became simply too much after several on-track incidents led Prost to part ways with the team in 1990. Prost went so far as to securing a contractual clause with his new team forbidding Senna from becoming a teammate again in the future. This bitter rivalry between Prost and Senna, which occupies much of the film's examination, seemed to finally cool off with the former's retirement and the latter's move to the Williams Team in 1994. In an effectively suspenseful way, Kapadia allows viewers to feel the growing concerns over safety that Senna had in the days leading up to his fatal crash and also to understand why he could not stop racing despite those concerns. *Senna* has grossed over $10 million worldwide and is one of the most successful British documentaries of all time.

Awards: 2011 Austin Film Critics Association: Best Documentary; 2011 British Independent Film Awards: Best Documentary, Best Technical Achievement for Editing (nominated: Chris King, Gregers Sall); 2011 Ghent International Film Festival: Best Film; 2011 International Documentary Association: Best Editing (Chris King, Gregers Sall); 2011 Los Angeles Film Festival: Best International Feature; 2011 Melbourne International Film Festival: Most Popular Documentary; 2011 Satellite Awards: Best Motion Picture, Documentary; 2011 Sundance Film Festival: World Cinema, Documentary Audience Award, World Cinema, Documentary Grand Jury Prize (nominated); 2011 Utah Film Critics Association Awards: Best Documentary Feature Film; 2012 BAFTA Awards: Best Documentary Film, Best Editing (Chris King, Gregers Sall), Best British Film (nominated); 2012 Australian Film Critics Association Awards: Best Documentary; 2012

U.S. Cinema Eye Honors Awards: Outstanding Achievement in Editing (Chris King, Gregers Sall), Audience Choice Prize (nominated), Outstanding Achievement in Nonfiction Feature Filmmaking (nominated); Outstanding Achievement in Original Musical Score (Antonio Pinto, nominated); 2012 Evening Standard British Film Awards: Best Documentary; 2012 Georgia Film Critics Association: Best Documentary; 2012 London Critics Circle Film Awards: Documentary of the Year, Technical Achievement of the Year for Editing (Chris King Gregers Sall, nominated); 2011 Awards Circuit Community Awards: Best Documentary Feature (nominated); 2011 USA National Board of Review: Top Five Documentaries (nominated); 2011 New York Film Critics Circle Awards: Best Nonfiction Film (2nd Place); 2012 Chlotrudis Awards: Best Documentary (nominated); 2012 Gold Derby Awards: Documentary Feature (nominated); 2012 International Cinephile Society Awards: Best Documentary (nominated); 2012 Irish Film and Television Awards: Best International Film (nominated); 2012 Online Film and Television Association: Best Documentary Feature Film (nominated); 2012 USA Writers Guild of America: Best Documentary Screenplay (Manish Pandey, nominated).

Shadow Boxers, 1999

Director: Katya Bankowsky; Running Time: 74 minutes; U.S.

One of the more unique sports documentaries prior to the explosion of the genre in the 21st century is filmmaker Katya Bankowsky's 1999 film *Shadow Boxers*. Using facets of both poetic and participatory mode documentaries, it explores women's boxing and specifically the career of rising star Lucia Rijker. Frequently shifting to grainy black and white and slow-motion cinematography, Bankowsky features many stylistic components similar to photographer Bruce Weber's boxing documentary from roughly a decade earlier, *Broken Noses*. The artistic look at the brutal sport and the top-notch female athletes competing in it is aided even further with a distinctive dance club-sounding score by Argentinian DJ Zoel. Even more compelling is the fact that Bankowsky's film takes place during the mid–1990s, when women's boxing was first being accepted as legitimate and gaining mainstream appeal. With women's mixed martial arts gaining popularity in the 2000s, much of that widespread appeal in the United States has fallen off, but the film still provides an interesting look at women's boxing in what could be considered its heyday.

A training sequence with the Dutch-born Rijker opens the film with her voice over explaining that she has been fighting since she was 12, beginning with karate and then moving on to kickboxing, in which she became the Dutch champion, European champion, and finally world champion. Rijker further explains that she became addicted to the lifestyle and adulation that came from winning, but she wanted a new challenge. After moving to Los Angeles and hooking up with trainer Freddie Roach, who would later become the head trainer for world champion Manny Pacquiao, Rijker turned down contract offers from Don King in order to sign with promoter Bob Arum. Arum, who had refused to get involved with women's boxing to that point, was reluctant at first, but was won over by Rijker's professionalism, talent, and charisma. Bankowsky next briefly visits Barbara Buttrick, who was a world champion of women's boxing in the 1950s, when willing opponents were hard to find, and later the founder and president of the Women's International Boxing Federation.

Bankowsky features some of the boxers at the 1995 Daily News Golden Gloves tournament at Madison Square Garden. A tradition dating back 68 years, the Golden Gloves finally opened its doors to women in 1995 and the women's matches were an immediate hit. Although not part of the film, Bankowsky herself even climbed into the ring for the first time for the occasion. With Jill Matthews, one of the more colorful participants, answering "a manicure and pedicure" to the question of how she prepared for the fight, the brief lighthearted venture into the amateur Golden Gloves competition ties in well with the more serious look at Rijker's preparation and career. A practicing Buddhist, Rijker prepares for an upcoming fight in her native Holland with chanting and moxibustion, and afterwards reveals more intimate details about her life. While also acknowledging that she may seek a career change before suffering any serious damage, Rijker articulately explains that the attention from her boxing success is addictive and tied to self-worth. After documenting Rijker's climb up the ranks for three years, Bankowsky's final scene is the 1997 WIBF title fight. In the years since the film's release, Rijker did in fact change careers and appeared in the 2004 Oscar-winning film *Million Dollar Baby*. After playing at a number of prestigious film festivals, Shadow Boxers was released on DVD in 2003 and is widely available for streaming.

Awards: 1999 CMJ Film and Music Festival: Best Music in Film, Best Editing; 1999 Florida Film Festival: Best Documentary First Feature Special Jury Award; 2000 Créteil International Women's Film Festival: AFJ Documentary Award; 2000 New Haven Film Festival: Kodak Cinematography Award, Audience Award; 2000 Santa Monica Film Festival: Best Documentary Moxie! Award.

Sherpa, 2015
Director: Jennifer Peedom; Running Time: 96 minutes; Australia/Nepal.

Australian filmmaker Jennifer Peedom (*Solitary Endeavor on the Southern Ocean*, 2008) set out to make a film about the Mount Everest climbing industry told from the Sherpas point of view in 2014, but she ended up with an even more dramatic film that cuts to the heart of the cultural clash between indigenous peoples and Western values. Her film came about after hardly-believable news broke of a brawl at nearly 22,000 feet between Western climbers and an angry mob of Sherpa guides in April 2013. The so-called "Everest brawl" was joked about in Western media, but Peedom viewed it as a political awakening that had been brewing for a long time, perhaps because of the way that the climbing industry commercializes the sacred mountain and accommodates tourists fulfilling their bucket list or perhaps simply because the highly-skilled Sherpa guides had grown tired of taking such risks for so little reward. In a 2016 interview with *The Guardian*, Peedom says that she could sense things reaching a tipping point: "It felt for me that where things were at politically, tension really was at the point where it felt like anything that was going to happen was going to be the straw that broke the camel's back" (Buckmaster, "Sherpa: Norbu Tenzing"). Taking place almost exactly a year after the Everest brawl, the proverbial straw that will likely forever change the Everest climbing industry was the April 18, 2014, ice avalanche that killed 16 Sherpas—what Peedom's award-winning 2015 film *Sherpa* refers to as "the darkest day in the history of Mount Everest."

When Sir Edmund Hillary became the first known person to summit Mount Everest in 1953, he and his mountaineering guide and partner Tenzing Norgay arguably became two of the most well-known people in the world. Norgay's fame has never been surpassed among other Sherpa people, but it probably was nowhere near the fame and credit that he actually deserved. As the film points out, Sherpa Tenzing had been to the mountain seven times already by the time that he guided Colonel John Hunt and Edmund Hillary on their famous 1953 expedition. Hunt and Hillary were both knighted after the expedition, whereas Norgay received the George Medal from the United Kingdom—quite an honor, but something of a "second-level award," according to the film. Interviewed in the film, Norbu Tenzing Norgay (Tenzing's son) points out that Sherpas and most people of Asia felt slighted by this. Sherpa Tenzing's fame also led to a sort of branding for the term "Sherpa." Most people in the Western world simply assume that a Sherpa is a mountaineering guide, rather than an actual

***Sherpa* (2015) looks at labor issues surrounding the Mount Everest climbing industry.**

ethnic group of people within Nepal. Peedom's primary themes emerging from the early part of the film are the commercialization of Everest and the discontent that modern Sherpas feel. Scenes of Sherpas setting up base camps stocked with books and a television provide an idea of just how much this one-time sacred adventure has morphed into more of a service industry for Nepalese tourism. The Sherpa guides have drastically changed as well. Sherpas are no longer uneducated and isolated from technological advances, and with the advances of formal education and mass media, demands for better treatment cannot be far behind.

A primary focus of the film is on Phurba Tashi, the most successful climbing Sherpa of his generation, and Russell Brice, a New Zealand mountaineer who operates an expedition company. The two had worked together many times since 1998 despite the fact that Tashi's family knows the danger and urges him to stop climbing. Tashi explains the rather simple reality of his continued climbing by pointing out that his entire community benefits from his work, including hotels and the many porters. The film's brilliant transition from the themes of Everest commercialization and Sherpas' livelihoods to a full-blown examination of labor relations and worker's rights is aided by footage of the 2013 brawl. While certainly not a melee, it clearly shows the tension that was present even a year earlier. When the dreaded disaster strikes, which it seems virtually everyone knew was coming because of the numerous times that the Sherpas are required to cross the dangerous icefall for a single expedition, the Sherpas stage a protest. Their anger is not toward the foreigners, but rather at the Nepalese government for under-payment in relation to the risks and especially for not providing better benefits for the families of Sherpas that have been killed. Brice now must explain to his clients that their expedition is over, and does so by suggesting that only a handful of Sherpas have threatened violence to any Sherpas who continue. There is no evidence of this claim and Tashi even denies that his group was threatened. The Sherpas effectively chose principle over money, but with Brice lecturing them about their ruined reputations for refusing to climb; it seems that the lack of Western respect for Sherpas remains. After a theatrical release in Australia and the U.S., *Sherpa* won numerous awards. It is currently available for streaming.

Awards: 2015 London Film Festival: Grierson Award; 2016 Australian Film Institute: Best Original Score in a Documentary(Partos), Best Feature Length Documentary (nominated), Best Editing in a Documentary (Christian Gazal, nominated), Best Cinematography in a Documentary (Renan Ozturk, Hugh Miller, Ken Sauls, nominated); 2016 Film Critics Circle of Australia Awards: Best Feature Documentary; 2016 Screen Music Awards Australia: Best Soundtrack Album (Anthony Partos); 2015 Adelaide Film Festival: Best Documentary (nominated); 2015 Melbourne International Film Festival: Best Documentary People's Choice Award (nominated); 2015 Philadelphia Film Festival: Best Documentary Feature Jury Award (nominated); 2015 Sydney Film Festival: Best Documentary Audience Award (nominated), Best Film (nominated); 2016 BAFTA Awards: Best Documentary (nominated); 2016 Palm Springs International Film Festival: Best Documentary Feature Audience Award (nominated).

The Short Game, 2013

Director: Josh Greenbaum; Running Time: 99 minutes; U.S.

The golfers competing for the 2012 U.S. Kids Golf World Championship come from all over. Viewers are introduced to golf prodigies from California, China, Florida, France, the Philippines, South Africa, and Texas, all making their way to Pinehurst, North Carolina, to attempt to add to their already well-stocked trophy cases. The tournament itself includes 1,250 of the best youth golfers in the world, but filmmaker Josh Greenbaum follows a path very similar to *Spellbound*, the 2002 Oscar-nominated film about the Scripps National Spelling Bee, by focusing in on only eight and allowing the many others to go nameless. These young golfers are clearly an extension of their parents (or "daddy caddies") on the course, but it's equally evident that they are seven and eight-year-olds who are very typical when not driving, chipping, and putting like professional golfers. For the most part, the kids seem to enjoy the pressure, and handle it better than their parents in many cases. As is the case with some examples of over-bearing parents pushing their children to athletic greatness, *The Short Game* makes clear that these children in the world of competitive golf seem to strive for that greatness and accept the coaching as part of the deal. Perhaps this is due to the fact that golf is an individual sport and more challenging mentally than physically.

In terms of just how much more difficult golf is than traditional sports for children, one Hall of Fame instructor explains that it's subtle and rhythmic, "like a waltz," instead of a sport where natural speed and strength matter. Keeping in mind that these are very young kids excelling at a very difficult sport, it is easy to find a favorite and a non-favorite among the children highlighted by Greenbaum. While some are simply adorable with infectious personalities, the PR-savviness of others is a little troubling. A few on-course meltdowns and tears could be expected from golfers so young, but hearing one talk about his goal of owning a golf club with a big hotel and a nice restaurant (a "huge, huge facility") while promoting Trump Ice brand bottled water is rather unexpected. Although fascinating that each one of these kids could be so good, and gripping in how they will finish their respective rounds, at times seeing such young kids taking part in swanky golf-club culture can remind viewers why the sport is sometimes criticized as being elitist. The film took home the prestigious Audience Award at the 2013 South by Southwest (SXSW) Film Festival and was short-listed for the Documentary Feature Academy Award after a theatrical run. Following this, the film became one of the first documentaries to be acquired by Netflix and streamed as a "Netflix Original."

Awards: 2013 Hampton International Film Festival: Best Documentary Feature; 2013 Maui Film Festival: Feature Documentary; 2013 South by Southwest Film Festival: Documentary Feature Audience Award, Documentary Feature Competition (nominated); 2013 Nantucket Film Festival: Best Feature (2nd place).

16 Days of Glory, 1986

Director: Bud Greenspan; Running Time: 145 minutes; U.S.

The official film of the XXIII Olympiad in Los Angeles should be mandatory viewing for anyone who has never seen the work of sports documentarian Bud Greenspan. What starts with an oddly-narrated look at the Parade of Nations and opening ceremony develops into an artistic and poetic record of the games, ending with a dedication to Greenspan's late wife, Cappy. This original *16 Days of Glory* would be followed by

Greenspan's similarly-titled International Olympic Committee-sanctioned films of the '88 Seoul Summer Games, '88 Calgary Winter Games, '92 Barcelona Summer Games, and the '94 Lillehammer Winter Games. Greenspan's 18 different camera crews shot nearly a million feet of film stock, which were later edited into a six-part television series as well. Many memorable moments, such as the Zola Budd-Mary Decker controversy and Carl Lewis's four gold medals, were left out of this 145-minute official IOC film and included in the televised series, but it still highlights a number of events and athletes in a way that the actual network broadcasts simply fail to do.

The film gives ample time, most in 10-minute segments, to a number of different events and athletes, but focuses in greater length and intensity on the decathlon, which reveals two-time British gold medalist Daley Thompson as one of the most engaging and best all-around athletes of a generation. In this 145-minute film, Greenspan clearly focuses his interest almost entirely on the many individual competitions, failing to mention the USA gold in men's basketball, considered by many to be one of the greatest amateur teams ever assembled, and the soccer competition (Gold to France), which drew unexpectedly large and enthusiastic American crowds. Also noteworthy but not treated in the film is the Soviet-led boycott, which was joined by 14 Communist-allied nations and was largely a response to the USA-led boycott of the 1980 Summer Games in Moscow. After a screening at the London Film Festival, *16 Days of Glory* had a limited theatrical release in 1986 and the edited television version could be seen for years on various cable channels. It can be found in VHS format or streaming online, but was never released on DVD.

Awards: 1985 International Documentary Association: IDA Award.

The Smashing Machine: The Life and Times of Extreme Fighter Mark Kerr, 2002

Director: John Hyams; Running Time: 93 minutes; U.S.

Originally titled *The Specimen* when it appeared at the inaugural Tribeca Film Festival in 2002, *The Smashing Machine: The Life and Times of Extreme Fighter Mark Kerr* is an up close and personal look at the early days of mixed martial arts fighting and one of the top performers in the burgeoning, violent combat sport. Filmmaker John Hyams, who would later direct two installments of the *Universal Soldier* movie franchise, follows former NCAA wrestling champion Mark Kerr as he turns to the world of ultimate fighting and seems to be a natural, but gets sidetracked dealing with issues of drug addiction. An early scene in the film documents Kerr at a doctor's office explaining to an older lady in the waiting area why he is sporting a black eye. Soft-spoken, articulate, and coming across nothing like the brawler viewers had heard and seen in the film's opening voice-over monologue set to violence, Kerr tells her that he's involved in ultimate fighting, a sport which pits athletes coming from different disciplines of combat sports (wrestling versus karate, for example) against one another. Aghast, the woman asks how he can take part in it; Kerr answers simply that you have to "treat it as a profession." Therein lies the true appeal of both Kerr's early MMA existence and the film itself. He reluctantly got into the sport as a means to income using his uniquely-honed skills and the film came about at a time when the general public knew little about the sport.

Hyams documents Kerr's first professional fights taking place at the World Vale Tudo Championship in Brazil in early 1997, in which he won the title after defeating three opponents. Kerr next enters The Ultimate Fighting Championships and wins back-to-back tournaments, but leaves the UFC to join the Pride Fighting Championships in Japan for more money. Relying on the MMA expertise of radio broadcaster Eddie Goldman, the film explains how the sport was accepted and lucrative in Japan in the late 1990s, but was incorrectly marketed as violent spectacle in the United States and subsequently relegated to pay-per-view events. Fairly early in the film, it becomes apparent that Kerr has a dependency on strong pain narcotics as he speaks candidly about knowing how to obtain them. Similarly, it becomes apparent that he is somewhat estranged from his family and has come to depend on his girlfriend, Dawn, for love and support. Another meaningful relationship for Kerr seems to be that of his friend and mentor, Mark Coleman, an aging fighter who also reluctantly continues as a means to large paydays. Following his first loss after 11 wins (later changed to a no contest, or draw, ruling) Kerr overdoses on pain medication and vows to get clean while hospitalized, later checking himself into a drug treatment facility.

As Kerr continues on the path of sobriety and begins training with legendary Dutch fighter Bas Rutten, Dawn continues to party and the couple separate. Kerr handily wins his fight, after which he and Dawn reconcile despite the warning from Rutten that his progress will be lost. The warning comes to fruition as Kerr takes a severe beating in his next fight and his career suddenly seems to now be on the downslide as he and Dawn decide to get married. Containing elements of both observational and participatory mode documentaries, the film came at time when the sport was undergoing major changes and first beginning to become legitimized in the United States. Hyams traces roughly a three-year period, 1997–2000, in which the "ultimate fighting" and "no holds barred" combat monikers began to be ditched for the more palatable name "mixed martial arts" and the sport veered away from the Brazilian Vale Tudo tradition of very few rules. While previous films dealing with the sport certainly existed, *The Smashing Machine* was perhaps the first to combine the inherent raw brutality with a character-led narrative and a sociological examination. Following its world premiere at the 2002 Tribeca Film Festival, the film was aired on HBO in 2003 as part of its long-running documentary series, *America Undercover*. It is widely available for streaming and was released in DVD format by Docurama that same year. The DVD special features include a commentary track with Hyams and producer Jon Greenhalgh, who was Kerr's wrestling teammate at Syracuse University, and *Fight Day*, a short film about legendary Brazilian fighter Renzo Gracie.

Awards: 2002 CineVegas International Film Festival: Pioneer Documentaries Selection; 2002 Tribeca Film Festival: International Showcase Selection.

Sons of Cuba, 2009

Director: Andrew Lang; Running Time: 88 minutes; U.K.

Since the 1970s, Cuba has dominated international amateur boxing in a way that few countries can claim with any sport. Since the Mexico City Summer Olympics in 1968, Cuba has won a total of 73 Olympic boxing medals, including 37 golds, and this despite not competing in the 1984 and 1988 games. Along with Hungarian Laszlo Papp, Cubans Felix Savon and Teofilo Stevenson are the only boxers to win gold three times. Two specific questions arise from Cuba's recent dominance in amateur boxing: First, how is it that the island nation of just over 11 million has come to be so dominant in this sport, and secondly, why is it that great Cuban amateurs like Savon and Stevenson never became professional champions? The first question is specifically explored by filmmaker Andrew Lang in his 2009 film *Sons of Cuba*, and the second question emerges as a major theme in the film. In fact, the two questions are closely related. From the early days of the Castro regime up until 2013, professional sports were banned in Cuba, so boxers remained amateurs despite great talent. Those who did want to box for fame and riches instead of Cuban pride had to defect away from the communist state. Lang examines how Cuba's great amateur boxers of tomorrow get started by following three youngsters during their time training and boarding at the Havana Boxing Academy, one of several such institutions designed to groom the nation's dominant Olympic boxing program.

Rising well before daybreak to put on tattered shoes and begin training, the children at the Havana Boxing Academy are fighting for a better future. The better future that boxing can bring them in Cuba comes primarily in the form of perks such as houses and cars for their families and from national fame and celebrity. The kids at the academy are sold on the idea that the relatively minor government-provided perks that await the ones who become champions will indeed mean a better future. That may well be true when compared to the type of bleak futures that await typical children in the totalitarian country. Even more than being sold on the notion of boxing as a means to a better future within Cuba, the kids at the academy are sold on the ideals of national pride and using their boxing ability to be "pioneers for communism." As the film begins, this concept is laid out as viewers see the pre-dawn academy with a voice-over coming from a famous Fidel Castro speech: "The revolution must concentrate on sport; it is of vital importance to the country. Youngsters with outstanding talent will be plucked from the masses and given the best possible training. On the frontline of sport the revolution will advance. Fatherland or death, we will win!"

While Lang's film is not overtly political, some political analysis is needed when, during the filming, Castro falls ill and ultimately cedes power and then three of Cuba's older, heroic boxing champions choose to defect in order to box professionally. Although it is certainly not surprising for hardline communist Cubans to declare this an evil act, it is rather surprising to hear the nine-year-olds at the academy declare it a betrayal. The children at the focus of *Sons of Cuba* include Christian, Santos, and Junior, who are all training for the national championships, in which various youth boxing clubs and academies compete against one another. This goes a long way in determining which of the young boxers take the next step to Olympic greatness. The training techniques are far from typical of higher-income nations, as the children are boarded at the academy for months at a time and subjected to physical, emotional, and even dietary regulations. Lang's examination of this training program shines a light onto why it is that Cuba has become the dominant nation in Olympic boxing, but the question may be left a bit open-ended when one wonders how much the national ethos, or communist indoctrination, has played into it. Following a strong festival run in 2009, the film was released in DVD format with special features including a commentary track with Lang and English subtitles.

Awards: 2009 Foundation on New Latin American Cinema: Best Documentary; 2009 Havana Film Festival: Best Foreign Language Film; 2009 London Latin American Film Festival: Audience Award; 2009 Los Angeles Latino International Film Festival: Best Documentary Jury Award; 2009 Rome Film Fest: Best Documentary; 2009 San Diego Latino Film Festival: Audience Award; Sheffield International Documentary Festival: Youth Jury Award; 2010 Malaga Spanish Film Festival: Audience Award; 2009 British Independent Film Awards: Best Documentary (nominated).

Speedo: A Demolition Derby Love Story, 2003
Director: Jesse Moss; Running Time: 88 minutes; U.S.

Some documentary films are successful because they tell a good story, but others succeed because they feature fascinating characters and fascinating real lives. Ed "Speedo" Jager, a Long Island, New York, mechanic, demolition derby racer, and devoted father, is such a character with such a life. Speedo is introduced while competing at Riverhead Raceway in May of 1999. Flying into a post-race tirade because he feels cheated out of a trophy, the fury of this man is as obvious as the aggression of the sport he loves. At the Garden City Exxon station where he works, he explains that working on cars is a real pleasure for him because it comes easy—he simply understands "how cars work from top to bottom." With the camera of filmmaker Jesse Moss (*The Overnighters*, 2014) intimately following Jager on and off the track during the 1999 demo season, viewers get a look at what the derbies are all about and the gearhead culture that surrounds them. As his family is introduced, it becomes clear that Speedo is equally passionate about being a good father to sons Michael and Anthony, but a clear tension is present with his wife, Linda, who can find no value in her husband's beloved hobby.

With the only tangible rewards he reaps from his success during the 1999 season being a few trophies, small cash prizes, and notoriety on the demo circuit, Speedo admits that he really dreams of racing stock cars for big money instead of smashing them up in demolition derbies. As his marriage completely disintegrates and he finally moves out of the family's house, it is also revealed that Speedo has developed a romantic relationship with Liz, a track official who shares his passion for demos and racing. He calls Liz his "one-woman pit crew," while she points out that he is no longer full of the rage that viewers had witnessed in the early scenes of the film. Using a handheld digital camera throughout, Moss captures the automobile expertise, the devotion of being a good father, the tribulations

Ed Jager, the subject of *Speedo* (2003), uses his skill as a mechanic to excel at a unique sport.

of a failing marriage, the budding new romance, and the overall infectious personality of Speedo in perfect cinéma vérité fashion. After capturing several festival wins in 2003, *Speedo* aired as part of the POV Film Series on PBS in 2004 and was released on DVD by Docurama. The DVD features include an entertaining commentary track with Moss and Speedo himself and three video updates, one of which is Anthony Jager's (or Speedo Junior's) first time competing in a derby.

Awards: 2003 Boston Independent Film Festival: Grand Jury Prize; 2003 Full Frame Documentary Film Festival: Audience Award; 2003 Hamptons International Film Festival: Best Long Island Film; 2003 Newport International Film Festival, Rhode Island: Best Documentary.

Spellbound, 2002

Director: Jeffrey Blitz; Running Time: 97 minutes; U.S.

Nominated for the Best Documentary Feature Academy Award in 2003, *Spellbound* is an entertaining look at the world of competitive spelling bees and a chronicle of the 1999 Scripps National Spelling Bee in

Washington, D.C. First-time feature filmmaker Jeffrey Blitz follows eight competitors from across the United States as they attempt to become the 72nd winner of the event that first began in 1925 and has been aired on ESPN since the mid–1990s. An intertitle early in the film reads that 9,000,000 children compete in school and city spelling bees across the country, but only 249 qualify for the Nationals in Washington, D.C. Over two days of competing, 248 of those children will misspell a word; the one who doesn't will become champion and follow in the footsteps of Frank Neuhauser, the bees first winner back in 1925. Neuhauser appears briefly in the film to talk about his experience, as do a few other past winners: Paige Kimble, the 1981 champion, who is now the director of the bee, explains that the media attention for the winner can be overwhelming. Jonathan Knisely, the 1971 champ, admits that it was a big deal to win, but also quips that "it didn't help him with his love life." Aside from the brief comments from these past winners, Blitz does not offer much history about the competition, but it really is not needed because the film works as a chronicle by zeroing in on the kids and the competition.

Representing a broad and diverse range of American children, *Spellbound* can be interpreted as an allegory for the American dream, or the immigrant experience, or perhaps just a film about kids finding a niche and fitting in. The first speller profiled is Angela Arenivar, from Perryton, Texas, whose parents are undocumented immigrants from Mexico and whose hard-working father ironically has not learned English. Nupur Lala, from Tampa, Florida, is the daughter of immigrants from India, who suggests that hard work is ingrained in her because second chances do not exist in India the way that they do in America. Soft-spoken and perhaps shy, Ted Brigham is from Rolla, Missouri, and seems to be more withdrawn than the others and more rurally-oriented. Emily Stagg, from New Haven, Connecticut, is a hard worker with supportive parents, but clearly exists in a socio-economic class that most children have no idea about. Far lower on the socio-economic ladder, Ashley White is from Washington, D.C., and representative of a child from a single-parent family who sees education as a tool for future success. The family of Neil Kadakia, from San Clemente, California, could be a poster for one experiencing the American dream. Also immigrants from India, the father speaks about American values of hard work equaling success as he provides a tour of their lavish home. April DeGideo, from Ambler, Pennsylvania, comes from a charming and quirky blue-collar family that may be the most typical, despite her atypical scholarly interests. And finally, Harry Altman of Glen Rock, New

Jersey, may be the most memorable because of his quirkiness and unrestrained nature.

Naturally, Blitz set out to document a diverse group of kids in terms of race and class, but that may not be as contrived as it appears. Despite making up less than one percent of school-aged children, Indian-American spellers have dominated the contest in recent years. In 1999, this trend of Indian-American children excelling at this was just taking shape. Likewise, the fact that the contest is made up of regional winners sort of dictates that class and race differences will exist. It is probably not by accident that when Angela is introduced, one of her practice words is "allegory." In the next scene, the rancher who employs her undocumented father praises his work ethic while Angela explains that the educational opportunity is the primary reason that her father took the risk of being smuggled into the country with his wife. As cringe-worthy as it is to hear Emily ask if the au pair will be coming with them to the nationals, it is just as heartwarming to see immigrants taking part and all the children, regardless of class, compete on a level playing field. Alex Cameron, the official word-pronouncer for the contest, describes how the bee is so intertwined with the immigrant story because so many see education and the hard work required to compete as the one thing that can create the level playing field. Although he wasn't the first, the blueprint laid out by Blitz in documenting individual competitors has been mimicked over and over by documentaries in the 21st century. Taking in nearly $6 million at the domestic box office, *Spellbound* is the second highest-grossing American film dealing with sports or competition. The film was released in DVD format following its successful festival run in 2003.

Awards: 2002 Hawaii International Film Festival: Documentary Feature Golden Maile Award; Los Angeles IFP West Film Festival: Best Documentary Audience Award, Special Jury Prize; 2002 South by Southwest Film Festival (SXSW): Documentary Feature Competition Award; Utah Film Critics Association Awards: Best Documentary Feature Film; 2002 Woodstock Film Festival: Best Documentary Jury Prize; 2003 Cleveland International Film Festival: Best Film; 2003 Durango Film Festival: Audience Award, Filmmakers Award; 2003 Melbourne International Film Festival: Most Popular Documentary; 2003 National Board of Review: Top Five Documentaries; 2003 Santa Barbara International Film Festival: Best Documentary; 2003 Sarasota Film Festival: Best Documentary Audience Award; 2003 Sydney Film Festival: Best Documentary Audience Award; 2004 American Cinema Editors: Best Edited Documentary Film (Yana Gorskaya); 2004 Golden Trailer Awards: Best Documentary; 2004

International Cinephile Society Awards: Best Documentary; 2002 Awards Circuit Community Awards: Best Documentary Feature (nominated); 2002 International Documentary Association: Feature Documentary (nominated); 2002 Tribeca Film Festival: Best Documentary Feature Jury Award (nominated); 2003 Academy Awards: Best Documentary Feature (nominated); 2003 Independent Spirit Awards: Truer Than Fiction Award (nominated); 2003 Seattle Film Critics Awards: Best Documentary (2nd Place); 2003 Village Voice Film Poll: Best Documentary (nominated).

Sumo East and West, 2003

Director: Ferne Pearlstein; Running Time: 85 minutes; U.S./Japan.

The national sport of Japan, sumo wrestling, dates back more than 2,000 years and is steeped in legend concerning ancient deities, religion, and rituals. As the 2003 film *Sumo East and West* begins, it also explains via intertitle that sumo has traditionally been extremely closed, adding after a pause "until the arrival of the Hawaiians." The filmmaking team of wife Ferne Pearlstein, as director, and husband Robert Edwards, as writer and producer, tackle the subject of sumo's tradition and its changing landscape as more and more foreign competitors take up the ancient sport and find success in the ring. Pearlstein's examination features broad themes of culture and tradition, but more precisely focuses on the question of whether this is an example of cultural appropriation, cultural appreciation, or simply cultural exchange. The questions are raised, and the story of sumo's recent transformation is seen, through the personal journey of Wayne Vierra, a Hawaiian who moved to Japan to train as an 18-year-old in 1990. While climbing up the ranks, Vierra was injured and Japanese rules do not allow one to re-enter the pro ranks after a certain time away from the sport. Training in Japan at the same time was another Hawaiian, Chad Rowan, who now goes by the name of Akebono. Whereas Vierra is now one of the top amateurs in the world and based in Hawaii, excelling at the westernized version of the sport, Akebono excelled in the traditional version and became the first non–Japanese-born yokozuna (or grand champion).

One interesting aspect relating to the notion of cultural appropriation or cultural exchange is that westerners are not only going to the East to compete in sumo, but sumo is coming to the West wrapped in a completely different package. As an American sumo journalist points out, the westerners who were most successful and accepted in Japan effectively Japanized themselves and upheld the traditions of sumo, meanwhile the amateur sumo that began to catch on in the USA during the 1990s was completely westernized, taking place with typical American flare. Pearlstein juxtaposes the decline in sumo participation and fandom in Japan in recent years with scenes depicting how Americanized Japanese culture at large has become over the same time. Pearlstein's well-made film sets itself apart from many others in that it approaches the topic by attempting to answer the cultural questions, but it goes the extra distance to fully examine the issues and goes even further in laying out the important historical facts. Sumo, in fact, has a long tradition in Hawaii (as evidenced by the archival film "Sumo in Hawaii," shot by Thomas Edison) and the tradition of Hawaiians coming to Japan to compete in sumo is much longer than most westerners might think. While some films may not take the time to educate viewers, *Sumo East and West* does the opposite and explains the important details of the sport for those not familiar. Following its festival run, the film was aired as part of the *Independent Lens* film series on PBS in 2004 and was also released in DVD format.

Awards: 2004 Director's View Film Festival: Feature Documentary, First Prize; 2003 Tribeca Film Festival: Best Documentary Feature Jury Award (nominated).

A Sunday in Hell (En Forarsdag i Helvede), 1977

Director: Jorgen Leth; Running Time: 111 minutes; Denmark.

On April 11, 1976, the 74th edition of the annual Paris-Roubaix bicycle road race was run and the resulting film of the event stands as one of the greatest sports documentaries of all time. Danish poet and filmmaker Jørgen Leth (*The Five Obstructions*, 2003) became a regular Tour de France television commentator in 1988, but his passion for the sport was exhibited more than a decade before that with his brilliant film *A Sunday in Hell*. The "Hell" that the title refers to is the course itself, which is 166 miles long, running through northern France and ending in the Roubaix Velodrome on the Belgian border. The first 100 miles of the course is run on smooth pavement, but the section known as "the Hell of the North" follows, in which several stretches are primitive roads made up of centuries-old cobblestones. What gives Paris-Roubaix the reputation as the hardest and most fascinating of all the prestigious "Monument" classic one-day races of Western Europe is the drama that comes from the final portion of the race over the cobbled stretches. Punctured tires, falls, and injuries are common here and the riders often come away covered in dust and mud with plenty of awful things to say about the tradition-rich race that is beloved by the European cycling fans of the region. The effective and dominant voice-over narration of Leth's expository mode documentary is provided by British cycling writer David Saunders. He describes the unique course as "a veritable Dante's Inferno, with incredible torture and even martyrdom," and prepares viewers before the start by pointing out that the finish is seven hours away, but how many riders will actually arrive can only be a guess.

The opening scenes capture meticulous preparation work by a bike mechanic and a massage session for one of the riders. Later in the film, Leth adds to his documentation of the race's atmosphere by capturing French cycling fans in a pub discussing the goings on and a large, very vocal demonstration by a group of citizens at the race protesting one of the sponsor's unfair labor policies (a French newspaper). At first glance, these scenes away from the actual racing may seem like nothing more than ordinary sporting event ambiance, but this is clearly something more with the Paris-Roubaix classic. The hostility of the labor protestors, which has also stopped auto traffic along the road, mixes with the urgency and doom that the racers exhibit as they mostly attempt to appease their anger. Those largely unfamiliar with European cycle racing will immediately notice the sport's proximity to its spectators and perhaps contrast that aspect to major American sporting events. It is in this vein that Leth's filming stresses the importance of the race on the community. In his 2014 book *The Sports Film: Games People Play*, author Bruce Babington points out that Leth closely follows the race in a linear fashion, but also emphasizes the event's commercial underpinnings in the community (36). As for the race, a primary focus is on rivals Eddy Merckx and Roger De Vlaeminck, both Belgians and two of the top cyclists in the world. Belgians Freddy Maertens and Marc Demeyer are heavily featured as well, as is Francesco Moser, the lone Italian hopeful. Often offered as a special screening at film festivals all over the world, the film is available in DVD format and can be found for online streaming as well.

Awards: 1996 International Documentary Film Festival Amsterdam (film selected); 2003 Bergen International Film Festival (film selected); 2007 Adelaide Film Festival (film selected); 2009 Athens International Film Festival: Honorary Award (Leth).

Sunshine Superman, 2014

Director: Marah Strauch; Running Time: 100 minutes; U.S.

A common misconception about BASE jumping is that "BASE" is actually an acronym for building, antenna, span, earth, rather than a "base" being part of the activity. The acronym refers to the four categories of objects from which one can parachute in order to take part in this adrenaline-rushing activity. Up until the late 1970s, choosing to parachute from a fixed structure such as a bridge, building, or cliff rather than a plane had primarily only been attempted as one-off stunts or as a way of testing early parachutes. However, when Carl Boenish made BASE jumping his lifelong passion and effectively became the sport's father by filming a series of jumps from El Capitan in Yosemite National Park in 1978, this new death-defying recreational activity soon had a name and a chief promoter. A cinematographer by trade and an avid skydiver, Boenish worked for Hughes Aircraft and was asked to shoot the aerial free-fall filming sequences of John Frankenheimer's 1968 movie *The Gypsy Moths*. Boenish soon became known as an innovator of free-fall cinematography and always considered himself a filmmaker first and skydiver second.

It was through the many films Boenish made of skydiving that led to the organizational concept of BASE jumping. Specifically, the jumps from El Capitan in 1978, which Boenish filmed from a homemade perch protruding out 20 feet from the top of the 3,600-foot cliff, served as the seminal moment for BASE jumping. Director Marah Strauch spends quite a bit of time on the El Capitan jumps, while also exploring the fallout due to the fact that these jumps, and many future jumps from other locales, were illegal. Creating a unique biographical film about a rare individual who almost single-handedly developed a new sport, Strauch also probes deep into the love story that developed between Boenish and his wife, Jean. Over a seven-year period examined in the film, BASE jumping went from being mostly outlawed to being featured on a Guinness Book of World Records television special with David Frost. Carl and Jean Boenish successfully made the televised record-breaking double jump from Norway's Troll Wall in 1984, but left a mystery behind as well. By equally exploring both the activity itself and its founding father, the biographical aspect of *Sunshine Superman* works in two ways. The DVD special features include two of Boenish's short film-poems.

Awards: 2015 Montclair Film Festival: New Jersey Films Competition; Portland International Film Festival: Best Documentary, Best New Director (Strauch); 2015 Cleveland International Film Festival: Best Documentary (nominated); Edinburgh International Film Festival: Best Documentary Feature Film (nominated).

Surfwise, 2007
Director: Doug Pray; Running Time: 93 minutes; U.S.

The competition of surfing takes a back seat to the turbulent family relationships in this fascinating story about Dorian "Doc" Paskowitz, his wife, and nine children, collectively known as the first family of surfing. Leaving a successful medical practice and two failed marriages behind, Doc Paskowitz simply left it all and began the search for a more holistic life experience, centered primarily on sex and surfing. After finding the appropriate bearer of his children (eventually eight boys and a girl), the entire family lived a bizarre nomadic lifestyle in a series of used traveling campers. The children never attended school, never ate refined sugar, or even had clothes of their own, but they won surfing competitions one after another and worked at the Paskowitz Surf Camp, which is still in existence today. It is a voyeuristic treat to watch, but at times the unconventional lifestyle that Paskowitz enacted upon his family is a little disturbing. A few of the children pull no punches in airing the resentment that they harbor, and filmmaker Doug Pray handles the touchy subject fairly and openly. As it becomes clear that each of the siblings remain dedicated to the sport of surfing, even those who do not look back fondly on their eccentric father and bizarre upbringing, one can realize how *Surfwise* is indeed a film about surfing as much as it is a biographical film about the patriarch of the Bohemian first family of surfing. The film was released in DVD format in 2007 and was theatrically released by Magnolia Pictures the following year.

Awards: 2008 Gen Art Film Festival: Best Feature Audience Award; 2008 Golden Trailer Awards: Best Documentary (nominated); 2009 Chlotridus Awards: Best Documentary (nominated); 2009 Cinema Eye Honors Awards: Outstanding Achievement in Graphic Design or Animation (Lasse Jarvi, nominated).

Through the Fire: Sebastian Telfair's Defining Year, 2005
Director: Jonathan Hock; Running Time: 103 minutes; U.S.

Exploring the theme of African American youths using basketball as a means to escape poverty, and the surrogate family members who also depend on those dreams, *Through the Fire: Sebastian Telfair's Defining Year* is a fly-on-the-wall chronicle of a year in the life of a high school basketball star. Sebastian Telfair is somewhat of a playground prodigy and Coney Island basketball legend by the time he is 17 years old. He is also the cousin of former NBA star Stephon Marbury and brother of former Providence College standout Jamel Thomas. Telfair has led his Lincoln High team to two straight New York City titles and is one of the most heavily recruited players in the nation. His decision to attend the University of Louisville brings national media attention, but by the season's end, after Telfair has become the city's all-time scoring leader, the attention has also brought NBA scouts, sports agents, and the lure of instant fame. Only ten years earlier, the same story would have likely had a different focus. What was once only a decision of which college to attend is now a decision whether to attend at all. Considering the money that an NBA contract can bring, and the repercussions of not succeeding while losing any future college eligibility, that decision is indeed a heavy one.

After working in production for the NBA, then with NFL Films, and writing and editing the blockbuster IMAX documentary *Michael Jordan to the Max*, Jonathan Hock has become one of the preeminent nonfiction filmmakers dealing strictly with sports. Having lived in Brooklyn, the story of another New York playground legend making it big was no doubt special to Hock, and he treats Telfair's tumultuous season in such a way. The focus is solidly on the recruitment and pressure of the young star's decision, perhaps missing an opportunity to more closely examine the controversy surrounding the larger issue at the time: the dichotomy of amateurism and corporatism in big-time basketball. Beginning in 1995, at least one high school player was selected in the first round of the next ten NBA Drafts. By 2004, the NBA Draft in question with Telfair, the number of prep stars choosing to forgo college in favor of NBA riches was eight. Sensing that the trend would hurt college basketball and create a perception problem for the league, the NBA—free market capitalism be dammed—instituted eligibility requirements to stop the practice after the 2005 draft. Following a strong critical reception at several 2005 film festivals, *Through the Fire* received a limited theatrical release, was aired nationally on ESPN, and has went over 100,000 in DVD sales.

Awards: 2005 AFI Fest: Best Documentary; 2005 Urbanworld Film Festival: Best Documentary; 2007 Krasnogorski International Film Festival: Best Documentary; 2005 Tribeca Film Festival: Spotlight Selection.

Tokyo Olympiad, 1965
Director: Kon Ichikawa; Running Time: 170 minutes; Japan

Like many other Olympic films, the official documentary of the 18th Summer Olympiad differs from other nonfiction sports films in many ways, but primarily in that it offers a more artistic look at the competition. These films are typically poetic mode documentaries, often forsaking the news and statistical element of sport for the tiny details of athleticism and competition. *Tokyo Olympiad* takes the viewer to the 1964 Summer Games, not as a fan or even someone concerned with the outcome, but rather as the athlete dedicated to a very specific craft. An athlete who participates in a single event (the shot put, for example) spends years preparing for the few moments of that specific Olympic competition. Understanding this fact leads to a better understanding of films which capture minute details in an artistic fashion. One of Japan's most distinguished filmmakers, Kon Ichikawa (*The Burmese Harp*, 1956), was commissioned to document the 18th Olympiad, held in 1964 in Tokyo, and his brilliant filmmaking specializes in those minute details of athleticism. While Ichikawa's final product is now revered as a masterpiece and true work of art, the original unedited film drew fire from the Japanese government because of its focus on athletes and the details and techniques of their craft rather than competition and records in a historical sense.

Ichikawa begins his filming of the events with arguably one of the most important moments in Olympic history—the men's 100 meter, won by USA sprinter and future Pro Football Hall of Famer Bob Hayes. In what would be the fastest time ever recorded, earning Hayes the title of the

Kon Ichikawa's *Tokyo Olympiad* (1965) features beautiful cinematography, a trademark of poetic mode documentaries.

"world's fastest human," Ichikawa holds a shot of the competitors on the starting block then goes wide in slow motion as the race unfolds. Other highlighted events and athletes include future heavyweight champion Joe Frazier, who won gold in boxing, Australian swimmer Dawn Fraser, and Czechoslovakian gymnast Vera Caslavska, who won three gold medals and moved past Soviet Larisa Latynina as the world's dominant female gymnast. Latynina, whose five medals won in 1964 pushed her career total to 18, would hold the record for the most medals until broken by Michael Phelps in 2012. Ethiopian runner Abebe Bikila, who became the first person to win the marathon twice, is heavily featured as well. Bikila had captivated the world four years earlier when he won gold in Rome while running barefooted. The one athlete to receive a focus that stands apart is Ahamed Isa, a runner from Chad. Perhaps Ichikawa focuses in on him because African athletes were largely new to the Olympics at the time, or he may find it interesting that many African athletes are there encountering certain technologies of the modern world for the first time.

These were the first Olympics held in Asia, but the importance was even greater for the nation of Japan, whose infrastructure had almost been completely destroyed by the atomic bombings that ended World War II just 19 years before. The economic and humanitarian recovery that Japan had made was remarkable and Ichikawa's film stresses this, even narrating that the Tokyo Olympics were a symbol of regeneration and acceptance for Japan. Because of the devastation to Japan from the atomic bombing, one unique aspect is that these games featured new, state of the art facilities rather than older ones typically used. While the edited 125-minute version of the film can be found for online streaming (with an English narration track), the original 170-minute version is difficult to locate in DVD format in non–Asian countries. Film historian and Olympics buff Peter Cowie provides a must watch/hear commentary track for the Criterion Collection DVD, which was released in 2002, but has since gone out of print. Cowie begins his commentary by stressing the importance of the film as it compares to the other official Olympic documentaries. Cowie argues that "film buffs and sport enthusiasts alike agree that just two Olympic documentaries stand out from the pack: the extraordinary, emotive, and arguably fascistic *Olympia*, made by Leni Riefenstahl during the games in Berlin in 1936 and Kon Ichikawa's *Tokyo Olympiad*, celebrating the 1964 Olympiad." The Criterion Collection DVD also features a 1992 interview with Ichikawa, in which he discusses his focus and theme: "sports are a wonderful manifestation of human culture."

Awards: 1966 BAFTA Awards: Flaherty Documentary Award, UN

Award; 1966 Mainichi Film Concours: Best Film Score (Toshiro Mayuzumi), Best Sound Recording; 1966 American Cinema Editors: Best Edited Feature Film (Richard L. Van Enger, nominated); 1989 National Society of Film Critics Awards, USA: Best Documentary (3rd Place).

Top Spin, 2014

Director: Sara Newens, Mina T. Son; Running Time: 80 minutes; U.S.

Table tennis became an Olympic sport in 1988 for both men and women, and since that time, the medal podium has been dominated by Asia. In men's singles, all but one gold medal has been won by either China or South Korea and all but six of the total 25 medals have been won by Asian countries. In women's singles, all eight golds have been won by China and no non–Asian nation has ever medaled. Three American teenagers were determined to change that in 2012. As the three teens, Ariel Hsing, Michael Landers, and Lily Xhang, attempt to make it to the London Olympics, filmmakers Sara Newens and Mina T. Son document their efforts in *Top Spin*. Rather than spending too much time exploring the particulars of the unique, lightning-fast sport, the film simply follows these three athletes as they train, compete, and balance the other demands of their high school lives. All three kids seem to be classic overachievers who play this demanding sport because they enjoy it, rather than because they are prodded to by over-bearing parents or coaches—an all-too-common theme in many youth sports.

The film briefly attempts to answer the question as to why America is not competitive on the world stage, which boils down to the fact that in America the sport is not taken seriously and carries little importance. As one of the top American players explains in the film, prize money for "beer pong" in the USA dwarfs that of ping-pong, but he also adds that it is slowly coming out of the garages and into mainstream sports. A comparison made by an ex–Olympian in the film is that table tennis is to China what soccer is to Brazil. Indeed, as one of the teens chooses to train for a period in China, viewers see giant facilities, museums, and even playing tables in the public parks. Newens and Son uniquely mix the very personal stories of the three teens with just enough information about the sport to make their attempts to become Olympians a very compelling narrative. Following a successful run at scores of film festivals and a limited theatrical release, the DVD was released in late 2015.

Awards: 2015 CAAMFest: Best Documentary Audience Award, Best Documentary Jury Award (nominated); 2015 Los Angeles Asian Pacific

Film Festival: Best Editing in a Documentary Feature (Newens, Summers Henderson), Best Documentary Feature (nominated); 2015 Nashville Film Festival: Documentary Competition (nominated).

Touching the Void, 2003
Director: Kevin MacDonald; Running Time: 106 minutes; U.K.

Two confident and adventurous British mountain climbers, Joe Simpson and Simon Yates, set out to conquer uncharted territory in 1985. What resulted was an amazing story of disaster and survival that led to an international bestselling book three years later and the award-winning film of the same title in 2003. Director Kevin MacDonald (*One Day in September* 1999, *The Last King of Scotland*, 2006) uniquely crafts the story of Simpson and Yates, the two climbers who had mastered various summits of the Alps and now wanted to tackle the yet-unclimbed West face of Siula Grande, a 21,000-foot peak in the Peruvian Andes. Tied together, using the Alpine style of climbing, which is a quick ascent in a single push while carrying all equipment without the use of fixed ropes or stocked camps, Simpson and Yates reached the summit in three days. On the way down, however, things went terribly wrong when Simpson fell and suffered a ghastly broken leg. Instead of leaving his partner for certain death, Yates decided to lower Simpson down the mountain 300 feet at a time. Aside from the excruciating pain, the descent was going well, but then Yates unknowingly lowered Simpson over a cliff, dangling in mid-air above a huge crevasse. Slowly sliding toward the cliff himself, not knowing his partner's status and his muscles failing, Yates was faced with an incredible decision—cut the rope or follow the climber's ethical code and remain tied to your partner.

The fact that Simpson found the courage to survive is only one facet of the now-famous story; his staunch and steadfast defense of Yates's decision is what has made it mountaineering legend. MacDonald wanted to make a film about the harrowing adventure, but knew that the story simply could not be translated as a narrative feature (two climbers who are not verbal or in contact with one another for the film's majority), so he decided on making a documentary, using a rare technique which he admittedly despises—dramatic recreations. MacDonald cast actors to play Simpson and Yates in recreations (Brendan Mackey and Nicholas Aaron), but remained true to the documentary form by using cut-away interviews with the actual climbers throughout. Indeed, *Touching the Void* is the rare documentary film that has a narrative feel and is able to keep viewers gripped to the unfolding drama rather than allowing cinéma vérité to capture real life events or historical storytelling to sink in.

As if the amazing story of tragedy and survival is not satisfying enough for nonfiction enthusiasts, the behind-the-scenes story of the film's production in 2002 and the tribulations of its characters make for great viewing as well. The DVD features three must-see mini-documentaries: *The Making of...*, *What Happened Next*, and *Return to Siula Grande*. Accounting for theatrical releases in Great Britain and the United States and DVD sales, *Touching the Void* is one of the most profitable sports-related documentaries of all time. In fact, few nonfiction sports films have earned the sort of critical acclaim that MacDonald's has. Despite this, the film did draw some criticism due to its usage of dramatic recreations and its classification as a true documentary. Often misclassified as a "pseudo-documentary," the authenticity of the happenings on Siula Grande in 1985 have never been in question, but rather the notion that entire event was recreated was clearly concerning for some documentary purists. Although aspects of expository and reflexive mode documentary filmmaking are present, film scholar Bill Nichols would likely classify MacDonald's unique technique as participatory mode, in which the interaction between filmmaker and subject are emphasized through interviews (34).

Awards: 2004 BAFTA Awards: Outstanding British Film; 2004 British Independent Film Awards: Best Documentary, Best Technical Achievement (Mike Eley), Best Director (MacDonald, nominated); 2004 Evening Standard British Film Awards: Best Film; 2004 Seattle Film Critics Awards: Best Documentary; 2005 International Cinephile Society Awards: Best Documentary; 2004 Boston Society of Film Critics Awards: Best Documentary (2nd place); 2004 Golden Trailer Awards: Best Documentary (nominated); 2005 Gold Derby Awards: Documentary Feature (nominated); 2005 Online Film and Television Association: Best Documentary Picture (nominated); 2005 Online Film Critics Society Awards: Best Documentary (nominated); 2005 Satellite Awards: Best Motion Picture, Documentary (nominated).

T-Rex, 2015

Director: Zackary Canepari, Drea Cooper; Running Time: 91 minutes; U.S.

T-Rex is the nickname for Claressa Shields, the American boxer who won gold in both the 2012 and 2016 Summer Olympics in the middleweight division. She became the first American boxer, regardless of gender, to capture gold in consecutive Olympics. In their 2015 film *T-Rex*, filmmakers Zackary Canepari and Drea Cooper follow Shields as she competes in the 2012 games, which was the inaugural Olympiad for the sport of women's boxing. Although women's boxing has seen surges in popularity in the United States in the 1990s, and elsewhere in more recent years, the aspect that the sport was new to the Olympics creates a unique opportunity for examination through nonfiction film. The examinations of race, class, and gender in a nontraditional sport are present in *T-Rex*, but the film works more deliberately as a biographical story of the Olympic champion from Flint, Michigan. The gritty, economically-depressed city of Flint is a perfectly fitting backdrop for the story of a young fighter overcoming great odds and accomplishing the highest goals by pure determination and hard work. Without too much detail in the film, viewers get a clear picture that Shields's home life has not been the best environment. That, however, may not be atypical for kids from Flint, a city with extraordinarily high rates of crime and poverty.

As the film begins, Shields has just turned 17, is virtually unknown, and is boxing in her first international tournament. This is where viewers are introduced to Jason Crutchfield, her coach and trainer. He admits that he wasn't in favor of women's boxing when Shields first started showing up at his gym, but her work ethic and talent soon changed his mind. Shields moves in with Crutchfield and his family, but still has her own family close by. Her traditional family seems to be depending on her fame and possible riches from boxing way more than should be the case with any 17-year-old. For an amateur boxer, those riches will only come by either turning professional or getting endorsement deals, which are very common for gold medal-winning athletes. The examinations of race, class, and gender in the film come specifically from the lack of endorsement deals that other athletes seem to get immediately. With one public relations consultant even suggesting that she try to soften her image by discontinuing the practice of explaining her love of boxing as "I like to beat people up," one has to wonder if the lack of endorsement opportunity has to do more with the fact that Shields does not fit the typical advertising mold. Journalist Sue Jaye Johnson, who also produced the film, suggests that because boxing was the last male-only Olympic sport, women in the ring is a stretch for many advertisers and promoters. Following a successful festival run in 2015, the film was broadcast as part of the Independent Lens series on PBS just prior to the 2016 Summer Olympics.

Awards: 2015 San Francisco International Film Festival: Best Documentary Feature Audience Award, Bay Area Documentary Feature Jury

Award, Documentary Feature Golden Gate Award (nominated); 2015 Sidewalk Film Festival: Best Documentary; 2015 Traverse City Film Festival: Roger Ebert Prize; 2015 Woods Hole Film Festival: Best Documentary Feature Jury Award.

The Trials of Muhammad Ali, 2013
Director: Bill Siegel; Running Time: 86 minutes; U.S.

In the 2002 Oscar-nominated documentary film *The Weather Underground*, directors Sam Green and Bill Siegel examine the anti–Vietnam war movement through the actions of the radical left-wing organization of the same name. Naturally, it is the controversial anti-war stance of Muhammad Ali during the same time, and the ensuing legal battle relating to that stance, that occupies the lion's share of Siegel's 2013 film *The Trials of Muhammad Ali*. Retrospectively, the common belief is that Ali was such a divisive figure because he so openly spoke against the war and that he had affiliated himself with the highly-controversial Nation of Islam, but in reality those aspects only added to the list for much of America, which viewed the champ as far too brash and arrogant. Considering that successful American politicos at the highest level operate with the exact same sort of bravado, self-promotion, and braggadocio nowadays, Ali's trash-talking ways during the 1960s and 70s should probably be re-examined and maybe understood differently. Siegel concentrates on the backlash that Ali faced from his conversion to Islam and refusal to serve in the military during the Vietnam War, but the way that those aspects shaped his persona and boxing career are the primary examinations. Many other films have covered the same ground, but Siegel does it in a way that better illuminates the cost that came with Ali's convictions. Although Ali clearly wasn't bothered by the court of public opinion price that he had to pay, or even the monetary loss from not being allowed to fight or travel outside the U.S., the real cost of his convictions may be best understood when one considers that his exile from boxing lasted nearly four years, 1967–1970, well before he turned 30 years old.

The film begins with Ali receiving the Presidential Medal of Freedom from President George W. Bush in 2005 with commentary from the controversial current leader of the Nation of Islam Louis Farrakhan, indicating both that his legacy has indeed been re-evaluated by many Americans and also the reason why he was the target of such animosity at one time. While it is difficult to gauge today, Ali's conversion to Islam was extremely provocative at the time. The group's call for black separatism was in complete contrast to the calls for integration by leaders of the Civil Rights Movement, whom many white Americans supported. At the same time, his career was affected even more greatly when he was stripped of his title, denied a boxing license, and faced up to five years in prison because he refused to be drafted into the military. With Ali's death in 2016, it was clear to all generations that he had become a cultural icon that transcended sports, but Siegel shows that he wasn't always thought of that way. In his 2005 book "What's My Name, Fool?" (the title refers to Ali's in-ring taunt to Ernie Terrell, who insisted on using his former name), author Dave Zirin explains that Ali has now been absorbed by the establishment as a legend, but the ragged truth is that "no athlete has been more reviled by the mainstream press and more persecuted by the U.S. government than Muhammad Ali" (53). While William Klein's 1974 film *Muhammad Ali: The Greatest* should be considered the definitive primary source film on Ali because it documents the champ in the moment, Siegel's 2013 film is quite necessary viewing as well because it takes a much more thorough look at the socio-political ramifications of Ali's greatness. In 2014, the film was aired on the PBS documentary series Independent Lens and released in DVD format. It can also be viewed in streaming format.

Awards: 2013 International Documentary Association: Video Source Award; 2014 FOCAL International Awards: Best Use of Sports Footage; 2015 News and Documentary Emmy Awards: Outstanding Historical Programming, Long Form, Best Documentary (nominated), Outstanding Individual Achievement in a Craft: Cinematography (Aaron Wickenden, nominated); 2014 Black Reel Awards: Outstanding Documentary (nominated); 2014 Image Awards: Outstanding Independent Motion Picture (nominated); 2014 Krakow Film Festival: Best Feature Length Documentary Silver Horn Award (nominated); 2015 Seattle International Film Festival: Documentary Award (nominated).

The 25,000-Mile Love Story, 2013
Director: John Davies; Running Time: 86 minutes; U.S.

In miles, the circumference of earth is 24,901 miles. What would provoke someone to attempt to run that distance, how long it would take, and what sort of complications they would encounter are questions that now have an answer thanks to the 2013 documentary film *The 25,000 Mile Love Story* and the preceding 2012 book of the same title. Of course, the man who set out to accomplish this in 2000 is no ordinary man. His name is Serge Roetheli and he may the greatest endurance athlete ever.

Born in 1955, Roetheli was a six-time national boxing champion in his native Switzerland, but later in life took up running, climbing, biking, and rowing. As a mountain climber, he has summited the highest peaks on four continents; he has biked across North America; in 2011 he tandem-rowed across the Atlantic Ocean in a canoe; and in his 1995 "American Challenge" he ran over 14,000 miles of the Pan American Highway, from the tip of Argentina to Fairbanks, Alaska. Likewise, the woman who joins Roetheli on his World Tour via motorcycle and serves as his lone support crew, his wife Nicole, is no ordinary woman either. For nearly three years in the mid–1990s she was by his side when he conquered the Pan American Highway and came to be known as the "Swiss Forrest Gump."

In what might be considered the most expansive travelogue ever, filmmaker John Davies pieces together an 86-minute film out of more than 90 hours of footage shot by the Roetheli's from 2000 to 2005 during their epic run. Davies makes good use of graphics and map sequences explaining the route and some of the deviations that were required due to various issues. One somewhat clumsy aspect with the low-budget filmmaking, however, is that Nicole's voice has been dubbed over to English, but the technical aspects of this film take an obvious backseat to the unfolding drama and adventure anyway. Narrated by Oscar-winning screenwriter John Ridley (*12 Years a Slave*), the film immediately dives into answering the question as to what their motivations were—athletic achievement, charitable mission, and love of adventure. In the 2012 book that was the basis for the film, Roetheli describes their decision to sell their home, leave behind their two children, and embark on their journey as being one with the goal of not only adventure and freedom, but also of "seeing and exposing the tender aspects of earth." In particular, Roetheli wanted to help children in need in developing nations and knew that his tour could do that by raising money. By traversing the world, according to Roetheli, they could tell the story of the people they met and how they could best be helped (16).

Just as one may expect, the journey is full of roadblocks, injuries, unpredictable weather, and downright scary situations. Departing Europe into Western Africa, the first major challenge occurs when they are forced to change their route due to the Sierra Leone Civil War. Just over a year into their run, Nicole contracts cerebral malaria and needs to be hospitalized and the 9/11 terrorist attack in the United States forces their route to be altered throughout certain areas of the Middle East. After two years, the worst possible scenario occurs when their sponsor, Terre des Hommes, an international children's charity, withdraws their support, but Serge is able to gain a new sponsor in year three as the couple heads to Australia and New Zealand. Through South America and into Miami, they then face the deadly 2004 hurricane season, but complete North America by the end of 2004 and head back to Europe via Portugal. After six continents, 35 countries, 64 pairs of shoes for Serge, 101 tubes of lipstick for Nicole, and 1,200 nights spent in a pup tent, the Roetheli's raised $400,000 for children's centers across the world. The film ends with an odd twist, however, as it divulges that the love story of Serge and Nicole ended not long after their tour and the couple divorced. The love of running, adventure, and altruism, on the other hand, no doubt endured. Following a successful film festival run in 2013 and 2014, the film was released in streaming and DVD format.

Awards: 2013 Atlanta International Documentary Film Festival: Audience Choice Award; 2013 Downtown Film Festival Los Angeles: Feature Audience Favorite Award; 2013 Moondance International Film Festival: Best Feature Documentary; The People's Film Festival of New York 2013: Best Humanitarian Documentary; 2013 Red Rock Film Festival: Best Documentary Audience Choice Award; 2013 Rome International Film Festival (Georgia): Best Feature Documentary; 2014 All Sports LA Film Festival: Best Documentary; 2014 CineTrofa—International Festival of Cinema and Literature: Best Feature Documentary; 2014 Costa Rica International Film Festival: Best Documentary Feature; 2014 International Family Film Festival: Best Feature Documentary; 2014 Rincon International Film Festival: Certificate of Excellence; 2014 Temecula Valley International Film Festival: Best Documentary; 2013 Gold Panda Awards Sichuan TV Festival: Best Long Form Documentary (nominated); 2013 Peace and Sport Organization: Special Jury Award (nominated); 2014 Idyllwild International Festival of Cinema: Best Documentary (nominated), Best Director, Documentary (nominated).

The Two Escobars, 2010

Director: Jeff, Michael Zimbalist; Running Time: 104 minutes; U.S./Colombia.

Brothers Jeff (*Favela Rising*, 2005) and Michael Zimbalist set out to make a film about Andrés Escobar, the talented center back for the Colombia national football team who was murdered after committing the on-field mistake of scoring an "own goal" in the team's second match of the 1994 World Cup. Their 2010 film, *The Two Escobars*, turns out to be a far deeper examination into the circumstances of his murder and the type of society that developed in Colombia during the 1990s, when politics, crime, and sport all came crashing together. The title refers to Andrés, the star soccer player who was captain of the 1994 team and known as "the gentleman of football," and Pablo Escobar, the powerful narcotics kingpin who headed the Medellín Cartel of Colombia and was once one of the wealthiest and most wanted criminals in the world. With one churchgoing and peaceful and the other a murderous criminal, the two unrelated men were very different individuals, but they will forever be linked together by more than their shared name—they were both instrumental in Colombia becoming one of the best teams in the world in the 1990s. Likewise, the two men represent both the rise and fall of what came to be known as "narco-soccer." Visiting a common theme of sports documentaries, the relationship of sports to community, the Zimbalist brothers use a wealth of archival footage and interview segments with former players, law enforcement officials, politicians, and family members of both Escobars to explain the concept of narco-soccer and how Colombia's favorite sport became so intertwined with drug trafficking.

In short, purchasing professional soccer teams served as a way for Pablo Escobar and other drug lords to launder and legalize their drug money by falsifying ticket sales and player salaries. As a notorious Medellín Cartel hitman explains in the film, "soccer became a tug of war among the drug lords," and it wasn't exactly a secret to the players or the fans what was going on. In the case of Pablo, the players were paid and treated well, and for many of them who had grown up in the slums, they had Pablo to thank for the entire careers as he had been financially supporting them since their youth. When players with long connections to Pablo began guiding the Colombian national team up the international rankings ahead of the 1994 World Cup, a blind eye was turned to its connections with drug money because they were altering the nation's image of crime and narcoterrorism that was taking place in the drug war at the same time. The Zimbalists bring home the irony that Pablo, the lethal drug lord responsible for a wave of terrorism in order to remain atop the illicit drug trade, was being hunted down by the government, but he had played a huge part in building the very team that was now restoring the nation's image through soccer. According to Francisco Maturana, Colombia's manager in 1993 and 1994 when the team reached a top five world ranking, the drug money brought the best players in and kept them from leaving.

Setting off a new era of lawlessness in Colombia as rival drug lords and sports gamblers now had the ability to reach inside the sport, the manhunt for Pablo Escobar ended with his death seven months before the 1994 World Cup began in the United States. Despite being one of the Cup favorites, Colombia lost its opening match to Romania as the players had their minds on the violence back home spiraling out of control as the new drug lords sought power. This led to death threats from gamblers who had lost money and even a threat from one club owner in Colombia if his player was not inserted for the next game. That next game was against the United States, whom Colombia had beaten 11 times in a row in friendly matches prior to the '94 Cup. Considering the pressure resulting from threats of violence, a loss to the U.S. was not too surprising, but when Andrés Escobar, a player who had recently signed with Italian powerhouse club AC Milan to escape his troubled homeland, committed the infamous own-goal, it was clear that Colombia was off its game. The filmmakers and some of the interview subjects give rise to the notion that Andrés Escobar's murder a month later likely would not have taken place if Pablo had still been in charge of the Colombian underworld. Regardless of how true that notion is, both the rise and fall of narco-soccer in Colombia would be impossible to explore without looking at both men. Following a festival run including Cannes and Tribeca, the film was aired as part of ESPN's award-winning *30 for 30* film series. It is available in DVD and streaming format.

Awards: 2011 Tacoma Film Festival: Best Documentary Film; 2011 New York Festivals International TV & Film Awards: Grand Trophy—History and Society (ESPN); 2010 Sao Paulo International Film Festival: Best Documentary International Jury Award (nominated); 2010 Tribeca Film Festival: Best Documentary Feature Jury Award (nominated); 2010 Writers Guild of America: Best Documentary Screenplay (nominated); 2010 Zurich Film Festival: Best International Documentary Film (nominated); 2011 Sports Emmy Awards: Outstanding Sports Documentary (nominated).

Undefeated, 2011

Director: Daniel Lindsay, T.J. Martin; Running Time: 113 minutes; U.S.

Starting right guard: shot, no longer in school; starting linebacker: shot, no longer in school; two players fighting while the coach speaks; starting center: arrested. For most coaches that would be a "career's worth of crap to deal with," but for one Memphis high school football coach it was just two weeks as he tries to prepare the Manassas Tigers for the upcoming 2009 football season. This is how the Academy Award-winning film *Undefeated* begins, with the coach addressing his team and explaining that he knew what he was signing up for, but he stays because he loves the program. It would be easy to see that speech as self-aggrandizing if it were coming from anyone other than this particular coach, but Bill Courtney drips with authenticity and sincerity. As he continues his lecture, he wears a Classic American Hardwoods T-shirt, which happens to match the school's colors exactly and happens to be Courtney's actual paying job, a small-business owner of a lumber company. The head coaching gig he does strictly as a volunteer. In the few years that he has been at the helm of the Manassas program, the team has improved only slightly from being the pushover opponent that other teams schedule for their homecoming game. The 2009 season, however, suddenly looks promising.

Directors Daniel Lindsay and T.J. Martin made a film about high school football, about Memphis, and about unity, but mostly it is about the charismatic man who teaches young people to be better. Lindsay and Martin craft a truly special film which could have easily diverted into a sociological examination of sports as an escape from inner-city realities, but instead they simply rely on cinéma vérité to allow the emotion to pour out. Viewers are introduced primarily to three team leaders as they interact with their unique force-of-nature coach. Chavis, a linebacker, has been

Winner of the Best Documentary Feature Academy Award, *Undefeated* (2011) follows the 2009 Manassas Tigers football team from Memphis, Tennessee.

in trouble due to anger issues and seems to need coach Courtney's guidance. O.C., an offensive lineman, has a certain collegiate football career ahead if he can qualify academically. Another offensive lineman, Montrail, is gifted academically, but suffers a knee injury that will derail any hopes of an athletic scholarship. One of the genuinely emotional moments of the film is when Montrail reacts to learning that a wealthy, unnamed friend of one of the coaches has offered to pay his college tuition to any school that he is accepted to academically. After premiering at the 2011 South by Southwest Film Festival, the film was picked up for distribution by The Weinstein Company, which has also suggested that a narrative feature film adaptation is possible. *Undefeated* is available in streaming and DVD format.

Awards: 2011 Chicago International Film Festival: Best Documentary Feature; 2012 Academy Awards: Best Documentary Feature; 2013 Christopher Awards: Feature Film; 2011 Houston Film Critics Society Awards: Best Documentary Feature (nominated); 2011 Philadelphia Film Festival: Audience Award (honorable mention); Southeastern Film Critics Association Awards: Wyatt Award (2nd place); 2011 South by Southwest Film Festival: Audience Award (nominated); 2012 Black Reel Awards: Best Documentary (nominated).

Up for Grabs, 2004

Director: Michael Wranovics; Running Time: 88 minutes; U.S.

In the 1998 Major League Baseball season, the single-season home run record was broken when St. Louis Cardinals slugger Mark McGwire hit 70, shattering the old mark of 61 hit by Roger Maris in 1961. Those respective home run balls, McGwire's 70th and Maris's 61st, are not the subjects of the witty and satirical 2004 documentary *Up for Grabs*, but they have lots to do with it. When the fan in Yankee Stadium who caught the 1961 record-breaker attempted to give the ball to the man who hit it, Maris instead suggested that he sell it for profit. By 1998, selling such an important souvenir from the ballpark was no longer an afterthought, and the price for such a ball had gone from $5,000 in 1961 to nearly $3 million in 1998. Obviously, in 2001, when San Francisco Giants slugger Barry Bonds was in the process of breaking McGwire's record, fans knew that those souvenirs could make them rich as well, with the final one being most valuable.

The story of what happened to that ball, Bonds's 73rd home run of

2001, is exactly what first-time director Michael Wranovics sets out to explore in his film. Bonds smacked number 73 on October 7, the final day of the regular season, in San Francisco's Pac Bell Park. The ball landed in the arcade section just past the right field bleachers, but who caught the ball, who ended up with it during the ensuing scrum of fans fighting for it, and who had a rightful claim to it is the question at hand. It was a question and mystery that, naturally, had to be answered in a court of law. The funny and slightly disturbing story plays out with a number of eyewitnesses more than willing to offer their account of what happened, a Zapruder-like film of the event, the possibility of a second baseball, and an all-out media circus. Although Wranovics treats both fairly, the plaintiff comes off looking attention-starved and the defendant comes off looking greedy, and considering that the event took place less than a month after the devastating 9/11 terrorist attack, sports fandom in general, and the big-business aspect of American sports in particular, looks bad as well. The DVD was released in 2007.

Awards: 2004 Los Angeles IFP/West Film Festival: Best Documentary; 2004 Phoenix Film Festival: Best Documentary; 2005 Gen Art Film Festival: Best Documentary.

Valley Uprising, 2014

Director: Peter Mortimer, Nick Rosen; Running Time: 86 minutes; U.S.

The evolution of rock climbing in California's Yosemite National Park is traced in this 2014 film by Peter Mortimer and Nick Rosen. Because of the many different climbers that it profiles, and the 60-year time frame in which they climbed, the subject matter is extremely broad. Nevertheless, the filmmakers cope with this fact by not spending too much time on any one climber and instead break down the climbing activity to three specific eras: the pioneers, who first began climbing the huge granite walls of Yosemite in the late 1950s, the "Stonemaster" era, whose members pushed both the rock climbing envelope and counterculture vibe to a new level in the 1970s and 80s, and finally the modern era (or "Stone Monkeys"), whose membership consists of the most noteworthy climbers today. The examination of the pioneering era primarily focuses on the not-so-friendly rivalry of Royal Robbins and Warren Harding, who had competing ideals of safety and rules versus danger and adventure. The group known as the Stonemasters moved from aid and traditional climbing to free and free solo climbing. Notable in this group included Jim Bridwell, the unofficial leader, John Long, who became a best-selling author, Lynn Hill, who became one of the best known sport climbers in the world, and John Bachar, who was widely regarded as the greatest free solo climber in history until his death from a fall in 2009. The primary modern era climbers profiled are Dean Potter, who became legendary for his risks and was killed while wingsuit flying in Yosemite only eight months after the film was released, and Alex Honnold, who is widely regarded as the world's top climber today despite not exactly fitting the traditional "dirtbag climber" mold.

The film offers a prolific soundtrack, but might go unnoticed because, like the climbers themselves, it largely rejects anything mainstream. Much in the same way that the soundtrack features some music probably known only to certain types of adventurers, the climbers seem to belong to a members-only club as well. Perhaps this comes more from the fact that death deifiers of this type are so rare rather than from counterculture elitism. Regardless, with the risks that some climbers have been taking since the 1980s, it obviously requires a certain type of personality. While this sort of factionalism amongst the self-proclaimed "dirtbag climbers" is perfectly understandable due to the fact that so very few people actually partake in the activity, it sharply narrows a film's audience and appeal. Keeping in mind that non-climbers are seemingly not the audience for *Valley Uprising*, it is still an interesting examination if for no other reason than seeing people take unthinkable chances with their lives, and that can be very tough to watch at times. The examinations that really exist in *Valley Uprising* are the development of ideas and the development of rock-climbing as more than just a countercultural pastime. Although the notion of actual climbing competitions (sport climbing) and corporate sponsorship flies in the face of mainstream rejectionist ideals, it did eventually get to that point. Mortimer and Rosen cover both a wide swath of history and a modern view of rock climbing in a frantic pace, but their film does provide those already interested in climbing with a nice reference and may even spark interest in future climbers. In addition to streaming, the film was released in DVD format in 2014.

Awards: 2014 Autrans Mountain Film Festival: Special Mention of the Jury; 2014 Banff Mountain Film Competition: Grand Prize; 2014 Bilbao International Festival of Documentary and Short Films: Audience Award for Best Film, Documentary Grand Prix; 2014 San Sebastian International Film Festival: Savage Cinema Prize; 2014 Wild & Scenic Film Festival: Most Inspiring Adventure Film; 2015 Sheffield Adventure Film Festival: Best Film Bronze Award; 2016 News and Documentary Emmy Awards:

Outstanding Graphic Design and Art Direction (Barry Thompson), Outstanding Individual Achievement in a Craft (Thompson).

Visions of Eight, 1973

Directors: Milos Forman, Kon Ichikawa, Claude Lelouch, Yuri Ozerov, Arthur Penn, Michael Pfleghar, John Schlesinger, Mai Zetterling; Running Time: 110 minutes; U.S.

The most unique among the official Olympic films might be *Visions of Eight*, covering the 1972 Summer Games in Munich. American producer David L. Wolper sought out eight internationally renowned directors to take part, with each one focusing on a specific aspect or event of the games. In order of their specific segments in the film, the eight different visions in this poetic mode documentary include Russian Yuri Ozerov, whose segment "The Beginning" documents various aspects of the Olympics prior to actual competition, Swedish actress and director Mai Zetterling, whose segment "The Strongest" offers a stylized and symbolic view of the weightlifting events, American Arthur Penn (*Bonnie and Clyde*, 1967), whose segment "The Highest" focuses on pole vaulting, and German Michael Pfleghar, whose segment "The Women" highlights various women's events. Japanese director Kon Ichikawa, whose 1965 film *Tokyo Olympiad* is considered the best of the genre, documents the 100 meter event at the film's midway point with the short segment titled "The Fastest." From there, Czech director Miloš Forman (*Amadeus*, 1984) offers his view of the decathlon event with the segment of the same title and French director Claude Lelouch (*A Man and a Woman*, 1966) uniquely focuses on the agony of defeat rather than any one specific event in his segment "The Losers." Finally, Oscar-winning English director John Schlesinger (*Midnight Cowboy*, 1969) documents the culminating marathon in the segment "The Longest."

Because of the film's anthology approach of using eight different filmmakers covering eight different aspects, much of the historical interest in the games in terms of the actual athletes is sacrificed in favor of art, but the film still ranks as a classic when considering it in such a way. When examining how this film compares to the other Olympic documentaries, it may be important to set aside the poetic mode versions such as *Visions*, *Tokyo Olympiad*, and *Olympia* (1938) specifically as artistic ventures into the aesthetics of sport while allowing the more straightforward versions such as *The Grand Olympics* (1961) and *The Olympics in Mexico* (1969) to cater more to typical sports fans. Film scholar David Scott Diffrient seems to suggest that the film has crossover appeal into the study of narrative films, arguing that it can be situated into the "narratological context" of episode films as well, which had become popular in European and Asian cinema during the 1960s. As virtually all of the official Olympic documentaries do, *Visions* attempts to steer clear of any political or social aspects of the respective Olympics, with the 1972 Munich massacre being the obvious aspect in the case of these games. Only Schlesinger's segment "The Longest" alluded to the terrorist attack in which 11 Israeli athletes and a German police officer were taken hostage and eventually murdered. The film, with the beautifully-composed score by Henry Mancini, was finally released in DVD format in 2011 by Olive Films. Online streaming is also available for the film, but lacks the English soundtrack and subtitles.

Awards: 1974 Golden Globe Awards: Best Documentary Film.

Weekend of a Champion, 1972

Director: Frank Simon, Roman Polanski; Running Time: 93 minutes; U.K./Monaco.

Also known as *Afternoon of a Champion* when it screened at European film festivals in 1972, *Weekend of a Champion* is a documentary film following British Formula One driver Jackie Stewart during the happenings at the 1971 Monaco Grand Prix in Monte Carlo. The film's credited director is Frank Simon, but the real force behind the project is its producer and co-director, Academy Award-winning director Roman Polanski (*Chinatown*, 1974, *The Pianist*, 2002). Polanski, several years before he became a worldwide controversial figure due to an American statutory rape conviction, took the opportunity of his friendship and solid rapport with the Scottish-born Stewart to follow the champion, converse with him away from the course, and document the spectacle of the event over a continuous four-day period. Stewart, the 1969 Formula One champion and runner-up the previous season, was already considered one of the best drivers in the world, but not quite the legend that he would become over the two ensuing years. In that regard, the film offers a unique and very personal glimpse into a sport's top athlete during the pinnacle of his career as he goes through the familiar motions of his craft. Similarly, as Polanski is heavily involved in a participatory mode fashion, the film also offers a glimpse into a filmmaker's vision and craft during what might be considered the pinnacle of his respective career.

Beginning with scenes of the bustling resort destination preparing for the famous race that makes up one leg of the Triple Crown of Motorsport, the film quickly shifts into technical mode as Stewart taxis Polanski through the course in what appears to be a golf cart, explaining the intricate details and how to handle each turn. Following a brief view of rain-soaked practice sessions, the film cuts to a swanky champagne brunch with adoring fans who have won a contest for the right to rub elbows with Stewart. Winning pole position on Friday, Stewart next has an in-depth and jovial conversation with Polanski about racing safety and his wife speaks for the first time about her concerns and the many deaths that have occurred. As the start of the race approaches, Polanski takes some artistic liberties to mix in the sound of a heartbeat while Stewart walks toward the course and speaks in voice-over about his safety concerns. *Weekend of a Champion* had a theatrical release in Europe in 1972, but had been out of circulation since that time until Polanski decided to restore the film and add an interesting epilogue segment to the film in 2013. The epilogue, which features an artistic cut from the original film's conclusion to Stewart and Polanski viewing the original in present day, is primarily a continuation of their conversation from 40 years ago about driver safety and life in general. While the film will have a clear appeal to F1 fans, its greatest appeal may be to those interested in filmmaking or archival time capsules of the early 1970s. The restored and extended version is available in DVD and streaming format.

Awards: 1972 Berlin International Film Festival: Documentary Special Recognition, Golden Berlin Bear Award (nominated); 2013 Cannes Film Festival: Film Presented.

When We Were Kings, 1996

Director: Leon Gast; Running Time: 86 minutes; U.S.

The story of the 1974 championship boxing match between George Foreman and Muhammad Ali was forever immortalized by filmmaker Leon Gast in his 1996 Academy Award-winning feature *When We Were Kings*. The film documents the hoopla surrounding the fight known as "The Rumble in the Jungle," cementing the legacy of Ali as he is seen at his charismatic best, winning over an entire African nation. The film also revisits an aloof, long-since-forgotten George Foreman—years before his transformation into an affable and beloved public figure. At the same time that Ali was serving a three-year ban from boxing for his refusal to be drafted during the Vietnam Conflict, George Foreman was winning the gold medal at the 1968 Olympics and soon ripping through the heavyweight ranks. In Ali's return to the ring and quest to regain his title, he suffered two major losses: to Joe Frazier in 1971 and to Ken Norton in 1973. Although he won rematches against both fighters within a year, it was clear that Ali was not the same boxer who had first won the title in 1964. Foreman, by 1974, had become the most dominant boxer in the world, compiling a 40–0 record with brutal knockouts of Frazier in 1973, to win the title, and Norton a year later. Despite his brash confidence, few experts thought the now 32-year-old Ali could withstand the power of Foreman.

While it is now considered to be one of the greatest sports films of all time, and proved to be a commercial success, its release came more than 20 years after the event, allowing time for a drastic change in the public opinion of both legendary fighters. The very same dogma that had made Ali such a controversial figure in 1974 had turned him into a heroic icon by 1996. Foreman, on the other hand, was seen as menacing and standoffish in 1974, but had become a truly beloved American icon himself by 1996. The cultural and political impact of holding the fight in Zaire, under the dictatorship of Mobutu Sese Seko, is only touched on briefly and clearly does not have the same importance as it would have had with a release in the tumultuous 1970s. Now known as The Democratic Republic of the Congo, Zaire had been economically and politically unstable since gaining its independence from Belgium in 1960, and had essentially become a police state under Seko. Despite the scarce resources of his nation, but seeking an international spotlight, Seko offered to pay the $10 million price required by promoter Don King to host the bout. In the

Muhammad Ali enjoyed strong support from native Zairians in *When We Were Kings* (1996).

opening scenes, Gast contrasts archival footage of Belgian Congo and Zairian officers brutalizing citizens with similar scenes from the American Civil Rights Movement of the same time. Interspersed among the footage are clips of the younger, controversial Muhammad Ali and just enough of a televised news clip to introduce General Mobutu, perhaps symbolizing another contrasting element of the film.

The story behind the motion picture and its 20-years-in-the-making production is about as unique as it comes with films of such magnitude. Gast traveled to Zaire in 1974 to film the boxers, but primarily to film a soul music festival organized in conjunction with the championship fight. Some footage of the Zaire '74 Music Festival, featuring acts like James Brown, B.B. King, The Spinners, and popular African musicians, can be seen in *When We Were Kings,* but many more hours were edited into another film, *Soul Power,* which was released in 2008. Using his unprecedented access to Ali and Foreman, and seeing hordes of Africans following the chant "Ali, bomeya" ("Ali, kill him"), while not embracing the quiet and somber Foreman, Gast changed his focus to the unfolding drama of the fight itself. Legal issues and funding problems held up the film's release for two decades, during which time the significance of the fight and the cultural importance of Ali have taken on new meanings. Two of America's foremost writers at the time of the fight, Norman Mailer and George Plimpton, are interviewed years later to provide keen retrospective insight to the event. Their insight becomes even more valuable when the footage from 1974 shows the much younger-looking writers interacting with the boxers and taking in the action. Also with the passage of time, the documentation of promoter Don King in action, with this being his first time on the big stage, takes on a different meaning than it would have had in 1974.

Awards: 1996 Los Angeles Film Critics Association Awards: Best Documentary/Nonfiction Film; 1996 New York Film Critics Circle Awards: Best Nonfiction Film; 1996 Sundance Film Festival: Special Recognition, Documentary Grand Jury Prize (nominated); 1997 Academy Awards: Best Documentary Feature; 1997 Broadcast Film Critics Association Awards: Best Documentary; 1997 Independent Spirit Awards: Truer Than Fiction Award; 1997 National Society of Film Critics Awards: Best Documentary; 1997 Directors Guild of America: Outstanding Directorial Achievement in Documentary (Gast, nominated); 1998 Image Awards: Outstanding News, Talk, or Information Special (nominated).

Word Wars, 2004
Director: Eric Chaikin, Julian Petrillo; Running Time: 80 minutes; U.S.

"The game you are about to see is not your grandmother's game of Scrabble," so begins *Word Wars*, the 2004 award-winning film by directors Eric Chaikin and Julian Petrillo. The filmmakers follow four competitors as they prepare for the 2002 U.S. National Scrabble Championships in San Diego, in which nearly 700 players were contending for the $25,000 first prize. One in a long line of documentary films made in the 2000s about gaming competitions ranging from classic arcade and modern video games to brain games such as spelling bees and board games such as Scrabble, *Word Wars* stands out not only because of the more formalized nature of the competition, but also because the sustained popularity of Scrabble might rank only behind chess and checkers among board games. Similar to *The King of Kong: A Fistful of Quarters*, Seth Gordon's fantastic 2007 documentary about classic arcade gaming competitors, Chaikin and Petrillo focus in on truly unique characters who could easily be exploited for the sake of entertainment, but instead simply seem to be either naturally gifted with the English language or obsessed with the game of Scrabble.

Invented in the 1930s, Scrabble became a craze in the 1950s, and by the 1970s game rooms in New York City were featuring all night Scrabble marathons. Some history of how these big-money Scrabble tournaments developed is provided, but is really not needed because of the focus on the players, their personalities, and their interaction with one another. The four subjects include Joe Edley, the reigning champion and top-ranked player, Matt Graham, a stand-up comedian who enjoys gambling on Scrabble games, Marlon Hill, a self-described "pre–Mecca Malcolm," and Joel Sherman, who plays Scrabble tournaments for a living and seems a bit neurotic about some medical issues. With the possible exception of Edley, perhaps because he appears to be the only one with a family, the players seem to fit together in a community of both friends and rivals. With this being the first feature film for either director, Chaikin and Petrillo skillfully explore the overarching theme of community and provide access to a unique world of specialized competition. Following a limited theatrical release and festival run in 2004, the film was released in DVD format the following year.

Awards: 2004 Full Frame Documentary Film Festival: Audience Award; 2004 Sedona International Film Festival: Best Documentary; 2004 International Documentary Association: Feature Documentaries IDA Award (nominated); 2004 Sundance Film Festival: Documentary Grand Jury Prize (nominated).

Bibliography

Aitken, Ian. *Encyclopedia of the Documentary Film 3-Volume Set*. New York: Routledge, 2013.

Babington, Bruce. *The Sports Film: Games People Play*. New York: Columbia University Press, 2014.

Bernstein, Mark F. *Football: The Ivy League Origins of an American Obsession*. University Park: University of Pennsylvania Press, 2001.

Bledsoe, Gregory H. "Mixed Martial Arts." *Combat Sports Medicine*, edited by W. Angus Wallace, Randall R. Wroble, Nicola Maffulli, Ramin Kordi. London: Springer London, 2009, pp. 323–330.

Buckmaster, Luke. "Sherpa: Norbu Tenzing on the Everest 'Circus' and the Inevitability of Another Disaster." *The Guardian*, Guardian News and Media Limited, 29 Mar. 2016, https://www.theguardian.com/film/2016/mar/30/sherpa-norbu-tenzing-on-the-everest-circus-and-the-inevitability-of-another-disaster. Accessed 19 Aug. 2016.

Derby, Rick. Personal Interview. 6 February 2017.

Diffrient, David Scott. "An Olympic Omnibus: International Competition, Cooperation, and Politics in Visions of Eight." *Film & History: An Interdisciplinary Journal of Film and Television Studies* 35.2 (2005): 19–28.

Downing, Taylor. *Olympia*. Basingstoke: Palgrave Macmillan, 2012.

Frazier, Eric, and Michael Gordon. "Going the Extra Yard." *The Charlotte Observer* [Charlotte, North Carolina], 23 Nov. 2008. Local.

Fuchs, Jeremy. "Best of Film." *Sports Illustrated*. 5 Dec. 2016.

Jeffries, Stuart. "The Saturday Interview: Asif Kapadia." *The Guardian*, Guardian News and Media Limited, 8 July 2011, www.theguardian.com/theguardian/2011/jul/09/asif-kapadia interview-ayrton-senna. Accessed 5 Nov. 2016.

Johnson, Sue Jaye. "For Olympic Boxer Claressa Shields, Round 2 Brings New Expectations." *The Torch: NPR's Olympic Coverage*. National Public Radio. 27 July 2016. Web. 19 Oct. 2016.

Kilkenny, Katie. "A Conversation with 'Prescription Thugs' Director Chris Bell." *Pacific Standard*, Miller-McCune Center for Research, Media and Public Policy, 27 Jan. 2016, https://psmag.com/a-conversation-with-prescription-thugs-director-chris-bell-6b08725ad92f#. Accessed 25 Feb. 2016.

Mailer, Norman. "The Eleventh Presidential Paper—Death: Ten Thousand Words a Minute." *The Presidential Papers*. New York: G.P. Putnam's Sons, 1963, p. 244.

McDonald, Ian. "Situating the Sports Documentary." *Journal of Sport & Social Issues* 31.3 (2007): 208–225.

Mooney, Michael J. "The Man in the Middle of Bountygate." *GQ*, Condé Nast, 19

Sept. 2012. http://www.gq.com/story/nfl-bountygate-saints-sean-pamphilon. Accessed 25 July 2016.
Nichols, Bill. *Introduction to Documentary*. Bloomington: Indiana University Press, 2001.
Niemi, Robert. *History in the Media: Film and Television*. Santa Barbara: ABC-CLIO, 2006.
"No Wonder They're Called Mavericks." *Eugene Register-Guard* [Eugene, Oregon], 28 July 1973, p. 1B.
Polsky, Gabe. "Red Army Explores How the Cold War Played out on Ice." *All Things Considered*. National Public Radio. 22 Jan. 2015. Accessed 19 Aug. 2016.
Roetheli, Serge. *The 25,000 Mile Love Story: The Epic Story of the Couple Who Sacrificed Everything to Run the World*. New York: Dunham Books, 2012.
Sammond, Nicholas. *Steel Chair to the Head: The Pleasure and Pain of Professional Wrestling*. Durham: Duke University Press, 2005.
Streible, Dan. *Fight Pictures: A History of Boxing and Early Cinema*. Berkeley: University of California Press, 2008.
Thompson, Howard. "Screen: Great Athletes: 'The Grand Olympics' Recalls '60 Games." *The New York Times*, 22 April 1964.
United States Anti-Doping Agency. *U.S. Postal Service Pro Cycling Team Investigation*. 10 Oct. 2012. http://cyclinginvestigation.usada.org/. Accessed 4 Apr. 2016.
Vogan, Travis. *Keepers of the Flame: NFL Films and the Rise of Sports Media*. Urbana: University of Illinois Press, 2014.
Zirin, Dave. *What's My Name, Fool? Sports and Resistance in the United States*. Chicago: Haymarket, 2005.

Index

Aaron, Hank 69–70
Aaron, Nicholas 168
AAU basketball 101
ABC 4, 88, 124, 134
Abidin, Dino 62
Aboriginal Peoples Television Network 138
AC Milan 176
Academy Award, Best Documentary Feature 4, 11, 20, 24, 28, 30, 37, 39, 41, 58–59, 66–67, 81, 90, 93, 96, 99, 103–104, 112–113, 113–114, 114–115, 156, 171, 177, 183–185
Academy of Motion Picture Arts and Sciences 8
Academy of Motion Picture Arts and Sciences Film Archive 96
Adams, Jay 34–35
Agee, Arthur 76–78
Agee, Bo 77–78
Agrelo, Marilyn 92–93
Aiken, Ian 5
Alaska 65–66, 95; Anchorage 65; Fairbanks 173; Nome 65
Alberto, Carlos 116
alcoholism 19, 109
Alfaro, Manuel 134–135
Ali, Muhammad 39–40, 102–103, 171–172, 183–185
All American Girls Professional Baseball League 15
The Alps 168
Altai Mountains 37
Altman, Harry 157–158
Altman, Robert 68, 126
Alva, Tony 34–35
Amadeus 181
Amazing Journey: The Story of the Who 115
Amazon Studios 58
Ambler, Pennsylvania 157
America Undercover 153
American Dream 41
American League MVP Award 91
American League Rookie of the Year Award 86
American Samoa 107–108
American Samoa National Football Team 107–108
Amy 143
amyotrophic lateral sclerosis 58, 139–140
Andreu, Betsy 12
Andreu, Frankie 12
"Angel by the Wings" (song) 37
Anker, Conrad 97–99
anti–Semitism 91–92
arcade competition 88–90; *see also* Donkey Kong
Arcade/Gaming: *The King of Kong: A Fistful of Quarters* 88
Archibald, Tiny 36
Arenivar, Angela 157
Argentina 173
arm wrestling 123–125; *Pulling John* 123
Armstrong, Lance 11–12, **12**
The Armstrong Lie 11–13
Arum, Bob 146
Assmann, David 46–47
Assmann, Marlene 46–47
Associated Press College Football Poll 73
Atenzi, Giovani **120**
Atlanta, Georgia 69, 105
Atlanta Braves 69–70
Atlantic Crossing 28
The Atomic Café 74
Auerbach, Stephen 21
August, Robert 39
Austin, Steve 75
Australia 96, 108, 142, 174; Perth 100; Melbourne 52
Australia National Cricket Team 44
auto racing 26–27, 128–129, 143–144, 155–156, 182–183; *Chasing the Horizon* 26; *Racing Dreams* 128; *Senna* 143; *Speedo* 155; *Weekend of a Champion* 182; *see also*

Index

demolition derby; Formula One; kart racing; NASCAR; off-road racing
Avila, Glena 59–60

Babington, Bruce 161
Bachar, John 180
The Bachelor 68
Badwater Ultramarathon 140–141
BAFTA Awards 28
Bagent, Travis 123
Baghdad, Iraq 126
Baja California Peninsula 27
Baker, Chet 24
Ball Four (book) 16
ballet 45–46; *see also* dance competition
ballroom dancing 6, 92–93; *see also* dance competition
Baloh, Marko 21
Bankowsky, Katya 145–146
The Barkley Marathons 13–14
The Barkley Marathons: The Race That Eats Its Young 13–14
Bar-Lev, Amir 70–71
Barnes, Annabeth 129
Barrera, Antonio 63–64
BASE jumping 161–162; *Sunshine Superman* 161, 190
baseball 14–15, 15–17, 69–70, 85–86, 91–92, 108–109, 178–179; *Baseball Girls* 14; *The Battered Bastards of Baseball* 15; *Hank Aaron: Chasing the Dream* 69; *Jose Canseco: The Truth Hurts* 85; *The Life and Times of Hank Greenberg* 91; *No No: A Dockumentary* 108; *Up for Grabs* 178; *see also* softball
Baseball (film) 5, 9, 14
Baseball America 85–86
Baseball Girls 14–15
basketball 35–36, 76–78, 101, 117–118, 126–127, 137–138, 163–164; *Doin' It in the Park: Pickup Basketball, NYC* 35; *Hoop Dreams* 76; *More than a Game* 101; *The Other Dream Team* 117; *Quantum Hoops* 126; *Rocks with Wings* 137; *Through the Fire: Sebastian Telfair's Defining Year* 163; *see also* H-O-R-S-E; street basketball; twenty-one
The Battered Bastards of Baseball 15–17
Battle of Khe Sanh 74
BBC 5, 52, 138
beach party films 39, 132
Beamon, Bob 113
The Beatles 102
Beattie, Jim 5
Beaver Stadium 71
Beckenbauer, Franz 116
beer pong 167

Beesley, Bradley 109–110
Begin, Menachem 50
Beitar Jerusalem Football Club 50–51
Belgium 160, 184
Bell, Chris 22–23, *23*
Bell, Mark 22
Bell, Mike 22–23
Bell, Otto 36–38
Belman, Kristopher 101
Bending Steel 17–19
Berger, Ron 133–135
Berkow, Ira 92
Beverly Hills Tennis Club 92
Beyond the Mat 19–21
Bicycle Dreams 21–22
Big Brother 68
The Big Guy 5
Bigger, Stronger, Faster* 22–23
Bikila, Abebe 64, 166
Bindler, S.R. 67–68
Bingham High School 85
Blaustein, Barry 19–20
Blindsight 28
Blitz, Jeffrey 156–158
Blood in the Face 74
Bloom, Howard 83
Bloomer Girls 15
Bloomfield, Leva 85
Bloomfield, Vita 85
board games 186; *Word Wars* 186; *see also* Scrabble
bodybuilding 22–23, 56–57, 125–126; *Bigger, Stronger, Faster** 22; *Generation Iron* 56; *Pumping Iron* 125
Boenish, Carl 162
Boenish, Jean 162
Bonanza (TV Show) 16
Bonds, Barry 178–179
Bonnie and Clyde 181
"bountygate" scandal 58
Bouton, Jim 16
Bowe, Riddick 114
Bowerman, Bill 100
bowling 121–122; *Pin Gods* 121
Bowling for Columbine 6
boxing 24, 39–40, 41–42, 90–91, 102–103, 114–115, 133–135, 145–146, 153–154, 169–170, 171–172, 183–185; *Broken Noses* 24; *Facing Ali* 39; *Fallen Champ: The Untold Story of Mike Tyson* 41; *Legendary Champions* 90; *Muhammad Ali, The Greatest: 1964–1974* 102; *On the Ropes* 114; *Ring of Fire: The Emile Griffith Story* 133; *Shadow Boxers* 145; *Sons of Cuba* 153; *T-Rex* 169; *The Trials of Muhammad Ali* 171; *When We Were Kings* 183
Boyer, Jacques 135–136
Brazil 152, 167

Brazilian Grand Prix 144
Brees, Drew 58
Breland, Mark 114
Brett, Mike 107–108
Brice, Russell 148–149
Bridwell, Jim 179–180
Brigham, Ted 157
Broken Noses 24, 145
Brooklyn Castle 24–25
Brooklyn Dodgers 134
Brown, Bruce 39, 113–114
Brown, Dana 39, 114
Brown, James (musician) 185
Brown, Milo 26–27
Brown University 61
Brunt, Stephen 40
Bruschelli, Gigi 120
Brushy Mountain State Penitentiary 13
Brzenk, John 123, **124**
BSV Al-Dersimspor 47
Budapest, Hungary 52–54
Budd, Zola 151
Buddhism 146
bullfighting 63–64; *Gored* 63
The Burmese Harp 165
Burns, Ken 5, 14
Burstein, Nanette 114–115
Bush, George W. 74, 171
Butler, George 56, 125–126
Buttrick, Barbara 146

California 34, 46, 132, 149; Badwater Basin 140; Death Valley 140; Los Angeles 146, 150–151; Pasadena 80, 127; San Clemente 157; San Diego 21, 186; San Francisco 132–133, 138–139; Santa Monica 134; Venice 125; Whitney Portal 140
California Institute of Technology 126–128
California State Girls Cross Country Championship 138–139
Calvin Klein (clothing) 24
Cambodia 54
Cameron, Alex 158
Canada Cup International Fast-Pitch Championships 15
Canary Islands 95
Canepari, Zackary 169–170
Cannes Film Festival 176
Canseco, Jose 85–87
Canter, Markus 26–27
Canter, Mason 26–27
Canton McKinley High School 61
Cantrell, Gary 13–14
Cape Epic 136
Caribbean Islands 44–45
Carlos, John 113, 141–143
Carlson, Katrina 62
Carlson, Kenneth 61–62

Carny 33
Carroll, Dave 17–19
Carson City, Nevada 3
Caslavska, Vera 166
Cassius le Grand 102
Castro, Fidel 153–154
Catholicism 88
"Cat's in the Cradle" 90
CBS 4
Cefn Fforest, Wales 31
Central Meru Peak 97–99, **98**
Chaikin, Eric 186
Chapin, Harry 4, 90–91
Chaplin, Charlie 91
Charlotte Observer 80
Chase, Kelly 82
Chasing the Horizon 26–27
Chechnya 50
Cheshire Academy 80
chess 25–26; *Brooklyn Castle* 25
Chicago, Illinois 76–78
Chichester, Sir Francis 32
child sexual abuse 70–71, 136
Chin, Jimmy 97–99
China 149, 167
Chinaglia, Giorgio 116
Chinatown 182
Chollima Movement 55
Chomičius, Valdemaras 117
Chuvalo, George 40
Cincinnati Reds 109
cinéma vérité 4, 37, 69, 93, 102, 115, 125, 156, 177
Civil Rights Movement 69–70, 141–143, 172, 185
Clancy, Gil 134
Clark, Jeff 132–133
Classic American Hardwoods 177
Cloud Cult (band) 43
Code Red DVD 34
Cohn, Erika 84–85
Cold War 52–54, 54–55, 118, 129–131, 153–154
Coleman, Mark 152
Colombia 46, 174–176
Colombia National Football Team 174–176
colonialism 44, 87–88, 135
Colorado 21
Colorado Silver Bullets 15
Columbia Pictures 42
communism 54–55, 130–131, 153–154
community 17–19, 30–31, 48–49, 60, 70–71, 84–85, 87–88, 88–90, 103–104, 119, 148, 160–161, 186
competitive soaring 5
concussions 83
Connecticut 80, 126; New Haven 157
The Conquest of Everest 4, 28

Contrade of Siena 119–120
Cooper, Drea 169–170
Cooper, Henry 40
Corbett, James J. 3
The Corbett-Fitzsimmons Fight 3
Cort, Bud 126
Corteo Storico 119
Cote, Riley 82
Cotton, Sian 101
Coughlin, Charles 91
Coughlin, Tom 139
Couliau, Kevin 35–36
Courtney, Bill 176–178
Cowie, Peter 166
The Crash Reel 28–30
Crazy Love 134
cricket 43–45; *Fire in Babylon* 43
Criterion Collection DVD 166
Croft, Colin 44
Cronkite, Walter 4
cross country running 138–140; *see also* track and field
cross-country skiing 42
Crossing the Line 55
Crowder, Paul 115–117
Crowhurst, Donald 30–31, 32–33
Crutchfield, Jason 170
Cuba 153–154
cultural appropriation 159–160
cultural assimilation 44, 49
culture 35–38, 39, 47–48, 49, 84–85, 87–88, 109–110, 119–120, 122–123, 125, 137–138, 159–160
Cumberland Mountains 13
Curry, Marshall 128–129
cycling 11–12, 21, 135–136, 160–161; *The Armstrong Lie* 11; *Bicycle Dreams* 21; *Rising from Ashes* 135; *A Sunday in Hell* 160
Czechoslovakia 142

Daily News Golden Gloves Tournament 146
D'Amato, Cus 41
dance competition 45–46, 92–93; *First Position* 45; *Mad Hot Ballroom* 92; *see also* ballet; ballroom dancing
Dark Horse: The Incredible True Story of Dream Alliance 30–32
Dartmouth College 73
Davies, Howard 31
Davies, John 172–174
Davis, Ron 72–73
Day, Walter 89
dead ball Era 91
Dearborn High School 49
Decker, Mary 151
Deep Water 30–31, 32–33, 95
defection of Soviet/Eastern Bloc athletes 54, 131, 154

DeGideo, April 157
Degortes, Andrea 120
Dekker, Laura 94–95
De Leyer, Harry 72–73
Dellamaggiore, Katie 25
Demeyer, Marc 161
Democratic Republic of the Congo 102–103, 184–185; *see also* Zaire
demolition derby 155–156; *see also* auto racing
Dempsey, Patrick 27
Derby 33–34, 67
Derby, Rick 137–138
Dershowitz, Alan 92
Detroit Tigers 91–92
Devenish, Ross 62
De Vlaeminck, Roger 161
Diffrient, David Scott 181–182
Dillon, Matt 117
Docurama 62, 153, 156
Dogtown 34
Dogtown and Z-Boys 34–35, 132
Doin' It in the Park: Pick-Up Basketball, New York City 35–36
Dominican Americans 93
Donkey Kong 88–90
Doonesbury 74
doping 11–12, 22–23, 86–87; *see also* performance-enhancing drugs; steroids
Douglas, Buster 41
Dow, Roy 127
Dower, John 115–117
Dowling, Brian 74
Down syndrome 29
Downing, George 132
Downing, Taylor 111
Dream Alliance (horse) 31
Drew, Robert 4
Drew Associates 4–5
drone photography 37
drug abuse 20, 23, 40, 66, 77–78, 108–109, 115, 129, 152
Duchovny, David 127
Dundee, Angelo 102
Dutch Resistance of World War II 72
Dye, Charles 42–43

eagle hunting 36–38; *see also* falconry
The Eagle Huntress 36–38
Earp, Wyatt 91
East Carolina University 80
Ecclestone, Bernie 144
Edelman, Ezra 9
Edison, Thomas 91, 160
Edley, Joe 186
Edwards, Harry 142
Edwards, Robert 159
Ehrlich, Judd 87–88

Index

Einstein, Albert 25
El Capitan 162
Ellis, Dock 108–109
Encyclopædia Britannica 77–78
The Endless Summer 39, 113
The Endless Summer II 39
endurance competition 67–69; *Hands on a Hard Body* 67
enforcer (hockey) 82–83
Engbloom, Skip 34
England 62–63; London 28; Middlesbrough, North Yorkshire 54–55
Enron: The Smartest Guys in the Room 11
equestrianism 4, 72–73, 81–82; *Harry and Snowman* 72; *The Horse with the Flying Tail* 81; *see also* horse racing; show jumping
Erving, Julius 36
Escobar, Andrés 174–176
Escobar, Pablo 174–176
ESPN 7, 9, 24, 88, 157, 164, 176
Eusebio 55, 63
The Exorcist 4
Extreme Championship Wrestling 19–20
extreme sports 6, 28, 28–30, 34–35, 96, 97–99, 147–149, 168–169, 179–180; *see also* mountaineering; rock climbing; skateboarding, snowboarding

fa'afafine 107
"face" (wrestling) 75
Facets DVD 103
Facing Ali 39–40
Facing Ali (book) 40
Fadlallah, Imad 48–49
Fahrenheit 9/11 6
falconry 36–38; *see also* eagle hunting
Fallen Champ: The Untold Story of Mike Tyson 9, 41–42
La Familia 50–51, **51**
Farman, Slim 18
Farrakhan, Louis 171
Favela Rising 174
FBI 69
feats of strength 17–19
Fedoruk, Todd 82
Ferrigno, Lou 56, 125–126
Festival of the Beauty 110
Festival of the Nations 110
Fetisov, Slava 130–131
Field, Todd 16
FIFA 48, 54–55, 62, 107–108
Fight Day 153
Fight of the Week 134
FilmRise 64
Finding Traction 42–43
Fiore, Robert 125–126
Fire in Babylon 43–45
First Position 45–47

fishing 109–110; *Okie Noodling* 109; *see also* noodling
Fitzsimmons, Bob 3
The Five Obstructions 160
The Flaming Lips 110
Float Like a Butterfly, Sting Like a Bee 102
Florida 81, 149; Miami 5, 102, 141, 174; Tampa 157
Foley, Mick 20
football 48–49, 57–59, 70–71, 73–75, 79–81, 84–85, 176–177; *Fordson: Faith, Fasting, Football* 48; *Gleason* 57; *Go Tigers!* 61; *Happy Valley* 70; *Harvard Beats Yale 29–29* 73; *The Hopeful* 79; *In Football We Trust* 84; *Undefeated* 176
Football Under Cover 47–48
Ford, Henry 91
Fordson High School 48–49
Fordson: Faith, Fasting, Football 48–49
Foreman, George 40, 102, 183–185
Forever Pure 50–52
Forman, Milos 181
Formula One 143–144, 182–183; *see also* auto racing
Formula One safety 143–144, 183
Forrest Gump 105
Forsyth, Ed 114
Fosbury, Dick 113
Fotiu, Nick 82
Four Christmases 90
Four Corners (region) 137
Four Days in November 141
Fox, Terry 106
foxtrot (dance) 93
France 108, 142, 149, 160
Frankenheimer, John 162
Fraser, Dawn 166
Frazier, Joe 40, 166, 184
Freedom's Fury 52–54
The French Connection 4
Friedkin, William 4
Frontiere, Dominic 114
Frontiere, Georgia 114
Frost, David 162
Fuchs, Jeremy 83
Fujita, Scott 58
Full Frame Film Festival 71
Fun Spot Arcade 89
Funk, Terry 20

Gaines, Charles 125
Galaxy Entertainment 141
Galvin, John 25
The Game of Their Lives 54–56, 63, 131
Ganges River 97
Garcia, Bobbito 35–36
Garden City Exxon 155
Garner, James 27

Garner, Joel 44
Gary, Jerome 56
Gast, Leon 6, 103, 183–185
Gates, Curtis 77–78
Gates, William 76–78
Gaydamak, Arcadi 50–51
Gazdik, Luke 82
gender equality 36–38, 42–43, 47–48, 94–95, 146, 169–170
Generation Iron 56–57
George Medal 147
Germany 47, 52; Berlin 110; Kreuzberg 47; Munich 181
Ghazi, Rashid 48–49
Giants Stadium 116
Gibney, Alex 11–12
Gibraltar (British Territory) 94
Gidget 132
Gillies, Clark 82
Givens, Robin 41
Glanville, Brian 62
Gleason 57
Gleason 57–59
Gleason, Michel 58
Gleason, Rivers 58
Gleason, Steve 57–59
Glena 59–61
Go Tigers! 61–62
Goal! The World Cup 62–63
Goat Park 36; *see also* Happy Warrior Playground
Golden Eagle Festival 37
Golden State Warriors 118
Goldman, Eddie 152
Gold's Gym 125
Goldstein, Ruby 134
golf 149–150; *The Short Game* 149
GoPro camera 43
Gorbachev, Mikhail 131
Gordon, Daniel 54–55, 63
Gordon, Robby 27
Gordon, Seth 88–90, 186
Gore, Al 74
Gored 63–64
Gracie, Renzo 153
Graham, Matt 186
Grammy Awards 35, 90
The Grand Olympics 4, 64–65, 181
Granger, Michelle 15
The Grateful Dead 118
Gray, Colin Keith 52–54
The Great Alone 65–66
The Great American Cowboy 66–67
Great Capes 32
Green, Sam 171
Green Mountains 42
Greenbaum, Josh 149–150
Greenberg, Hank 91–92
Greene, Kai 56
Greenhalgh, Jon 153
Greenspan, Bud 150–151
Greenstein, Joseph 19
Greenwald, Rick 126–127
Grierson, John 7
Griffith, Emile 133–135
Grizzly Man 95
The Guardian 143–144, 147
Guinness Book of World Records 89, 162
The Gypsy Moths 162

H-O-R-S-E (game) 36; *see also* basketball
Haines, Tommy 82, 122–123
haka 84
Hal 9000 96–97
Hamill, Pete 134
Hamilton, Laird 133
Hands on a Hard Body 8, 67–69
Hands on a Hard Body Contest 67–69
Hands on a Hard Body: The Musical 69
Hank Aaron: Chasing the Dream 69–70
Happy Valley 70–72
Happy Warrior Playground 36; *see also* Goat Park
Harding, Warren (rock climber) 179
Harewood, Dorian 70
Harlan County, USA 41
Harold and Maude 126
Harry and Snowman 72–73
Hart, Brett 75–76
Harush, Ariel 51
Harvard Beats Yale 29–29 73–75
Harvard Crimson 73
Harvard Stadium 74
Harvard University 73–74
Harvey, Brett 82–83
Hary, Armin 64–65
Hauser, Robin 138–139
Havana Boxing Academy 153–154
Hawaii 39, 132, 159–160
Hawkins, Connie 36
Hayes, Bob 100, 165
HBO 30, 153
Heath, Phil 56–57
"heel" (wrestling) 75
Heisman Trophy 74, 80
Henn, Karl 13–14
Hercules in New York 126
Herne, Tsieboo 88
Herzog, Werner 95, 131
Highland High School 85
Hill, Calvin 74
Hill, Lynn 180
Hill, Marlon 186
Hillary, Sir Edmund 4, 28, 147
Himalayas 97–99
Hitchcock, Sue 106

Index

Hitchcock, Terry 105–106
Hitler, Adolph 110–112
Hitman Hart: Wrestling with Shadows 75–76
Ho, Jeff 34
Hobson, Josh 128–129
Hock, Jonathan 163–164
hockey: *Ice Guardians* 82; *Pond Hockey* 122; *Red Army* 129
Hockey: A People's History 9
Hoffman, Paul 143
Hogan, Hulk 22
Holding, Michael 44
Holmes, Larry 40
Honnold, Alex 180
Hoop Dreams 5, 6, 76–79
The Hopeful 79–81
Horrible Bosses 90
horse racing 30–31, 119–121; *Dark Horse: The Incredible True Story of Dream Alliance* 30; *Palio* 119; *see also* equestrianism
The Horse with the Flying Tail 4, 81–82
Hsing, Ariel 167
Huff, Sam 4
Hughes Aircraft 162
human growth hormone 23
Hungarian Men's National Water Polo Team 52–54
Hungarian Revolution of 1956 52–53
Hunt, John 28, 147
Hunter High School 85
hunting: *The Eagle Huntress* 36
Hurricane Katrina 57
Hurst, Geoff 63
Hyams, John 151–153
Hyde Park (London) 62
Hynson, Mike 39

Ice Guardians 82–84
ice hockey 82–83, 122–123, 129–131
Ichikawa, Kon 165–166, 181
Iditarod Trail 65–66
If a Tree Falls: A Story of the Earth Liberation Front 128
IFC Films 46, 62
Iltis, Annika 13–14
IMAX 164
immigration 156–158
In Football We Trust 84–85
In the Bedroom 16
The Incredible Hulk (TV) 125
Independent Lens (TV series) 51–52, 85, 160, 170, 172
India 97–99, 157
Indianapolis, Indiana 41
Indianapolis 500 5
IndiePix Films 124
Intermediate School 318 25–26, **26**
International Basketball Federation 117

International Cycling Union 12
The International Jew (book) 91
International Olympic Committee 142
Into the Wild (book) 97
Into Thin Air (book) 97
Iran 46–47
Iranian Revolution 48
Iranian Women's National Football Team 47
Iranol 48
Irvine, Sandy 28
Irwin, Dave 61
Isa, Ahamed 166
Isaac, Alberto 112–113
Isaacs, Gregory 45
Islam 47–48, 48–49, 102, 171
Israel 50–51
Israeli Premier League 50–51
Italy 46, 96; Imola 143; Rome 64; Siena, Tuscany 119–121
Ivy League 73–74

Jack Long Nissan 67–68
Jacobsen, Jaime 42–43
Jager, Ed 155–156, **156**
James, Jesse 91
James, Joni 24
James, LeBron 101
James, Steve 6, 76–79
Jamison, Steve 107–108
Japan 108, 152, 159–160; Tokyo 62, 165–166
Jay, Paul 75–76
Jeff Ho Surfboards and Zephyr Productions Shop 34
Jeffries, James J. 3
Jerome, Harry 99–101
Jerome, Valerie 100
Jerome, Wendy 100
John Marshall High School 76–78
Johnson, Dwayne 20
Johnson, Jack 3, 91
Johnson, Jimmie 27
Johnson, Rafer 64
Johnson, Sue Jaye 170
Johnstone, T.C. 135–136
Jones, Ben 140
Jones, Tommy Lee 74
Jose Canseco: The Truth Hurts 85–87
Joyce, Dru, II 101
Judaism 91–92
"Juiced: Wild Times, Rampant 'Roids, Smash Hits & How Baseball Got Big" 86

Kadakia, Neil 157
Kadiyev, Dzhabrail 50–51
Kane, Timothy James 13–14
Kapadia, Asif 143–144
Kargman, Bess 45–46

kart racing 128–129; *see also* auto racing
Kasatonov, Alexi 130
Katz, Mike 125–126
Kaufusi, Fihi 85
Kaylor, Robert 33–34
Kazakhs 36
Keepers of the Game 87–88
Keith, Cody 79–81
Keith, Greg 80–81
Keith, India 80–81
Keitt, Harry 114–115
Kempner, Aviva 91–92
Kennedy, Robert F. 74
Kerr, Mark 151–153
KGB 131
Kharlamov, Valeri **130**
Khonsari, Vassiliki 123–125
The Kid Stays in the Picture 114
Kim, Duk-Koo 133
Kimball, Nikki 42–43
Kimble, Paige 157
King, B.B. 185
King, Don 41, 146, 184
King, Martin Luther, Jr. 13, 74
King George Cup V 81–82
The King of Kong: A Fistful of Quarters 6, 88–90, 186
Kino International 24
Kirkland, Pee Wee 35
Kirsch, Brendan 79–81
Klein, William 100, 102–103, 172
Klores, Dan 133–135
Knisely, Jonathan 157
Knox-Johnson, Robin 33
Knoxville, Tennessee 13
Kohs, Greg 65–66
Kopple, Barbara 41–42
Korean War 54
Korenfein, Itkiz 51
Koryo Tours 55
Krakauer, John 97
Krutov, Vladimir 130
Kubrick, Stanley 96–97
Kukoč, Toni 117
Kurtinaitis, Rimas 117

La Familia 50–51, *51*
lacrosse 87–88; *Keepers of the Game* 87
Lake Calhoun (Minnesota) 123
Lala, Nupur 157
Lampley, Jim 118–119
Landers, Michael 167
Lang, Andrew 153–154
Langi, Harvey 84–85, ***84***
Lansburgh, Larry 81
Larionov, Igor 130
The Last King of Scotland 168
Latynina, Larisa 166

Lawwill, Mert 114
Lazore, Jacelyn 87–88
Lazore, Mimi 87–88
Leacock, Richard 4
A League of Their Own 15
Lee, Annabelle 15
Lee, Bill 15
Lee, David 58
Legendary Champions 4, 90–91
Lelouch, Claude 181
Leth, Jørgen 160–161
Let's Get Lost 24
Levin, Carl 92
Lewis, Carl 151
Lietman, Ruth 49
The Life and Times of Hank Greenberg 91–92
Lincoln High School 164
Lindbergh, Charles 91
Lindsay, Daniel 176–178
Lipscomb, James 4
Listen to Me Marlon 43–44
Liston, Sonny 102
Lithuania 117
Lithuanian Men's National Basketball Team 53, 117–119
Little Children 16
Liu, Lucy 54
Lloyd, Clive 44
Lloyd, Jeff 26–27
Locke, Larry 121–122
London Film Festival 151
Long, John 180
The Long Goodbye 126
Long Trail 42–43
Longview, Texas 67–68
Lowe, Alex 99
Lowe, George 28
Luebke, Allen 60
Lyle, Ron 40
Lyne, Phil 66–67

MacDonald, Kevin 168–169
Mackey, Brendan 168
Mackey, Lance 65–66
Mad Hot Ballroom 6, 46, 92–94
Madison Square Garden 146
Maertens, Freddy 161
Magnolia Pictures 163
Mahan, Larry 66–67
Maidentrip 94–96
Mailer, Norman 133–134, 185
Maine 102
Major League Baseball 14–15, 15–17, 22, 69–70, 74, 85–86, 91–92, 108–109, 178–179
Makarov, Sergei 130
Malcolm X 102
Mallory, George 28, 97
A Man and a Woman 181

The Man Who Skied Down Everest 96–97
Manassas High School 176–178
Mancini, Henry 182
Mancini, Ray 133
Manigault, Earl 36
Manley, Effa 14
Manson, Tyrene 114–115
Mantle, Mickey 69
Maranatha High School 80
marathon 13–14, 42–43, 105–106, 140–141, 172–174; *see also* ultramarathon; trail-running
Marbury, Stephon 164
Marcellini, Romolo 64
Marčiulionis, Šarūnas 117–118
Maris, Roger 178
Markevicius, Marius 117–119
Marley, Bob 45
Marquette University 78
Martin, T.J. 176–178
Martinez, Victor 56
Marx, Frederick 77–78
Maryland 46
Massachusetts 42
Massena Central High School 88
matador 63–64
Matossain, Sevan 123–125
Matthau, Walter 92
Matthews, Jill 146
Maturana, Francisco 175
Mavericks (California) 133
Mays, Willie 69
Maysles, Albert 4
McAdams, Bill, Jr. 85–87
McCain, John 60
McCormack, Pete 39–40
McCrea, Joel 66
McCready, Mike 58
McDonald, Ian 5
McGee, Willie (basketball) 101
McGrattan, Brian 82
McGwire, Mark 178
McLaren Racing 144
McMahon, Vince 20, 75–76
McQueen, Steve 27, 114
Medellín cartel 175
Memphis, Tennessee 176–178
Men of the Tall Ships 5
Merckx, Eddy 161
merengue (dance) 93
Merrill, Keith 66–67
Meru 97–99
Mexico 27, 63–64, 112–113; Mexico City 100, 141
Michael Jordan to the Max 164
Michaels, Shawn 75–76
Michigan 128; Dearborn 48–49; Detroit 91; Flint 170
Midnight Cowboy 181
Mighty Jerome 99–101
Mikhailov, Boris **130**
military occupation 52, 118; *see also* Soviet satellite states
Miller, Warren 6
Million Dollar Baby 146
Milwaukee, Wisconsin 69
Minneapolis, Minnesota 123
Minor League Baseball 15–16, 85–86
Minsker, Andy 24
Minton-Small, Ty 58
Miramax Films 117
Mr. Olympia 56, 125–126
Mr. Universe 125–126
Mitchell, Billy 88–90, **89**
Miura, Yuichiro 96–97
mixed martial arts 59–60, 151–153; *Glena* 59; *The Smashing Machine: The Life and Times of Extreme Fighter Mark Kerr* 151; *see also* Ultimate Fighting Championship; World Vale Tudo Championship
Mizrachi Jews 50
Mizrahy, Ido 63–64
Mohawk Territory 87–88
Moitessier, Bernard 33
Monaco Grand Prix 182–183
Monday Night Football 57
Monte Carlo, Monaco 182–183
"Montreal screwjob" 76
Mooney, Michael 58
Mooney vs Fowle 5
Moore, Ellery 61
Moore, Michael 6
moral codes 47–48; *see also* Iran; morality police; religious fundamentalism
morality police 48; *see also* Iran; moral codes; religious fundamentalism
More Than a Game 101–102
Morgen, Brett 114–115
Mormonism 84–85
Mortimer, Peter 179–180
Moser, Francesco 161
Moss, Jesse 155–156
motorcycle sport 113–114; *On Any Sunday* 113
Mount Everest 28, 65, 96–97, 97, 147–149
Mount Fuji 96
Mount Scott Boxing Club 24
mountaineering 28, 96, 97–99, 147–149, 168–169; *The Conquest of Everest* 28; *The Man Who Skied Down Everest* 96; *Meru* 97; *Sherpa* 147; *Touching the Void* 168; *see also* rock climbing
Mudcats 110
Muhammad Ali, the Greatest: 1964–1974 100, 102–103, 172
Munich massacre 182

Murderball 103–105
Murphy's Irish Stout 141
Murray, Derick 40
My Own Private Idaho 33
My Run 105–107
Myers Park High School 80

Najafi, Ayat 46–47
"narco-soccer" 175–176
NASCAR 27, 43, 128–129; *see also* auto racing
National Baseball Hall of Fame 14–15
National Basketball Association 117, 164
National Film Board of Canada 14–15, 75–76, 99–101
National Film Registry at the Library of Congress 78
National Football League 4, 57–58, 74, 84–85
National Hockey League 82–83, 130–131
National Public Radio 131
nationalism 50, 75
Native American sports mascots 88
Native Americans 87–88, 137–138
Nautical (horse) 81–82
Navajo Nation 137–138
nazism 4, 110–112
NBC 41
NCAA football 70–71, 79–81
NCAA softball 15
Negro Leagues 14
Nelson, Donnie 118
Nepal 28, 148; Katmandu 96
Nesmith, Michael 27
Netanyahu, Benjamin 50
Netflix 17, 150
The Netherlands 72, 94–95
Neuhauser, Frank 157
New Bed-Stuy Boxing Center 114
New Hampshire 89
New Holland, Pennsylvania 72
New Jersey 21, 157–158; Atlantic City 21; Glen Rock 157–158
New Line Cinema 90
New Mexico 137–138
New Mexico Highlands University 81
New Orleans, Louisiana 57
New Orleans Saints 57–59
New Orleans Superdome 57
New York (state) 87–88; Akwesasne 87–88; Fort Covington 87–88; Johnstown 41
New York City 6, 17, 35–36, 45–46, 116–117, 134; Bensonhurst 92–93; The Bronx 92; Brooklyn 25, 92–93, 114, 164; Coney Island 18–19, 164; Harlem 102; Long Island 155; Manhattan 92–93; Queens 92–93; Tribeca 92–93; Washington Heights 92–93

New York Cosmos 115–117
New York Giants (baseball) 134
New York Giants (football) 139
New York Times 65, 141
New York Yankees 25, 117
New Zealand 28, 39, 174
Newens, Sara 167
Newman, Paul 27
newsreel 5, 61–62
Next Goal Wins 107–108
NFL Films 4, 164
NHL Expansion 83
Niblett, Simon 37
Nichols, Bill 169
Niekro, Phil 15
9/11 terrorist attacks 48–49, 93, 173, 179
1924 British Mount Everest Expedition 28
1928 Summer Olympics 100
1930 FIFA World Cup 62
1936 Summer Olympics 3, 110–112
1948 Summer Olympics 112
1952 Summer Olympics 112
1953 British Mount Everest Expedition 28
1956 Summer Olympics 52–54, 64–65
1960 Summer Olympics 64–65, 100
1962 British Empire and Commonwealth Games 100
1964 Summer Olympics 62, 100, 165–166
1966 British Commonwealth Games 100
1966 England National Football Team 63
1966 FIFA World Cup 54–55, 62–63, 116
1966 Italian National Football Team 55, 63
1966 North Korean National Football Team 54–55, 63
1966 Portugal National Football Team 55, 63
1966 West German National Football Team 63
1967 Pan-American Games 100
1968 Cultural Olympiad 112–113
1968 Summer Olympics 100, 112–113, 141–143, 153, 183
1968 *Sunday Times* Golden Globe Race 30–31, 32–33, 95
1972 Presidential Election 73
1972 Summer Olympics 181–182
1975 Del Mar Nationals Skateboard Championships 34
1976–77 California drought 34
1980 Winter Olympics 130
1984 Summer Olympics 150–151
1986 NBA Draft 117–118
1988 Summer Olympics 117, 151
1988 Winter Olympics 151
1992 Summer Olympics 53, 117–119, 151
1992 United States Men's Basketball Team 117
1994 Winter Olympics 151
1994 World Cup 174

Index

1994–95 MLB strike 14, 69
1996 Summer Olympics 105
1997 New York Golden Gloves Tournament 114–115
Nixon, Richard 73
Niyonshuti, Adrien 136
No No: A Dockumentary 108–109
Noll, Greg 132
nomadic societies 36
noodling (fishing) 109–110; *see also* fishing
Norgay, Norbu Tenzing 147
Norgay, Tenzing 28, 147
Norman, Matt 113, 141–143
Norman, Peter 113, 141–143
North American Scrabble Championship 6, 186
North American Soccer League 62, 115–117
North Carolina 129; Charlotte 79–80; Pinehurst 149
North Korea 54–55, 63
North Vancouver, British Columbia 100
Northwest League 17
Norton, Ken 40, 184
Norway 162
Noyes, Dan 138–139
Nugent, Ted 27
Nurgaiv, Aisholpan 36–38
Nyznik, Bruce 96–97

Oakland Athletics 86
O'Connell, Charlie 34
Odjick, Dino 82
Oerter, Al 113
off-road racing 26–27; *see also* auto racing
Officer, Charles 99–100
Ohio 33–34; Akron 101; Massillon 61–62
O.J.: Made in America 9
Okie Noodling 109–110
Okie Noodling II 110
Oklahoma 109–110
Olgii, Mongolia 37
Olive Films 182
Ollie's Army 115
Olympia 3, 110–112, 166, 181
Olympia (book) 111
Olympic Project for Human Rights 142–143
Olympic Stadium (Berlin) 111
Olympics: *The Grand Olympics* 64; *Olympia* 110; *The Olympics in Mexico* 112; *Salute* 141; *16 Days of Glory* 150; *Tokyo Olympiad* 165; *Visions of Eight* 181
The Olympics in Mexico 4, 7, 112–113, 181
Omak Stampede 66
O'Mara, Toby 26–27
On Any Sunday 39, 66–67, 113–114
On Any Sunday: The Next Chapter 114
On Any Sunday II 114
On the Pole 5

On the Ropes 114–115
Once in a Lifetime: The Extraordinary Story of the New York Cosmos 115–117
One Day in September 168
Oregon 59; Portland 16, 24, 59
Oregon Veteran's Home 60
Osmond, Louise 30–31, 32–33
The Other Dream Team 53, 117–119
Over the Top 124
The Overnighters 155
Owens, Jesse 111
Ozerov, Yuri 181
Ozturk, Renan 97–99

Pac Bell Park 179
Pacific Islander Americans 84–85
Pacific Ocean Park 34
Pacquiao, Manny 146
Pageant 72
Palio 119–121
Palio di Siena 119–121
Pamphilon, Sean 58
Pan American Highway 173
Papp, Laszlo 153
Paret, Benny 133–134
Park City, Utah 29
Parker, Scott 82
Parros, George 82
Paskowitz, Dorian 163
Pastrana, Travis 27
Paterno, Joe 70–71
Patrick, Nigel 62
Pavelchak, Sonny 122
PBS 5, 14, 26, 51–52, 78, 85, 128, 138, 156, 160, 170, 172
Pearce, David 29
Pearce, Kevin 28–30
Pearl Jam 58
Pearlstein, Ferne 159–160
Peedom, Jennifer 147–149
Pelé 116
Penn, Arthur 181
Penn, Sean 35
Penn State University 70–71
Pennebaker, D.A. 4
Peralta, Stacy 34–35, 132–133
perestroika movement 131
performance-enhancing drugs 11–12, 22–23, 57, 86–87; *see also* doping; steroids
Perkins, Benny 68
Perryton, Texas 157
Peruvian Andes 168–169
Peters, Frank 16
Peters, Sibil 56
Petrillo, Julian 186
Petrov, Vladimir **130**
Petrović, Dražen 117
Pfleghar, Michael 181

Phelps, Michael 166
Philadelphia, Pennsylvania 46
The Philippines 149
The Pianist 182
Piazza del Campo 119
Pickens, Slim 82
Pin Gods 121–122
Pingatore, Gene 77
Pittsburgh Pirates 109
Pizza Hut 78
Plimpton, George 185
Polamalu, Troy 84
Polanski, Roman 182–183
Pollard, Fritz, Jr. 112
Polsky, Gabe 129–131
Pond Hockey 82, 122–123
Pope John XXIII 64
Portland Beavers 16
Portland Mavericks 16–17
Portland Trailblazers 117–118
Portugal 174
Potter, Dean 180
POV (film series) 26, 128, 156
poverty 25, 77–78, 92–93, 115, 137–138, 154, 163–164, 169–170, 177
powerlifting 22
Prague Spring 142
Pray, Doug 163
Prescription Thugs 23
Presidential Medal of Freedom 171
Pride Fighting Championships 152
Prince Albert, Saskatchewan 100
Pro Football Hall of Fame 165
Pro Football: Mayhem on a Sunday Afternoon 4
Procuna, Luis 4
Professional Bowlers Association 121–122
professional wrestling 19–20, 22, 75–76
Prost, Alain 144
Providence College 164
public school funding 25, 61, 87–88
Public School 115 92–93
Public School 150 92–93
Public School 112 92–93
Pulling John 123–125
Pumping Iron 56, 67, 125–126
Pumping Iron (book) 125
Pumping Iron II: The Women 126

quad rugby 103–104; *see also* wheelchair rugby
Quantum Hoops 126–128
Queen Elizabeth II 28

Race Across America 21
Racing Dreams 46, 128–129, **129**
racism 44, 46, 50–51, 77–78, 85, 93, 100, 137–138, 142, 170

Radice, Jeff 108–109
Radio 69
Rafferty, Kevin 73–74
Rain, Douglas 96–97
Ramadan 49
Raney, Megan 52–54
Raw Iron 126
Ray, James Earl 13
Rector, Enoch 3
Red Army 129–132
religious extremism 50–51
religious fundamentalism 47–48
Reynolds, Holland 138–139
Richards, Viv 44
Richardson, Jerry 137–138
Richert, William 33–34
Richmond, Mitch 117
Rider, Chris 17–18
Riding Giants 132–133
Ridley, Daisy 37
Ridley, John 173
Riefenstahl, Leni 3, 110–112, 166
Rijker, Licia 145–146
Riley, Stevan 43–45
Ring of Fire: The Emile Griffith Story 133–135
"Ripley's Believe it or Not" 19
Rising from Ashes 135–136
Ritchey, Tom 135–136
Riverhead Raceway 155
Roach, Freddie 146
Robbins, Royal 179
Roberts, Andy 44
Roberts, Jake 20
Robič, Jure 21
Robinson, David 117
Robinson, Jackie 91–92
Rock, Chris 68
rock climbing 179–180; *Valley Uprising* 179; *see also* mountaineering
Rocks with Wings 137–138
rodeo 66–67; *The Great American Cowboy* 66
Roetheli, Nicole 172–174
Roetheli, Serge 172–174
Rogers, Dennis 19
Rolla, Missouri 157
roller derby 33–34, 67; *Derby* 33
Rongen, Thomas 107–108, **108**
Roosevelt, Theodore 91
Rosamilia, Tony 121–122
Rosen, Nick 179–180
Ross, Steve 116–117
Rothwell, Jerry 32–33
Roubaix Velodrome 160–161
Rourke, Mickey 57
Rowan, Chad (Akebono) 159–160
Rubin, Alex 103–104
Rucker Park 36

Rudolph, Wilma 64
rumba (dance) 93
Running for Jim 138–140
Running on the Sun: The Badwater 135 140–141
running/trekking/marathon: *The Barkley Marathons: The Race That Eats Its Young* 13; *Finding Traction* 42; *My Run* 105; *Running on the Sun: The Badwater 135* 140; *The 25,000 Mile Love Story* 172
Russell, Bing 16
Russell, Kurt 16
Rust Belt 34, 61
Ruth, Babe 69, 91
Rutten, Bas 152
Rwanda 135–136
Rwandan genocide 135–136

Sabol, Ed 4
Sabonis, Arvydas 117–118
Sachs, Eddie 5
Sadayev, Zaur 50–51
Saelua, Jaiyah 107–108
sailing 32–33, 94–95; *Deep Water* 32; *Maidentrip* 94; *see also* yachting
St. Joseph High School 76–78
St. Lawrence Valley 87–88
St. Louis Cardinals 178–179
St. Paul, Minnesota 105
St. Vincent-St. Mary High School 101
Salapu, Nicky 107
Salmon River Central School 87–88
Salt Lake City, Utah 85
Salute 113, 141–143
Salvation Army Church 142
Salvino, Carmen 122
Sammond, Nicholas 76
Samoan Americans 84–85
San Diego Padres 108–109
San Francisco Giants 178
San Jose State University 142
San Marino Grand Prix 143
Sandusky, Jerry 70–71
Santiago, Noel 114–115
Saunders, David 161
Savon, Felix 153
Schaap, Dick 92
Schiller, Lawrence 96–97
Schlesinger, Jillian 94–95
Schlesinger, John 181
Schoeck, Chris 17–19, **18**
Schultz, Dave 82
Schwarzenegger, Arnold 22, 56, 125–126
SCORE Baja 1000 26–27
Scrabble (game) 6, 186
Scripps National Spelling Bee 6, 93, 149, 156–158
Seattle, Washington 107

Seko, Mobutu Sese 184
Semenko, Dave 82
Senna 143–145
Senna, Ayrton 143–144
separation of church and state 49
Sewell, Amy 93
sexual assault 41, 136
sexuality 107–108, 133–134
Shadow Boxers 145–146
Shapiro, Dana Adam 103–104
Shavers, Earnie 40
Sherman, Joel 186
Sherpa 147–149, **148**
Sherpas 28, 96, 97, 147–149
Shields, Claressa 169–170
Shiprock 137
Shiprock High School 137–138
Shiprock Productions 138
Shoemaker, Don 114
"shoot" (wrestling) 76
The Short Game 149–150
show jumping 72–73, 81–82; *see also* equestrianism
Showtime 60
Sia 37
Siegel, Bill 171–172
Siegel, Lois 14–15
Sierra Leone 46
Sierra Leone Civil War 46, 173
Silverwood, Victoria 82–83
Simon, Frank 182
Simpson, Joe 168–169
Siula Grande 168–169
16 Days of Glory 150–151
Skateboarder Magazine 34
skateboarding 34–35l *Dogtown and Z-Boys* 34
Slamdance Film Festival 60
sled dog racing 65–66; *The Great Alone* 65
The Smashing Machine: The Life and Times of Extreme Fighter Mark Kerr 151–153
Smith, Earl 77
Smith, Malcolm 27, 114
Smith, Tommie 113, 141–143
Snell, Mike 33–34
snow skiing 96–97
snowboarding 28–30; *The Crash Reel* 28
Snowman (horse) 72–73
Soares, Joe 103–104
soccer 47–48, 50–52, 54–56, 62–63, 107–108, 115–117, 174–176; *Football Under Cover* 47; *Forever Pure* 50; *The Game of Their Lives* 54; *Goal! The World Cup* 62; *Next Goal Wins* 107; *Once in a Lifetime: The Extraordinary Story of the New York Cosmos* 115; *The Two Escobars* 174
social class 30–31, 33–34, 67–68, 77–78, 93, 134, 157–158, 170, 177

softball 14–15; *see also* baseball
Softball City Sports and Entertainment Complex 15
Solitary Endeavor on the Southern Ocean 147
Son, Mina T. 167
Sons of Cuba 131, 153–155
Sony Pictures 26
Soul Power 185
South Africa 39, 136, 149; Pretoria 125
South African rebel tours (cricket tours) 44
South by South West Film Festival 95, 124, 150, 178
South Jordan, Utah 85
South Korea 167; Seoul 117
South Mecklenburg High School 80
Southern California Intercollegiate Athletic Conference 127
Southern Discomfort (book) 14
Southern Ocean 32–33
Soviet satellite states 52; *see also* military occupation
Soviet Union 52, 64, 117–118, 129–131
Soviet Union National Basketball Team 117–118
Soviet Union National Ice Hockey Team 129–131
Spain 63–64; Barcelona 117–118
Speaker's Corner (London) 62
Speedo: A Demolition Derby Love Story 155–156
Speirs, Greg 118
Spellbound 6, 46, 93, 149, 156–159
spelling bee 156–158; *Spellbound* 156
Spender, Cosima 119–121
Spinks, Leon 40
The Spinners 185
Spitz, Mark 53
Spokane, Washington 16
The Sports Film: Games People Play 161
Sports Illustrated 83
sports scandal 11–12, 22, 32–33, 41–42, 58, 70–71, 76, 86, 94–95, 178–179
Stagg, Emily 157–158
Stalin, Joseph 130
Stallone, Sylvester 22, 124
Star Wars: The Force Awakens 37
State College, Pennsylvania 70–71
A State of Mind 55
Stay Hungry 126
Stecyk, Craig 34
"Steel Chair to the Head: The Pleasure and Pain of Professional Wrestling" 76
steroids 22–23, 57, 86; *see also* doping; performance-enhancing drugs
Stevenson, Teofilo 153
Stewart, Jackie 182–183
Storyville (TV series) 51–52, 138

Strauch, Marah 161–162
Streep, Meryl 68, 74
street basketball 35–36, 78
Street Fight 128
strongman/feats of strength: *Bending Steel* 17
Stuart, Mel 140–141
Studer, Danny 61
Sullivan, John L. 91
Sumo East and West 159–160
"Sumo in Hawaii" 160
Sumo Wrestling: *Sumo East and West* 159
The Sun Ship Game 5
Sundance Film Festival 17, 23, 24, 31–32, 59, 62, 71, 85, 99, 109, 115, 132
A Sunday in Hell 160–161
The Sunday Times 32
Sunshine Superman 161–162, 190
Super Bowl 139
surf films 6, 39
surfing 8, 34, 39, 113, 132–133, 163; *The Endless Sumer* 39; *Riding Giants* 132; *Surfwise* 163
Surfwise 163
Surrey, British Columbia 15
Survivor 68
Swank, Hillary 68
swimming 52; *see also* water polo
swing (dance) 93
Swinton, Tilda 33
Switzerland 173
Syracuse University 153

T-Rex 169–171
table tennis 167; *Top Spin* 167
Tahiti 39
"Take Me Out to the Ballgame" (song) 91
tango (dance) 93
Tarantino, Quentin 54
Tarasov, Antoli 131
Tashi, Phurba 148
Tator, Charles 83
Taxi to the Dark Side 11
TBS 69
Team Gleason 58
Team Horizon 26–27
Team Lotus 144
Tebow, Tim 80–81
Teddy Stadium 50–51
Telfair, Sebastian 163–164
Terre des Hommes 173–174
Terrell, Ernie 40, 172
ThinkFilm 104
30-for-30 (TV Series) 7, 9, 176
Thomas, Isiah 77–78
Thomas, Jamel 164
Thompson, Daley 151
Thompson, Howard 65

Thornton, Billy Bob 68, 106
Thrilla in Manilla 115
Through the Fire: Sebastian Telfair's Defining Year 163–164
Tikhonov, Viktor 131
A Time to Die (book) 14
Tlatelolco massacre 113, 142
Tokyo Olympiad 4, 165–167, **165**, 181
Toleman Motorsport 144
Tollin, Mike 69
Tongan Americans 84–85
"Too Young" (song) 24
Top Spin 167–168
Torero! 4
Toronto International Film Festival 24
Toronto Raptors 118
Touchdown Town 61
Touching the Void 32–33, 168–169
Tour de France 11–12, 136, 160
track and field 99–101, 138–140; *Mighty Jerome* 99; *Running for Jim* 138; see also cross country running
Tracy, Jim 139–140
tradition vs. modernity 63–64, 87–88, 119–121, 159–160
trail running 13–14, 42–43; *see also* trekking; marathon; ultramarathon
traumatic brain injury 29
Travis, Romeo 101
trekking 13–14, 42–43; *see also* trail running
Trent, Buzzy 132
The Trials of Muhammad Ali 171–172
Tribeca Film Festival 54, 88, 108, 121, 153, 176
The Tribeca Trib 93
trimaran (boat) 32
Triple Crown of Motorsport 182–183
Triumph of the Will 110
Troll Wall 162
Trophy Kids 23
Trudeau, Gary 74
Trump Ice Natural Spring Water 150
Tryon School for Boys 41
Tunney, Gene 91
Tweel, J. Clay 57–58
12 Years a Slave 173
The Twentieth Century (TV Series) 4
The 25,000 Mile Love Story 172–174
The 25,000 Mile Love Story (book) 172
twenty-one (game) 35; *see also* basketball
Twin Galaxies 89
The Two Escobars 9, 174–176
2001: A Space Odyssey 96–97
2002 Wheelchair Rugby World Championship 104
2004 Paralympic Games 103–104
2010 Winter Olympics 29
2011 NBA Draft 118
2012 Summer Olympics 169
2013 Iditarod Trail Sled Dog Race 65–66
2014 World Cup 107
2016 Summer Olympics 169
Tyson, Mike 41–42

Ultimate Fighting Championship 152; *see also* mixed martial arts
ultramarathon 13–14, 42–43, 105–106, 140–141, 172–174; *see also* marathon; trail-running
Undefeated 176–178, **177**
The Union: The Business Behind Getting High 82
United States Anti-Doping Agency 11
United States Bicentennial Celebration 5
United States Congress 86
United States Equestrian Team 82
U.S. Kids Golf World Championship 149
United States Men's National Ice Hockey Team 130
United States Men's National Soccer Team 176
United States National Wheelchair Rugby Team 103–104
United States Olympic Boxing Team 24
U.S. Pond Hockey Championships 123
U.S. Postal Service Pro Cycling Team 11
United States Soccer Federation 107
Universal Soldier 151
University High School (San Francisco) 138–139
University of California, Berkeley 139
University of Louisville 164
University of North Carolina at Charlotte 81
University of Oregon 100
Up for Grabs 178–179
Uruguay 62
USA Network 135

Vainuku, Tony 84–85
Valančiūnas, Jonas 118
Valley Uprising 179–181
Vancouver, British Columbia 29
VandeSteeg, Tim 105–106
Vasarhelyi, Elizabeth Chai 97–99
Vaudeville 17
Vedder, Eddy 58
Vermont 42–43
Very Much So Productions 56
Vesi, Bob 122
Viagra 22
The Victory of Faith 110
Vierra, Wayne 158–160
Vietnam War 74, 102, 142, 171, 183
Vigni, Silvano 120
The Violent World of Sam Huff 4

Virgin Islands 134
Visions Audience Award (SXSW) 95
Visions of Eight 181–182
Vokes, Brian 31
Vokes, Jan 31
Voyevoda, Alexy 124

Wailer, Bunny 45
Walker, Lucy 28–29
Waller, Ken 126
Walt Disney Productions 4, 81
Walton, Bill 118
Walton, George 114–115
Warner Communications 116
Warren, Branch 56
Warren, Brandon 129
Warsaw, Poland 124
Washington, D.C. 156–157
Waste Land 28
water polo 52–54; *Freedom's Fury* 52; *see also* swimming
Way, Chapman 15–16
Way, Maclain 15–16
The Weather Underground 171
Weber, Bruce 24, 145
Weekend of a Champion 182–183
West 4th Street Courts 36
West Indies Cricket Team 43–45
West Valley City, Utah 85
West Virginia 123
Westgarth, Kevin 82
"What's My Name, Fool?" 172
wheelchair rugby 103–104; *see also* quad rugby
wheelchair sports: *Murderball* 103
When We Were Kings 6, 103, 183–185
Whitaker, Forest 135
White, Ashley 157
White, Shaun 29
White Australia policy 142
Wide World of Sports 124
Wiebe, Steve 88–90, **89**
Wiley, Hugh 82
Williams, Greg 58
Williams, James 35
Williams, Percy 100
Williams, Walter Ray 121
Williams Racing 144
Willie Wonka and the Chocolate Factory 141

Winfrey, Oprah 11
Winklaar, Roelly 56
Wolf, Dennis 56
Wolper, David L. 4, 181
Women's International Boxing Federation 146
Wooden Bike Classic 136
Word Wars 6, 186
"work" (wrestling) 76
World Championship Wrestling 75–76
World Karting Association 128–129
World Series 25, 91
World Vale Tudo Championship 152; *see also* mixed martial arts
World War II 52, 72, 91, 111, 117, 166
World Wrestling Entertainment 19–20, 75–76
World Wrestling Federation 19–20, 75–76
Wranovics, Michael 178–179
wrestling: *Beyond the Mat* 19; *Hitman Hart: Wrestling with Shadows* 75

Xhang, Lily 167

yachting 32–33, 94–95; *see also* sailing
Yale University 73–74
Yamagishi, Hidetada 56
Yankee Stadium 178
Yates, Simon 168–169
Yiddish 91
yokozuna 159
Yosemite National Park 162, 179–180
Youth America Grand Prix 45–46
Yudin, Vlad 56–57
Yugoslavia 54
Yugoslavian National Basketball Team 117

Z-Boys (Zephyr Competition Team) 34–35
Zádor, Ervin 53–54, **53**
Zaire 102–103, 184–185; *see also* Democratic Republic of the Congo
Zaire '74 Music Festival 185
Zetterling, Mai 181
Zimbalist, Jeff 174–176
Zimbalist, Michael 174–176
Zinshtein, Maya 50–51
Zirin, Dave 172
Zloty Tour Cup 124
Zoel 145

www.ingramcontent.com/pod-product-compliance
Ingram Content Group UK Ltd.
Pitfield, Milton Keynes, MK11 3LW, UK
UKHW042006140426
5217IPUK00015B/1012